AN INDIAN RATIONAL THEOLOGY

The present work is a modest attempt to give a brief introduction to the doctrine of God as found in Udayana's works in general, in his Nyāyakusumāñjali in particular. The writer's aim has been to give as faithtul an interpretation of Udayana's ideas as possible in the given amount of space. How far he has succeeded in the realization of his aim should be left to the judgement of the critical reader. With a view to acquaint the reader with the manner of argumentation of the author of the Nyāyakusumāñjali, he has let Udayana himself speak by quoting him in translation wherever an important point was at issue.

PUBLICATIONS OF
THE DE NOBILI RESEARCH LIBRARY, VIENNA

Founded by
GERHARD OBERHAMMER

MOTILAL BANARSIDASS PUBLISHERS PVT. LIMITED,
DELHI, AUTHORIZED REPRINT SERIES

Edited by
KARIN PREISENDANZ

VOLUME I

AN INDIAN RATIONAL THEOLOGY

Introduction to UDAYANA'S NYĀYAKUSUMĀÑJALI

by

GEORGE CHEMPARATHY

MOTILAL BANARSIDASS
SINCE 1903 IN INDOLOGY

*First Indian Edition: Delhi, **2018***

Earlier published as Publications of the De Nobili Research Library
Volume I in 1972 by Indologisches Institut der Universität Wien,
Sammlung De Nobili, edited by Gerhard Oberhammer

ISBN: 978-81-208-4202-1

Also available at

MOTILAL BANARSIDASS

41 U.A. Bungalow Road, Jawahar Nagar, Delhi 110 007
1-B, Jyoti Studio Compound, Kannady Bridge, Nana Chowk, Mumbai-400 007
203 Royapettah High Road, Mylapore, Chennai 600 004
236, 9th Main III Block, Jayanagar, Bengaluru 560 011
8 Camac Street, Kolkata 700 017
Ashok Rajpath, Patna 800 004
Chowk, Varanasi 221 001

MLBD Cataloging-in-Publication Data
An Indian Rational Theology
Introduction to Udayana's Nyāyakusumāñjali
by George Chemparathy
Also Includes Appendix and Index
ISBN: 978-81-208-4202-1
I. Indian Philosophy, II. Nyāya-Vaiśeṣika
III. Nyāyakusumāñjali, IV. Udayana
V. Chemparathy, George

Published by
Motilal Banarsidass Publishers Private Limited
www.mlbd.com • mlbd@mlbd.com
Printed & bound at Nutech Print Services, India

MAGISTRIS AMICISQUE AUSTRIACIS

PRAESERTIM

FAMILIAE APUD QUAM

PROCUL A DOMO PROPRIA

NOVAM INVENI DOMUM

TABLE OF CONTENTS

PREFACE

In the Indian theistic schools of thought we can distinguish two distinct kinds of approach to the doctrine of God, the one based primarily on logical reasoning, the other on the authority of the sacred scriptures. The first mode of approach may be termed 'philosophical' or 'rational', the second 'theological' or 'scriptural'. Among the Brahmanical systems of the first millennium of our era that admitted the existence of God, the Nyāya-Vaiśeṣika doctrine of God can be said to represent the typical rational theology. No doubt, we come across stray references to theistic Sāṃkhyins and theistic Mīmāṃsakas even during this period, but we have little or no knowledge of their doctrine of God. Moreover, these are representatives of only small groups that have broken themselves off from the classical schools and made some modifications in the doctrines of their respective schools in order to assign a place, perhaps of no great importance, to God.

The Nyāya-Vaiśeṣikas have consistently pursued a rational approach to the doctrine of God whom they call Īśvara. A glance at the history of the origin and development of the Īśvara doctrine of the school shows that, whether it was a question of establishing his existence or his attributes, the adherents of this school have drawn their arguments primarily from reason. This rational approach of the Nyāya-Vaiśeṣikas to the doctrine of God is closely bound up with another important doctrine of theirs. In their view the Vedic scriptures do not derive their authoritativeness from intrinsic validity (*svataḥ prāmāṇyam*), as the non-theistic Mīmāṃsā and the theistic Vedānta schools had maintained. For according to them validity of truth was extrinsic (*parataḥ prāmāṇyam*), and in consonant with this theory, the validity of the very Vedic statements was derived from an extrinsic source. This source, they argued, could be no other than Īśvara, the omniscient and veracious author of the Veda. As the validity of the Veda was derived from the omniscience and veracity of Īśvara, it is quite clear that the Nyāya-Vaiśeṣikas could not have argued for the existence of Īśvara from the testimony of the Vedic scriptures without making themselves guilty of the logical fault of vicious circle. No doubt they quote scriptural passages now and then, but such scriptural references are, on the whole, very rare, and, when used, they are brought forward at the close of the rational discussion of the point at issue and only in a very subordinate role, namely in confirmation of the conclusion already arrived at through rational arguments. Such references were also intended to show that the conclusions reached by reason were not at variance with the statements in the Vedic scriptures, the validity of which was accepted by the Nyāya-Vaiśeṣikas without any reservation. The method followed by

Udayana reveals the predominant role ascribed to the human reason and the subservient role given to the Vedic scriptures in man's intellectual quest after God.

Udayana's doctrine of God can be said to be the culmination of a process of development of about a millennium, a process marked by rational controversy with the opponents of theism, notably the Buddhists and the Mīmāṃsakas, in which strict logical accuracy went hand in hand with greater precision of ideas and depth of thought. Due, in large measure, to the excessive and almost exclusive importance attached to the problems of epistemology, the successors of Udayana did not make — at least as far as the content is concerned — any substantial contribution to the doctrine of God. Udayana's rational or natural theology thus represents the acme of perfection attained by the Nyāya-Vaiśeṣikas in their rational search for God.

Moreover, we can say that in studying the doctrine of God as developed and perfected by Udayana we study the Indian rational or natural theology in general. For the only philosophical system other than the Nyāya-Vaiśeṣika that admitted the existence of God and developed a doctrine of God is the Vedānta system. But the method of approach pursued by the Vedāntins, whether they belonged to the school of monism or dualism or any other of the diverse intermediary sub-schools of the Vedānta, distinguishes itself from that of the Nyāya-Vaiśeṣikas in that it was the second kind of approach we spoke of at the beginning, namely the theological or scriptural. Their arguments were primarily based on the authority of the scriptural texts, while rational arguments were relegated to a subordinate place. The Vedāntins went even to the extent of saying that neither the existence nor the nature or attributes of God could be known without the help of the sacred scriptures. Since they admit the intrinsic validity (*svataḥ prāmāṇyam*) of the Veda, independent of God, such an approach is also consistent with the doctrines of their school.

The present work is a modest attempt to give a brief introduction to the doctrine of God as found in Udayana's works in general, in his Nyāyakusumāñjali in particular. The writer's aim has been to give as faithful an interpretation of Udayana's ideas as possible in the given amount of space. How far he has succeeded in the realization of his aim should be left to the judgement of the critical reader. With a view to acquaint the reader with the manner of argumentation of the author of the Nyāyakusumāñjali, he has let Udayana himself speak by quoting him in translation wherever an important point was at issue.

This study was originally planned to be published as the introductory volume to an English translation of the Nyāyakusumāñjali. It is hoped that the publication of the translation of the Nyāyakusumāñjali will follow in the near future.

It gives me great pleasure to express my indebtedness and gratitude to those who have in one way or other helped me to bring my present work to completion. I am greatly indebted, first of all, to Prof. Dr. E. FRAUWALLNER, Professor emeritus in Indology at the University of Vienna who introduced me into the study of Indian philosophical texts and in whose seminars I had the happiness of taking part for more than three years. Even after I left Vienna he has shown great interest in my work and encouraged me to study Udayana.

To Prof. Dr. J. Gonda I owe a debt of gratitude not only for inviting me to join the staff of his institute in the University of Utrecht, but also for his active interest and constant encouragement in my work. Besides reading the manuscript of the present work, he took all the trouble of going through my translation of the entire Nyāyakusumāñjali and offered many suggestions for improvement.

I am indebted to Prof. Dr. G. Oberhammer of the University of Vienna for all the help he gave me during my stay in Vienna and afterwards for following my work with friendly interest. He went through the manuscript of this book offering valuable suggestions for improvement. My special thanks are due to him for including this book in the "Publications of the De Nobili Research Library" of which he is the editor.

I am very grateful to Prof. Dr. L. Schmithausen of the University of Münster and Dr. T. Vetter of Utrecht University for their valuable help in understanding some difficult passages of Udayana's text. I express my thanks to Dr. T. Goudriaan and Dr. K. R. van Kooy, both of the University of Utrecht, for their kind help in reading the proofs. My sincere thanks go also to the staff of the libraries of the Institute of Oriental Languages in Utrecht and of the University of Utrecht for their willing and ready services.

Despite my great interest in Udayana and his works, I have not found him an easy author. What will be presented in this book is but one aspect of the contribution of Udayana to Indian thought. If my modest contribution will incite an interest in the study of Udayana and his works I shall deem myself amply rewarded.

Utrecht
8 September 1972

George Chemparathy

LIST OF ABBREVIATIONS AND BIBLIOGRAPHY

I. General Abbreviations

ALB	The Adyar Library Bulletin
ASS	The Asutosh Sanskrit Series
BI	Bibliotheca Indica
BSS	Benares Sanskrit Series
ChSS	The Chowkhamba Sanskrit Series
CSS	The Calcutta Sanskrit Series
GOS	Gaekwad's Oriental Series
HIP	History of Indian Philosophy
IHQ	Indian Historical Quarterly
JGJRI	The Journal of the Ganganatha Jha Research Institute
JORM	The Journal of Oriental Research, Madras
MIS	Mithila Institute Series
PWSBS	The Princess of Wales Sarasvati Bhavana Studies
TSWS	The Tibetan Sanskrit Works Series
VIJ	Vishveshvaranand Indological Journal
WZKM	Wiener Zeitschrift für die Kunde des Morgenlandes
WZKSO	Wiener Zeitschrift für die Kunde Süd- und Ostasiens und Archiv für indische Philosophie

II. Texts and Translations

AP — Tārkikaśiromaṇi śrīmadvidyānandasvāmiviracitā āpta-parīk ṣāsvopajñāptaparīkṣālaṅkṛti-ṭīkāyutā. Ed. with Introduction and Hindi translation by Paṇḍita Darbarilal Jain. (Virasevamandir Series, No. 8) Saharanpur 1949.

ATV — The Ātmatattvaviveka of Śrī Udayanāchārya with the (Nārāyaṇī) commentary of Śrī Nārāyaṇāchārya Ātreya & the (Bauddhadhikāra) Dīdhiti Commentary of Śrī Raghunātha Śiromani, with Bauddhādhikāra Vivṛti of Śrī Gadādhara Bhaṭṭāchārya . . . Edited with Critical Introduction, Index & Exhaustive foot Notes by Pandit Dhundhirâja Śâstri. (ChSS, No. 84), Benares 1940

ATV_1 — Ātmatattvaviveka or Bauddhādhikāra by Udayanācārya, with the commentaries of Śaṅkara Miśra, Bhagīratha Ṭhakkura, Raghunātha Tārkika Śiromaṇi, Mathurānātha Tarkavāgīśa, etc. Edited by Vindhyeśvarī Prasāda Dvivedin (BI, No. 170), Calcutta 1907—1939.

ATV_2 — Ātmatattvavivekaḥ mahāmahopādhyāya śrīmad udayanācāryaviracitaḥ. . . . [śrīyuta vāvu rasamaya dattamahodayānām anujñayā . . .] śrīyuta jayanārāyaṇa tarkapañcānanaiḥ pariśodhitaḥ . . . śrīmadanamohana tarkālaṅkāraiḥ saṃskṛtaḥ. Calcutta Samvat 1906.

ATVK — Ātmatattvavivekakalpalatā. Commentary of Śaṅkaramiśra on ATV. See ATV_1.

BAUp. — Bṛhadāraṇyakopaniṣad. In: The Principal Upaniṣads edited with Introduction, text, translation and notes by S. Radhakrishnan. London 1953.

BCA — Bodhicaryāvatāra of Śāntideva with the Commentary Pañjikā of Prajñākaramati. Edited by P. L. Vaidya (Buddhist Sanskrit Texts, No. 12), Darbhanga 1960.

Bh. Gītā Śrīmad-Bhagavadgītā. Edited and translated by S. K. Belvalkar (Hindu Vishvavidyalaya Nepal Rajya Sanskrit Series, Vol. I), Varanasi (1959).

Bṛh Bṛhatī by Prabhākara Miśra with the Commentary the Ṛjuvimalā of Śālikanātha Miśra, ed. by Chinnaswami Sastri. (ChSS No. 391) Benares 1929.

BSuBh Brahmasūtrabhāṣyam (Śaṅkara): The Brahmasūtra-Shāṅkarabhāṣyam with the commentaries Ratnaprabhā, Bhāmatī and Nyāyanirṇaya ... ed. by Rāmchandra Shāstrī Dhupakar and Mahādeva Śāstrī Bākre. Bombay 1934.

ChUp. Chāndogya Upaniṣad. In: The Principal Upaniṣads, see BAUp.

JMN Jñānaśrīmitranibandhāvalī (Buddhist Philosophical Works of Jñānaśrīmitra) ed. by A. Thakur (TSWS Vol. 5), Patna 1959.

KhKhKh Khaṇḍanakhaṇḍakhādya. kavitātārkikacūḍāmaṇi — śrīharṣapraṇītam. paṇḍita-śrīcaṇḍīprasāda-sukula-viracitabhāṣānuvādayuktam. Ed. by Śrīkṛṣṇapantaśāstri and Govinda-Narahari-Vaijāpurakara. Kāśi Samvat 2018.

Kir Kiraṇāvali (Udayana): The Aphorisms of the Vaiśeshika Philosophy by Kaṇâda, with the commentary of Praśastapâda, and the gloss of Udayanâchârya. Ed. by Vindhyeśvarî Prasâda Dvivedî and Dhuṇḍhiraj Śâstri. (BSS No. 9), Benares 1919.

Kir_1 Kiraṇāvalī by Udayanācārya. With the commentary of Vardhamānopādhyāya. Part I: Ed. by Śiva Chandra Sārvabhouma. Part II: Ed. by Narendra Chandra Vedantatirtha (BI No. 200), Calcutta 1911—1956.

LM Lakṣaṇamālā of Udayanācārya. Ed. by Sri Sasinatha Jha (MIS, Ancient texts Series, No. 13) Darbhanga 1963.

LV Lakṣaṇāvalī of Udayanācārya with the Prakāśa of Bhaṭṭakeśava. Ed. by Sri Sasinatha Jha. MIS, Ancient Text No. 14) Darbhanga 1963.

Maitri Up. Maitri Upaniṣad. In: The Principal Upaniṣads, see BAUp.

Manu Manusmṛti with the commentary Manvarthamuktāvalī of Kullūka, tenth edition. Ed. with critical & explanatory notes etc. by Nārāyaṇ Rām Āchārya "Kavyatirtha". Bombay 1946.

Mbh Mahābhārata. The Mahābhārata critically ed. by V. S. Sukthankar, Poona 1933ff.

MSu Mīmāṃsāsūtram (Jaimini). See ŚBh.

Nar Nārāyaṇī. See ATV.

NBh Nyāyabhāṣyam (Vātsyāyana): Nyāyadarśanam with Vātsyāyana's Bhāṣya, Uddyotakara's Vārttika, Vācaspati Miśra's Tātparyaṭīka & Viśvanātha's Vṛtti. Critically ed. with notes by Taranatha Nyaya-Tarkatirtha and Amarendramohan Tarkatirtha. Vol. I and II. (CSS Nos. 18 and 29), Calcutta 1936—1944.

NBhu Nyāyabhūṣaṇam (Bhāsarvajña): śrīmadācāryabhāsarvajñapraṇītasya nyāyasārasya svopajñaṃ vyākhyānaṃ nyāyabhūṣaṇam. Ed. by Svāmī Yogīndrānandaḥ (ṣaḍdarśanaprakāśanagranthamālā, 1) Vārāṇasī 1968.

NKand Nyāyakandalī (Śrīdhara): Praśastapādabhāṣya (Padārthadharmasaṅgraha) with commentary Nyāyakandalī of Śrīdharabhaṭṭa along with Hindi translation. (Gaṅgānātha-Jhā-Granthamālā, Vol. 1), Varanasi 1963.

NKus Nyāyakusumāñjali (Udayana): The Nyāya Kusumāñjali of Śrī Udayanāchārya with four commentaries—the Bodhinī, Prakāśa,

Prakāśikā (Jalada) and Makaranda by Varadarāja, Vardhamānopādhyāya, Megha Thakkura and Ruchidattopādhyāya and notes by Śrī Dharmadatta (Bachchā Jhā). Ed. by Sri Padmaprasāda Upādhyāya & Sri Dhuṇḍhirāja Śāstri. With Foreword by Gopināth Kavirāj. (KSS No. 30) Varanasi 1957.

$NKus_1$ Nyāyakusumāñjali: Udayanācārya's Nyāyakusumāñjali with the commentaries of Śaṅkara Miśra and Guṇānanda Vidyāvāgīśa Parts I and II. Ed. by Narendrachandra Vedantatirtha. (ASS No. 4) Calcutta 1954—1964.

$NKus_2$ Nyāyakusumāñjali: The Nyaya-Kusumanjali Prakaranam by Udayanāchārya. Parts I and II. Ed. by Chandrakānta Tarkalankar. (BI No. 123), Calcutta 1891—1895.

$NKus_3$ The Kusumánjali, or Hindu proof for the existence of a Supreme Being, by Udayana Ácharya, with the commentary of Hari Dása Bhaṭṭácharya, edited and translated by E. B. Cowell, assisted by Paṇḍita Maheśa Chandra Nyáyaratna. Calcutta 1864.

$NKus_4$ Nyāya Kusumāñjali (English Translation). PWSBS, ed. by Gaṅgā Nātha Jha and Gopī Nātha Kavirāja, Vol. 2. Benares 1923, pp. 159—191.

$NKus_5$ The Nyāyakusumāñjali of Udayanācārya. (A presentation of theistic doctrines according to the Nyāya System of philosophy). Translated into English by Swami Ravi Tirtha. Vol. I—Books i and ii. (The Adyar Library Series, No. 53), Adyar 1946.

NKusAm Nyāyakusumāñjalyāmoda. (Śaṅkaramiśra): See $NKus_1$.

NKusBo Nyāyakusumāñjalobodhanī (Varadarāja): See NKus.

NKusPr Nyāyakusumāñjaliprakāśa (Vardhamāna): See NKus.

NKusVi Nyāyakusumāñjaliviveka (Guṇānanda): See $NKus_1$.

NKusVy Kusumāñjalikārikāvyākhyā: Kusumāñjalikārikā of Udayanācārya with the commentary Kusumāñjalikārikāvyākhyā of Rāmabhadra Sārvabhauma and Sanskrit notes compiled by Chandidasa Nyaya-Tarkatirtha, ed. by Narendrachandra Vedantatirtha. (ASS No. 2) Calcutta 1944.

NM I Nyāyamañjarī, Part I: The Nyāyamañjarī of Jayanta Bhaṭṭa. Ed. with notes etc. by Śrī Sūrya Nârâyana Śukla. (KSS No. 106) Benares 1936.

NP Nyāyapariśista: Udayanācārya's Nyāyapariśiṣṭam with Vardhamāna Upādhyāya's Commentary Prākaśa. Critically ed. . . . by Narendra Chandra Vedantatirtha. (CSS No. 22), Calcutta 1938.

NR Nyāyaratnākara (Pārthasārathimiśra): See ŚV.

NSa Nyāyasāra (Bhāsarvajña): See NBhu.

NSu Nyāyasūtram. (Gautama): See NBh.

NV Nyāyavārttika (Uddyotakara): See NBh.

NVTP Nyāyavārttikatātparyapariśuddhi: Nyāya-Vārttika-Tātparya-Pariśuddhi by Udayanāchārya with a gloss called Nyāya-nibandhaprakāśa by Vardhamanopadhyaya. Ed. by Pandit Vindhyeśvarī Prasād Dvivedin and Pandit Lakshmana Sāstri Drāviḍa. (BI No. 205), fasc. I—VIII. Calcutta 1911—1924 (incomplete).

NVTT Nyāyavārtikatātparyaṭīkā (Vācaspatimiśra): See NBh.

PDhS Padārthadharmasaṃgraha (Praśastapāda): See Kir.

PrP Prakaraṇapañcikā of Sri Śālikanātha Miśra with Nyāya-Siddhi. Ed. with Introduction and Notes by Pt. A. Subrahmanya Sastri. (Benares Hindu University Darśana Series, No. 4) Benares 1961.

PV Pramāṇavārttikam (Dharmakīrti): Pramāṇavārtikabhāshyam or Vārtikālaṅkāraḥ of Prajñākaragupta (Being a commentary on Dharmakīrti's Pramāṇavārtikam) Deciphered and ed. by Rāhula Sāṅkṛtyāyana. (TSWS, Vol. I), Patna 1953.

RKN Ratnakīrtinibandhāvalī (Buddhist Nyāya Works of Ratnakīrti). Deciphered and ed. by Anantalal Thakur. (TSWS Vol. 3), Patna 1957.

ṚP Ṛjuvimalapañcikā (Śālikanātha): See Bṛh.

ṚV (Ṛgveda): Hymns of the Rig-Veda in the Samhita and Pada Texts. Reprinted from the editio princeps by F. Max Müller. Third edition. In 2 volumes. (KSS, No. 167), Varanasi 1965.

ŚBh Śabarabhāṣya (Śabara): The Aphorisms of the Mīmāṃsa by Jaimini with the commentary of Śavara-Svāmin ed. by Paṇḍita Maheśachandra Nyāyaratna. Vols. I and II (BI No. 45) Calcutta 1873—1889.

ŚD Śāstradīpikā (Pārthasārathimiśra): Sastra Dipika of Pârtha Sarathi Misra, with the commentary called Yuktisneha Prapûrani by Pt. Rama Krishna Misra. Ed. by Pt. Laxman Shastri Dravid. (ChSS No. 188—190, 225, 226), Benares 1916.

SDS Sarvadarśanasaṃgraha: Sarva-darśana-Saṃgraha of Sāyana Mādhava ed. with an original commentary in Sanskrit by Vasudev Shastri Abhyankar. Second edition (Government Oriental Series, Class A. No. 1), Poona 1951.

STK Sāṃkhyatattvakaumudī: The Tattva-Kaumudī (Vācaspati Miśra's Commentary on the Sāṃkhya-Kārikā). Ed. with English translation ... by Ganganatha Jha and ... Har Dutt Sharma. (Poona Oriental Series No. 10). Poona 1934.

ŚV Ślokavārtika: The Mîmânsâ-Sloka-Vârtika of Kumârila Bhatta. With the commentary called Nyâyaratnâkara by Pârtha Sârathi Miśra. Ed. by Râma Sâstri Tailaṅga (ChSS No. 3), Benares 1898.

TC Tattvacintāmaṇi: The Tattva-chintāmaṇi by Gangeśa Upadhyāya. Part II, Anumāna Khaṇḍa Vol. II. Īçvarānumāna. With the commentary of Jayadeva Miçra, ed. by Paṇḍit Kāmākhyā—Nātha Tarka-vāgiśa. (BI 98, 3), Calcutta 1897.

TS Tattvasaṅgraha of Ācārya Shāntarakṣita with the commentary 'Pañjikā' of Shrī Kamalashīla, critically ed. by Swami Dwarikadas Shastri. In two volumes. (Bauddha Bhārati Series, 1 and 2), Varanasi 1968.

TSP Tattvasaṃgrahapañjikā (Kamalaśīla): See TS.

VSu Vaiśeṣikasūtra of Kaṇāda with the commentary of Candrānanda. Critically ed. by Muni Śrī Jambuvijayaji. (GOS No. 136), Baroda 1961.

YBh Yogabhāṣya (Vyāsa): Patañjala-Yogasūtra-Bhāṣya Vivaraṇam of Śaṅkara-Bhagavatpāda. Critically ed. by Polakam Sri Rama Sastri and S. R. Krishnamurthi Sastri. (Madras Government Oriental Series No. 94), Madras 1952.

YD Yuktidīpikā. An ancient Commentary on the Sāṃkhya-Kārikā of Īśvarakṛṣṇa. Ed. by Ram Chandra Pandeya, Delhi 1967.

YSu Yogasūtram (Patañjali): See YBh.

III. Secondary Literature

BHATTACHARYA, D. C.: Date of Vācaspati Miśra and Udayanācārya. JGJRI, 2 (1945), pp. 349—356.

— Śrīvatsācārya, a long-forgotten Naiyāyika. IHQ, 22 (1946), pp. 152—154.

— Udayanācārya and Śrīharṣa. Siddha—Bhāratī or The Rosary of Indology ... in honour of the 60th Birthday of Dr. Siddheshwar Varma, ed. by Vishva Bandhu, Part II, Hoshiarpur 1950, pp. 138—143.

— History of Navya-Nyāya in Mithila MIS, No. 3, Studies No. 2), Darbhanga 1958 = HNNM.

— Tvantopādhyāya. (A long-lost name in the history of Navyanyāya.) JGJRI, 5 (1947), pp. 13—22.

Chemparathy, G.: The testimony of the Yuktidīpikā concerning the Īśvara doctrine of the Pāśupatas and Vaiśeṣikas. WZKSO, 9 (1965), pp. 119—146.

— The Īśvara doctrine of Praśastapāda. VIJ, 6 (1968), pp. 65—87.

— Two little-known fragments from early Vaiśeṣika literature on the omniscience of Īśvara. ALB, 33 (1969), pp. 117—134.

— Two early Buddhist refutations of the existence of the Īśvara as the creator of the universe. WZKSO, 12—13 (1968/1969) (Beiträge zur Geistesgeschichte Indiens. Festschrift für Erich Frauwallner, herausgegeben von G. Oberhammer), pp. 85—100.

Evans, D. D.: The logic of Self-involvement. A philosophical study of everyday language with special reference to the Christian use of language about God as Creator. London 1963.

Faddegon, B.: The Vaiçesika-System, described with the help of the oldest texts. (Verhandelingen der Koninklijke Akademie van Wetenschappen te Amsterdam, Afdeeling Letterkunde, Nieuwe reeks, Deel XVIII, No. 2), Amsterdam 1918.

Frauwallner, E.: Beiträge zur Geschichte des Nyāya. I. Jayanta und seine Quellen. WZKM, 43 (1936), pp. 263—278.

— Jñānaśrī. WZKM, 38 (1932), pp. 229—234.

— Beiträge zur Geschichte des Nyāya. I. Jayanta und seine Quellen. WZKM, 43 (1936), pp. 263—278.

— Zu den buddhistischen Texten in der Zeit Khri-sron-lde-btsan's. WZKSO, 1 (1957), pp. 95—103.

— Landmarks in the History of Indian Logic. WZKSO, 5 (1961), pp. 125—148.

— Geschichte der indischen Philosophie, Vol. II, Salzburg 1962 = Geschichte II.

Gonda, J.: Die Religionen Indiens. II. Der jüngere Hinduismus (Die Religionen der Menschheit, herausgegeben von C. M. Schröder, Vol. 12) Stuttgart 1963.

— Change and Continuity in Indian Religion. (Disputationes Rheno-Trajectinae, ed. by J. Gonda, Vol. 9), The Hague 1965.

— The Concept of a personal God in ancient Indian Religious Thought. Studia Missionalia, Vol. 17, Rome 1968, pp. 111—136.

— Āyatana. ALB, 33 (1969), pp. 1—79.

— Aspects of Early Viṣṇuism. Utrecht 1954.

— Viṣṇuism and Śivaism. A Comparison. (Jordan Lectures in Comparative Religion, IX), London 1970.

Hall, F. E.: A Contribution Towards an Index to the Bibliography of the Indian Philosophical Systems. Calcutta 1859.

Hacker, P.: Untersuchungen über Texte des frühen Advaitavāda. 1. Die Schüler Śaṅkaras. Akademie der Wissenschaften und der Literatur (Mainz). Abhandlungen der geistes- und sozialwissenschaftlichen Klasse, Jahrgang 1950, No. 26.

— Jayanta Bhaṭṭa und Vācaspatimiśra, ihre Zeit und ihre Bedeutung für die Chronologie des Vedānta. In: Beiträge zur indischen Philologie und Altertumskunde, Walther Schubring zum 70. Geburtstag. Alt- und Neu-Indische Studien, Vol. 7. Hamburg 1951, pp. 160—169.

HIRIYANNA, M.: Outlines of Indian Philosophy. London 1964.

INGALLS, D. H. H.: Materials for the Study of Navya-Nyāya Logic. (Harvard Oriental Series, Vol. 40), Cambridge/Massachussetts 1951.

JACOBI, H.: Die Entwicklung der Gottesidee bei den Indern und deren Beweise für das Dasein Gottes. Bonn und Leipzig 1923 = Gottesidee.

JHA, K. N.: Nyāyakusumāñjalau prācīnācāryaprabhāvaḥ. Ṛtam. Journal of Akhila Bharatiya Sanskrit Parishad, 1 (Lucknow 1969), pp. 1—9.

JOSHI, L.: Studies in the Buddhistic Culture of India. Delhi 1967.

KANE, P. V.: History of Dharmaśāstra, Vol. V, Part II (Government Oriental Series, Class B, No. 6), Poona 1962.

KAVIRAJ, G. N.: Gleanings from the History and Bibliography of the Nyāya-Vaiśeṣika Literature. (Reprint: Indian Studies Past & Present), Calcutta 1961 = Gleanings.

KEITH, A. B.: The Karma-Mīmāṃsā. (The Heritage of India Series), Calcutta 1921.

KIRFEL, W.: Die Kosmographie der Inder. Bonn und Leipzig 1920.

MISHRA, U.: History of Indian Philosophy, Vol. II, Allahabad 1966 = HIP II.

MOOKERJEE, S.: Nyāya-Vaiśeṣika, The Cultural Heritage of India. Ed. by H. Bhattacharyya, Vol. III. The Philosophies, Calcutta ²1953, pp. 91—124.

NIERMANN, E.: Article on 'Providence', Sacramentum Mundi. An Encyclopedia of Theology, ed. by K. Rahner and others. Vol. 5, London 1970, pp. 130—133.

OBERHAMMER, G.: On the Sources of Jayanta Bhaṭṭa and Uddyotakara, WZKSO, 6 (1962), pp. 91—150.

— Der Svābhāvika-Sambandha, ein geschichtlicher Beitrag zur Nyāya-Logik, WZKSO, 8 (1964), pp. 131—181.

— Zum Problem des Gottesbeweises in der indischen Philosophie, Numen. International review for the History of Religions, 12 (1965), pp. 1—34.

RADHAKRISHNAN, E. P.: A rare commentary on Nyāyakusumāñjali. Poona Orientalist, 4 (1940), pp. 170—173.

RADHAKRISHNAN, S.: Indian Philosophy, Vol. II (The Muirhead Library of Philosophy), second edition, London 1931, reprint 1951.

RAJA, K.: Indian Theories of Meaning (The Adyar Library Series, Vol. 91), Adyar 1963.

RENOU, L.: Religions of Ancient India. London 1953.

SASTRI, S. KUPPUSWAMI: A Primer of Indian Logic. Madras ³1961.

SCHMITHAUSEN, L.: Der Nirvāṇa-Abschnitt in der Viniścayasaṃgrahaṇī der Yogācārabhūmiḥ. (Österreichische Akademie der Wissenschaften, philosophisch-historische Klasse, Sitzungsberichte 264. Band, 2. Abhandlung. Veröffentlichungen der Kommission für Sprachen und Kulturen Süd- und Ostasiens, Heft 8), Wien 1969.

SHASTRI, D. N.: Critique of Indian Realism. A Study of the Conflict between the Nyāya-Vaiśeṣika and the Buddhist Dignāga School. Agra 1964.

SRINIVASAN, S. A.: Vācaspatimiśras Tattvakaumudī. Ein Beitrag zur Textkritik bei kontaminierter Überlieferung (Alt- und Neu-Indische Studien, herausgegeben vom Seminar für Kultur und Geschichte Indiens an der Universität Hamburg, 12), Hamburg 1967.

STEINKELLNER, E.: Die Literatur des älteren Nyāya. WZKSO, 5 (1961), pp. 149—162.

STRAUSS, O.: Indische Philosophie (Geschichte der Philosophie in Einzeldarstellungen, Vol. 2), München 1925.

SUALI, L.: Introduzione allo studio della filosofia indiana. Pavia 1913.

THAKUR, A.: Some Lost Nyāya Works and Authors. Proceedings and Transactions of the All Indian Oriental Conference, 17th Session, Ahmedabad, October—November 1953, pp. 385—394.

TUCCI, G.: Storia della filosofia indiana. Bari 1957.

TUXEN, P. and S. KONOW: Religions of India. Copenhagen 1949.

VETTER, T.: Erkenntnisprobleme bei Dharmakīrti. (Österreichische Akademie der Wissenschaften, philosophisch-historische Klasse, Sitzungsberichte 245. Band, 2. Abhandlung) Wien 1964.

WINTERNITZ, M.: Geschichte der indischen Literatur. Vol. I and III. Reprint Stuttgart 1968.

PART ONE

THE AUTHOR AND THE WORK

Chapter One

UDAYANA

1. Place of Birth and Date

Udayana, the illustrious exponent of the Nyāya-Vaiśeṣika philosophy, is rightly numbered by scholars among the great Indian thinkers of all times. Although he wrote several works, he is specially remembered for his two works, the Ātmatattvaviveka and the Nyāyakusumāñjali. As in the case of most of the earlier Indian philosophers, the details of his life are unknown, and the little that we know of him is either uncertain or borders on the legendary[1].

Scholars were for a time divided in their opinion as to the place where Udayana was born and lived. It is now commonly believed that he was a Maithilī[2]. On the basis of some hitherto unpublished portions of the Nyāyavārttikatātparyapariśuddhi D. C. Bhattacharya maintains that Śrīvatsa was the teacher of Udayana[3].

The controversy[4] about Udayana's lifetime seemed to have been settled by the discovery of the Lakṣaṇāvalī, the concluding verse of which states that it was written in Śāka era 906 (= 984—985 A. D.)[5].

D. C. Bhattacharya, however, has put forward a new date. His main arguments can be thus summarized: The date of the composition of the Nyāyasūcīnibandha of Vācaspati given in its concluding verse as *vasvaṅkavasuvatsare,* and interpreted hitherto by scholars as referring to the Vikrama era, should be taken as referring to the Śāka year 898 (= 976—977 A. D.). Hence Vācaspati should be placed, at the earliest, in the early part of the tenth century. On the other hand, the date of the composition of the Lakṣaṇāvalī of Udayana, given in the manuscript as well as in the printed editions as

[1] For two of these legends cf. D. C. Bhattacharya: HNNM, pp. 5—7 and A. Thakur's English Introduction to his edition of JMN, pp. 32—33. One of them is referred to below p. 28.

[2] Cf. U. Mishra: HIP, II, pp. 150ff.; D. C. Bhattacharya: HNNM, p. 5.

[3] Cf. D. C. Bhattacharya: HNNM, pp. 20—22; idem: Śrīvatsācārya, a long-forgotten Naiyāyika, pp. 152ff.; U. Mishra: HIP II, p. 145.

[4] Fitzedward Hall: A Contribution Towards and Index to the Bibliography of the Indian Philosophical Systems, p. 20 and E. B. Cowell: The Kusumánjali, p. X.

[5] This verse runs:

tarkāmbarāṅkapramiteṣv atīteṣu śakāntataḥ
varṣeṣūdayanaś cakre subodhām lakṣaṇāvalīm /
vidyāsandhyodayodrekādavidyārajanīkṣaye
yad udeti namas tasmai kasmaicid viśvatas tviṣe //

Śāka year *tarkāṃbaraṅka* (906 = 984—985 A. D.) and accepted hitherto as such by the scholars, is probably a scribal error for Śāka year *tarkasvaraṅka* (976 = 1054—1055 A. D.). Such a new interpretation of the dates is necessary in order to exclude "the close contemporaneity of Udayana and Vācaspati". Moreover the fact that there is a Bengali manuscript of the Lakṣaṇāvalī which does not contain the verse under discussion, raises the question of its very authenticity. With regard to the relative chronology of Śrīdhara and Udayana, BHATTACHARYA maintains that the author of the Kiraṇāvalī consulted the Nyāyakandalī which, according to its concluding verse, was composed in the Śāka year 913 (= 991—992 A. D.) and hence he should be dated a generation later. Studying the relative chronology of Udayana with that of the Buddhist author Jñānaśrī mentioned explicitly by name in the Ātmatattvaviveka and the Nyāyavārttikatātparyapariśuddhi, BHATTACHARYA maintains that, since the literary activity of Jñānaśrī continued up to about 1025 A. D., "Udayana could not have written any of his works before, say 1040 A. D.". Finally, according to BHATTACHARYA, the Vedāntic writer Śrīharṣa cannot be placed earlier than 1075 A. D. and must have written his works in the years 1125—1150 A. D. Since Udayana is believed to have challenged and defeated in philosophic controversy Śrīhīra, the father of Śrīharṣa, "he was removed only by a generation from the times of Śrīharṣa". On the basis of the above considerations BHATTACHARYA concludes that the date of composition of the Lakṣaṇāvalī, given as Śāka year 906, should be rejected and that "Udayana's period of activity might be placed in the second half (1050—1100 A. D.) of the 11th century A. D."[6].

Briefly, although BHATTACHARYA's arguments will serve as a good incentive for further inquiry into the date of Udayana, they are not sufficiently convincing, since they are based on rather unsure grounds. Whether the date of the Nyāyasūcīnibandha is to be interpreted as Śāka or Vikrama era is still a moot point among scholars[7]. Even granting that it should be taken as Śāka era (= 976—977 A. D.), there is the further question whether the date of the composition of the Lakṣaṇāvalī, and consequently the date of Udayana, require to be modified on that account. The fact that a Bengali manuscript of the Lakṣaṇāvalī does not contain this verse and that the verse in question is not commented upon by the author of the Nyāyamuktāvalī is not sufficient ground for repudiating this verse as unauthentic. In fact, as BHATTACHARYA himself points out in one place, all the manuscripts of the work should be carefully examined in order to find out the exact reading of the date in which

---

[6] I have picked out here only the more important points in the arguments of the author from his following publications: Date of Vācaspati Miśra and Udayanācārya, pp. 349—356; Udayanācārya and Śrīharṣa, pp. 138—143; HNNM, pp. 25—54.

[7] Cf. E. STEINKELLNER: Die Literatur des älteren Nyāya, pp. 157—158. See also P. HACKER: Jayantabhaṭṭa und Vācaspatimiśra, ihre Zeit und ihre Bedeutung für die Chronologie des Vedānta, pp. 160—169, and S. A. SRINIVASAN: Vācaspati Miśras Tattvakaumudī, pp. 54—63 both of whom defend the view that the year of the composition of the Nyāyasūcīnibandha is to be taken as Śāka era.

it is said to have been composed. Only a close study of all the manuscripts of the Lakṣaṇāvalī will allow one to decide whether the verse in question is authentic or not[8]. A modification of the reading *tarkāṃbaraṅka* into *tarkasvaraṅka* cannot be justified unless there are more serious reasons than that of excluding "the close contemporaneity of Udayana and Vācaspati". For, theoretically speaking, is it not possible to assume that the Nyāyasūcīnibandha belongs to Vācaspati's advanced age—in fact, since the Nyāyasūcīnibandha is not mentioned in nor mentions any other work of Vācaspati, there is no objection to its being considered as one of his later works—and that the Lakṣaṇāvalī is, as usually maintained by the scholars, Udayana's earliest work or at least one of his earliest works? Similarly, even if it is true that Udayana refers in his Kiraṇāvalī to the views of Śrīdhara, does it necessarily require a modification of the date of Udayana? For, being his last work (or, one of his last works), the Kiraṇāvalī could have been composed some years after the Nyāyakandalī, and there is no need to place Udayana's period of activity to the second half of the eleventh century in order to account for his referring to the views of Śrīdhara. In the same manner, BHATTACHARYA's conclusion of the date of Udayana from that of Śrīharṣa's father, Śrīhīra, with whom he is said to have had a philosophical contest does not carry conviction, since it is based on uncertain or, in any case, disputed premisses. Finally, the date of Jñānaśrī in relation to whom the author calculates Udayana's date is also debated by scholars[9].

Since there is thus some uncertainty as regards the arguments proposed by BHATTACHARYA, it seems to me better to adhere to the earlier view of those scholars who accepted the date given in the verse of the Lakṣaṇāvalī as authentic, until the unauthenticity of that verse or the incorrectness of the reading *tarkāṃbaraṅka* is established beyond doubt. Hence we might assume that Udayana wrote the Lakṣaṇāvalī as his first work (or one of his earliest works) in Śāka year 906 (= 984—985 A. D.) and that his more important works were written in the first half of the eleventh century[10].

---

[8] The authenticity or otherwise of the verse in question can be decided only after examining the nature of the manuscripts of the LV. The details known to me hitherto from publications are somewhat ambiguous. D. C. BHATTACHARYA says in one place that "the verse recording this date [i. e. of the composition of the LV] is not found in a Bengali Ms of 1621 Ś. belonging to the Cal. Sans. College Descr. Cat., (pp. 260—1) and is neither presupposed in the Nyāyamuktāvalī commentary" (cf. Date of Vācaspati Miśra and Udayanācārya, p. 353). In another place he observes that LV's "date of composition 906 Śaka (*tarkāmbarāṅka*) is recorded in one single Ms. dated 1708 Samvat (No. 594 of Sarasvati Bhavana)" (HNNM, p. 2).

[9] To mention the view of a few scholars, E. FRAUWALLNER thinks that Jñānaśrī must have lived in the first half of the tenth century (cf. his article: Jñānaśrī, pp. 232—233). L. JOSHI assigns to him (as teacher of Yamāri who lived between ca. 800—900 A. D.) a date too early to be acceptable (cf. his book: Studies in the Buddhist Culture of India, pp. 200 and 203). A. THAKUR places him in the first half of the eleventh century (cf. JMN, Introduction in English, pp. 1—3).

[10] It is on set purpose that I have abstained from a more approximate determination of the date of Udayana. The research which I have hitherto made on

2. The Works of Udayana

There is general agreement among scholars as to the number and the names of the works of Udayana. The only work concerning which there was some divergence of opinion in the past is the Lakṣaṇamālā[11], but now the problem of its authorship seems to be settled beyond doubt.

Seven works have been ascribed to Udayana. Two of them, the Lakṣaṇamālā and the Lakṣaṇāvalī, are short introductory manuals of the Nyāya and Vaiśeṣika systems. Three of his works are commentaries on the most important works of the same systems: the Nyāyavārttikatātparyapariśuddhi is a commentary on the Nyāyavārttikatātparyaṭīkā of Vācaspati; the Kiraṇāvalī comments on the Padārthadharmasaṃgraha of Praśastapāda and the Nyāyapariśiṣṭa is a commentary on the last chapter of the Nyāyasūtras. The remaining two works, the Ātmatattvaviveka and the Nyāyakusumāñjali, are independent treatises, or monographs as we would now call them.

Usually Udayana refers in his works to his previous treatises. From this fact one can conclude that the work mentioned is prior to the one which mentions it. This criterion has been followed in determining the chronological order of Udayana's works.

Unfortunately it cannot be applied to the two small introductory manuals, Lakṣaṇamālā and Lakṣaṇāvalī, as they neither mention, nor are themselves mentioned in any other work of Udayana. It is very probable that they were his earliest compositions. We have also no criterion to decide which of these two works was written first.

The chonological order of his other works can be determined with great probability. While the Ātmatattvaviveka does not mention any other work of Udayana, it is itself mentioned in the Nyāyakusumāñjali[12], the Nyāyavārttikatātparyapariśuddhi[13] and the Kiraṇāvalī[14], and hence it must have been written prior to these. The Nyāyakusumāñjali mentions only the Ātmatattvaviveka, but is itself mentioned in the Nyāyavārttikatātparyapariśuddhi[15] and the Kiraṇāvalī[16]. Consequently it was written after the Ātmatattvaviveka but before the Nyāyavārttikatātparyapariśuddhi and the Kiraṇāvalī. The chronological order of the Nyāyapariśiṣṭa is less certain;

---

this point raised so many problems that I thought it advisable to carry on further study before making a more definite statement about it. After that I hope to publish a paper on the problems regarding the date of Udayana and my own approach to solve them.

[11] Gopinath Kaviraj believed that the LM was the work of Śivāditya and that the ascription of that work to Udayana by Mallinātha was erroneous. Cf. Gleanings p. 22, footnote 49.

[12] NKus 502, 5.

[13] Mentioned in the unpublished part of the NVTP according to D. C. Bhattacharya: HNNM, p. 4.

[14] Kir 103, 8—9; 147, 22—23.

[15] Mentioned in the unpublished part of the NVTP according to D. C. Bhattacharya: HNNM, p. 4.

[16] Kir 103, 8; 147, 23.

for, though it is mentioned in the Nyāyavārttikatātparyapariśuddhi[17], it mentions no other works. Thus we can say that it was certainly composed before the Nyāyavārttikatātparyapariśuddhi. Since it is not mentioned in the Ātmatattvaviveka or the Nyāyakusumāñjali, we may assume that it was composed after these two works[18]. The Nyāyavārttikatātparyapariśuddhi mentions the Ātmatattvaviveka, the Nyāyakusumāñjali and the Nyāyapariśiṣṭa[19], and hence it must have been written after them; it is itself mentioned in no other work of Udayana. However, it is the Kiraṇāvalī which is generally accepted to have been his last work. Since it mentions the Ātmatattvaviveka and the Nyāyakusumāñjali, it must have been written after them. That it comes after the Nyāyavārttikatātparyapariśuddhi is probable; for, though the Nyāyavārttikatātparyapariśuddhi and the Kiraṇāvalī do not mention each other and are not mentioned in any other work of Udayana, yet the fact that complete manuscripts of only the Nyāyavārttikatātparyapariśuddhi have been found, favours the conclusion that the Kiraṇāvalī was his last work and that probably death prevented him from completing it.

Thus the probable chronological order of Udayana's works is as follows: Lakṣaṇamālā, Lakṣaṇāvalī, Ātmatattvaviveka, Nyāyakusumāñjali, Nyāyapariśiṣṭa, Nyāyavārttikatātparyapariśuddhi and Kiraṇāvalī. Interesting to note in this list is the fact that the two independent treatises, the Ātmatattvaviveka and the Nyāyakusumāñjali, were composed before the commentaries.

The Lakṣaṇamālā of Udayana is a short manual giving very clear definitions and the main divisions of the sixteen categories of the Nyāya and the six categories of the Vaiśeṣika system. The treatment of the Vaiśeṣika categories is inserted into the treatment of the Nyāya categories, namely after the category "object of cognition" (*prameyam*) which is the second in the Nyāya enumeration of categories.

The second manual, the Lakṣaṇāvalī, resembles the Lakṣaṇamālā in form, purpose and method of treatment. It differs from the latter in that it deals exclusively with the Vaiśeṣika categories and their subdivisions, representing reality as existent (*bhāvaḥ*) as well as non-existent (*abhāvaḥ*). A comparison of this work with the Lakṣaṇamālā shows that the treatment of the Vaiśeṣika categories here is not a mere reproduction of what is found in the Lakṣaṇamālā.

The Ātmatattvaviveka, also called Bauddhādhikāra or Bauddhadhikkāra, is an independent treatise (*prakaraṇaṃ*) consisting of four chapters of varying

---

[17] Cf. D. C. Bhattacharya: HNNM, p. 4.

[18] It should, however, be pointed out that the NP deals only with the last chapter of the Nyāyasūtras which, though interesting from the point of view of logic, do not offer much opportunity to be referred to in the other works of Udayana except perhaps the LM and the NVTP, and hence silence about this work in the author's other works cannot serve as a reliable guide in determining its relative chronology.

[19] The mention of these three works is found, according to D. C. Bhattacharya (HNNM, p. 4), in the unpublished part of the NVTP.

lengths. At the beginning of this work the author brings forward four theories of the opponents that aim at establishing the non-existence of a permanent soul (*ātmā*) such as conceived by the Nyāya-Vaiśeṣikas: 1) the theory of *kṣaṇabhaṅgaḥ* holds that whatever exists, exists only for a moment, 2) the theory of *bāhyārthabhaṅgaḥ* states no reality exists outside the act of cognition, 3) the theory of *guṇaguṇibhedabhaṅgaḥ* puts forward that there is no distinction between quality (*guṇaḥ*) and its subject (*guṇī*) and that consequently there is no soul distinct from cognition, 4) the theory of *anupalaṃbhaḥ* asserts that what is not perceived, does not exist, and since the soul is not perceived, it should be assumed to be non-existent. Each of these theories forms the subject-matter of the four respective chapters. After refuting these theories, Udayana establishes in the fourth chapter, by means of a number of arguments, the existence of permanent (*sthira-*), eternal (*nitya-*) and omnipresent (*vibhu-*) souls, distinct from the body. The reference to the sacred scriptures as an authority to show that the soul cannot be destroyed, and that knowledge of the soul as distinct from the body leads to the *summum bonum* gives Udayana an occasion to discuss and vindicate the authoritativeness of the sacred scriptures on the ground that they have a reliable (*āpta-*) author, namely Īśvara. In this connection Udayana gives a rather elaborate treatment of the Īśvara doctrine where he not only establishes his existence as the omniscient creator of the universe, but also as the author of the sacred scriptures, who is full of compassion towards the living beings. At the same time he rejects the theory of the eternity of the Veda as taught by the Mīmāṃsakas and the authoritativeness of the Buddhist scriptures, and establishes that the Veda alone is authoritative, since Īśvara is the author of that alone. A brief discussion on the nature of liberation (*mokṣaḥ*) which is the ultimate end of the soul brings this discussion to a close.

The Nyāyakusumāñjali is perhaps the best—in any case, the most famous—among the works of Udayana. We shall speak of this in detail in the next chapter.

The Nyāyapariśiṣṭa, also known as Prabodhasiddhi or Bodhasiddhi, deals exclusively with the Jātis and Nigrahasthānas[20], which form the subject-matter of the fifth chapter of the Nyāyasūtras.

The Nyāyavārttikatātparyapariśuddhi, also known as Nibandha or more often by the simple name of Pariśuddhi, is an elaborate commentary on the Nyāyavārttikatātparyaṭīkā of Vācaspatimiśra. Only a small portion of the text, extending up to the commentary on the first four Sūtras and on a part of the fifth Sūtra of the first chapter of the Nyāyasūtras, has been hitherto published. However, the manuscript of the complete text has been discovered and is expected to be published in the near future[21]. According to the informa-

[20] Jāti is a false objection to an argument through a wrong application of the similarity and dissimilarity of the example and the subject of the argument. Cf. NSu I, 2, 18. Nigrahasthāna consists in wrong understanding or not understanding of the nature of the object under discussion. Cf. NSu I, 2, 19.

[21] Cf. LV edited by SASINATHA JHA, Introduction by A. THAKUR, p. ii. The complete NVTP is planned to be published in the Mithila Institute Series, along

tion given by UMESHA MISHRA, the chapters of the Nyāyavārttikatātparyapariśuddhi are of varying length. The first chapter is not only the longest, but also considerably longer than the second, while the succeeding chapters are much shorter, each shorter than the preceding one[22].

The Kiraṇāvalī, which is believed to be the last work of Udayana, is a commentary on the Padārthadharmasaṃgraha of Praśastapāda. The portion of the text hitherto published ends with the commentary on a part of the section on *buddhiḥ*. Another portion of the manuscript of the Kiraṇāvalī has been discovered recently and is awaiting publication[23].

It may be pointed out here that, even in his commentaries, Udayana brings substantial contributions of his own on the problem discussed. This is especially true of the Kiraṇāvalī where the author gives his own views, sometimes in great detail, in several excurses.

3. ESTIMATE OF UDAYANA

Scholars are almost unanimous in declaring Udayana to be one of the greatest of Indian philosophers[24]. In the Nyāya-Vaiśeṣika school itself, to which he belongs, he occupies a singular position of authority and renown. Flourishing at the period of transition from the Older Nyāya to the New (Navya-Nyāya), he shines as an unrivalled master of the former and an inspiring herald of the latter. His importance in the history of Nyāya-Vaiśeṣika can be gauged by the attitude towards him of later writers, from his own school as well as from other schools. While he became for his own school a recognized authority who is often referred to by the mere title of Ācārya[25],

---

with NSu, NBh, NV and NVTT. After the manuscript of the present book was sent to the editor, I came to know of the publication of the first volume of the edition containing the NVTP up to the end of the first Adhāya in the MIS, Ancient Text No. 20, Darbhanga 1967.

[22] Cf. U. MISHRA: HIP, II, pp. 199—200.

[23] In his Introduction to SASINATHA JHA's edition of the LV (p. ii, Note 1) A. THAKUR informs us that J. S. JETLEY is preparing an edition of the Kir which will include a newly discovered portion of the work. Similarly D. C. BHATTACHARYA says in his HNNM (p. 4, footnote 1) that a further portion of the Kir has been recently discovered and is being edited by MUNI SRI JAMBUVIJAYAJI. How far the newly discovered portion of the Kir extends is not yet known to me.

[24] GOPINATH KAVIRAJ writes: "... Udayana, according to the unanimous verdict of all ancient and modern scholars, was one of the deepest, most learned, abstruse and authoritative of Indian Philosophers. His position in the history of Indian Philosophy is *as a specialist* (in Nyāya-Vaiśeṣika) certainly higher than that of Vāchaspati Miśra. His Ātmatattvaviveka, Nyāya Kusumāñjali, Kiraṇāvali and to some extent his Nyāyavārtikatātparyapariśuddhi bear upon them the stamp of his bright genius ..." (Cf. NKus$_4$, Prefatory Note, p. 159f.

[25] For example, Gaṅgeśa refers to Udayana simply as *ācāryāḥ*. To take only the Īśvarānumānam-section of his TC: p. 82, 9—12: *tad āhur ācāryāḥ : paramāṇvadṛṣṭādy* .... (= NKus 497, 1—2) and 178, 11—12: *ācāryyās tu : aśarīraṃ* ... (= Kir 11, 4—5). D. C. BHATTACHARYA observes:" From the 12th century onwards he [= Udayana] was looked upon as the greatest exponent of the Nyāya-Vaiśeṣika doctrines and was the greatest target of all scholars of the opposing camps" (HNNM, p. 37).

his style and method of argumentation seem to have had a remarkable influence upon the followers even of the other schools. For example, Śrīharṣa, the author of the Khaṇḍanakhaṇḍakhādya and the Naiṣadhacaritam, despite his having been a bitter opponent of Udayana, discloses in his works a style and method of argumentation that betray the influence of the author of the Nyāyakusumāñjali. Similarly, Madhusūdana Sarasvatī, one of the greatest of the later exponents of the Advaita Vedānta, as well as Rāmādvayācārya, the author of the Vedānta Kaumudī, not only quote often from his works, but also seem to have imitated his style and method of argumentation.

We shall now briefly examine to what extent Udayana deserves the place of importance that is accorded to him.

To start with a point of minor importance, Udayana is the author of two extensive independent monographic treatises, the Ātmatattvaviveka and the Nyāyakusumāñjali. Even leaving out of consideration for the moment the philosophic merits of these two treatises, Udayana deserves, in my opinion, a special place in the system for the simple fact that these two are, at least as far as we know at present, the first Nyāya-Vaiśeṣika monographs. For, looking back to the earlier Nyāya-Vaiśeṣika literature that is known to us, we find no work dedicated to the treatment of a single theme. Most of the works we possess up to the time of Udayana are the Sūtra works with their commentaries and sub-commentaries, while the remaining are manuals or handbooks on the important doctrines of the two systems, such as the Padārthadharmasaṃgraha of Praśastapāda with its commentaries, the Nyāyasāra with its recently published commentary called Nyāyabhūṣaṇam, both by Bhāsarvajña, or the Nyāyamāñjarī of Jayanta Bhaṭṭa. Even the lost Nyāya works of such significant thinkers as Śaṅkarasvāmin or Trilocana, however important they might be for the proper understanding of the development of the Nyāya-Vaiśeṣika thought, do not seem to have been such independent treatises as the Ātmatattvaviveka or Nyāyakusumāñjali. The Nyāya-Vaiśeṣika authors who preceded Udayana had dealt with the doctrine of Īśvara in brief excurses: the Naiyāyikas did so when commenting upon certain Sūtras[26], the Vaiśeṣikas when commenting upon the section on creation and dissolution of the universe in Praśastapāda's Padārthadharmasaṃgraha. Udayana, on the other hand, devotes to it an entire treatise of no mean dimensions as well as a good part of the fourth chapter of his Ātmatattvaviveka, not to speak of his commentary in the Kiraṇāvalī upon Padārthadharmasaṃgraha's section on creation and dissolution of the universe and his commentary in the Nyāyavārttikatātparyapariśuddhi upon Vācaspati's Ṭīkā on Nyāyasūtras IV, 1, 19—21. This fact itself earns for him a place of special honour among the Nyāya-Vaiśeṣika writers. Moreover these treatises reveal him to be an exceptional thinker. One who carefully goes through his works, especially the Nyāyakusumāñjali, cannot fail to discern in their author a systematic thinker, a sound logician

---

[26] NSū IV, 1, 19—21 is the *locus classicus* in Nyāya texts for the Īśvara doctrine. The section containing NSū II, 1, 49—68 have been used by some commentators to speak of Īśvara.

and an indefatigable controversialist. Neither the abstruse style nor the formulations that make the study of his works a difficult task can deprive him of the right to be counted as a great thinker and logician. Although we cannot dwell at length here on the merits of Udayana as a logician, it may be pointed out that he has made valuable contributions to the cause of Indian logic. Not only the Prabodhasiddhi, which deals specifically with *jātiḥ* and *nigrahasthānam,* two themes of Indian logic, and the Nyāyavārttikatātparyapariśuddhi, large portions of which are devoted to logical problems, but also his other works offer valuable material for the study of Indian logic. His explanation of the method of removing doubt about the presence of the *hetuḥ* in the *vipakṣaḥ* and of determining the invariable relation necessary for a valid inference[27] or his excursus on the nature and classification of the *aprayojakahetuḥ*[28] may be mentioned as two instances in point taken at random from the third Stabaka of the Nyāyakusumāñjali. The logical competency of Udayana seems to have been generally accepted. To mention but one Indian writer of the sixteenth century, Sāyana Mādhava, the author of the Sarvadarśanasaṃgraha, speaks of him not only as "one whose fame had spread everywhere" (*viśvavikhyātakīrtiḥ*), but also as "one who has seen the opposite shore of the ocean of the principles of logic" (*nyāyanayapārāvārapāradṛk*)[29], an epithet which aptly expresses his thorough knowledge of logic.

His contributions to Indian epistemology, too, deserve mention. The discussion on the validity of cognition (*prāmāṇyam*) in the second Stabaka, the discussion on the different means of valid cognition as found in the third Stabaka, or his refutation of the Mīmāṃsaka theory of cognizedness (*jñātatā*) as found in the fourth Stabaka are some examples from the Nyāyakusumāñjali alone.

It is, however, as the staunch defender of Nyāya-Vaiśeṣika theism that Udayana is most celebrated and cherished[30]. His Nyāyakusumāñjali stands out as the unequalled treatise of Indian philosophic theism, in which the existence of Īśvara is established through rational arguments. As S. Kuppuswami Sastri puts it: "In the history of Indian theism . . . Udayana's theistic contribution is of particular value in demonstrating the extent to which theism may press reason into service where revelation fails, as in the case of anti-Vedic Buddhists"[31].

---

[27] Cf. NKus 342, 7—365, 12.

[28] Ibid. 366, 1—371, 4.

[29] Cf. SDS 235, 8—9.

[30] S. Kuppuswami Sastri calls Udayana "the greatest champion of Nyāya theism" (A Primer of Indian Logic, p. 79). Similar statements can be found also in L. Suali: Introduzione allo studio della filosofia indiana, p. 63; H. Jacobi: Gottesidee p. 58; G. Tucci: Storia della filosofia indiana, p. 24.

[31] Cf. A Primer of Indian Logic, p. 85. According to Swami Ravi Tirtha "The Nyāyakusumāñjali of Udayanācarya is perhaps the most outstanding work in Indian philosophy dealing with the problem of God" ($NKus_5$, p. xi). Cf. also S. Mookerjee, Cultural Heritage of India, Vol. III, pp. 123—124; U. Mishra: HIP, II, p. 269.

For a proper appreciation of Udayana's contribution to the Īśvara doctrine of the Nyāya-Vaiśeṣika school, it is necessary to recall the philosophic and religious atmosphere of the period in which he flourished and composed his treatises. In the wake of the systematic and thoroughgoing attack on the Īśvara doctrine by Dharmakīrti, this doctrine assumed a more important place in the metaphysical controversies between the theists and their adversaries, notably the Buddhists, than was earlier the case. We know from the fragments handed down in Buddhist works that the Nyāya-Vaiśeṣika authors, whose works have not come down to us, continued to answer the assaults of the opponents and to defend the existence of Īśvara. But then there appeared in the field of controversy Jñānaśrī, the great Buddhist thinker. In defence of the Buddhist doctrines and against some of the important tenets of the rival schools, he composed several treatises of varying lengths. The second largest of these treatises was written to refute the Īśvara doctrine of the Nyāya-Vaiśeṣikas. After exposing the arguments of the Nyāya-Vaiśeṣika theists he refuted them in such a thorough manner as no one after Dharmakīrti had done. It was at this period when the Īśvara doctrine seemed to lose the battle with the Buddhists that Udayana entered the arena. His Ātmatattvaviveka and Nyāyakusumāñjali bear ample testimony to the fact that he proved himself equal to his opponent. Becoming "the leader of a caravan in order to protect the wayfarers (on the path towards liberation) who have become motionless through fear, in the long desolate road of darkness (in the form) of a large number of doctrines of the opponents"[32], to use his own words, Udayana dauntlessly met the objections of the adversaries with a thoroughness of thought and soundness of logic that apparently brought them to silence. Never again had Indian philosophic theism to meet such a dreadful foe as he had to face[33].

There is a legend which relates that, coming one day to the temple of Jagannātha in order to offer worship to his favourite deity, Udayana found the doors of the temple closed on all sides. Unable to restrain his feelings of anger at this apparent indifference of Īśvara, he is said to have exclaimed: "You are intoxicated by the pride of your lordship in that you (now) remain treating me with disdain. (But remember that) when the Buddhists approach (to attack), your existence is in my hands"[34]. We need not give credence to this legend; in fact, I for one doubt whether the author of the concluding verses of the Nyāyakusumāñjali would ever have had the audacity or haughtiness

---

[32] Cf. ATV 451, 9—10:
bahutaraparatantraprāntaradhvāntabhīti-
stimitapathikarakṣāsārthavāhena . . .

[33] No doubt, the decline of Buddhist philosophy in India as well as the gradual acceptance of the Īśvara doctrine by some non-theistic Brahmanic schools (v. g. Sāṃkhya and Mīmāṃsā) also account for the absence of such opposition to the Īśvara doctrine in the later period.

[34] The famous verse runs:
aiśvaryamadamatto'si māṃ avajñāya vartase /
upasthiteṣu bauddheṣu madadhīnā tava sthitiḥ //

to address such words to his Lord. But in any case this account serves to bring out very clearly the signal contribution of Udayana in defending the existence of Īśvara. It is very probable that it has been invented by a later writer with the purpose of eulogising Udayana for his significant role in defending the existence of Īśvara. Without fear of exaggeration it can be said that he defended the existence of Īśvara in a manner unparalleled before him and unexcelled after him. Hence we can subscribe to the view of H. JACOBI: „Bei den Indern gilt nun Udayanācārya für denjenigen, welcher der Beweisführung für das Dasein Gottes den höchsten Grad der Vollkommenheit verliehen habe. Jedenfalls ist er der letzte originelle Schriftsteller über diesen Gegenstand"[35].

Although the main purpose of the Nyāyakusumāñjali is to vindicate the existence of Īśvara against the opponents of theism by means of philosophical reasoning, one cannot evade the impression that Udayana shows himself here not only as a speculative philosopher, but also as an ardent devotee of Īśvara. This is seen in the introductory and concluding verses of his works, especially those of the Nyāyakusumāñjali. The "handful of flowers of logic" (*nyāyaprasūnāñjaliḥ*) whose composition he is about to begin is humbly placed at the feet of Īśvara; for it is, indeed, more as an act of worship than as pure philosophic speculation that he undertakes the logical treatment of Īśvara[36]. The concluding verse of each of the Stabakas gives expression to his sentiments of devotion and self-surrender to the Lord. In the concluding verse of the first Stabaka he entreats Īśvara to bring delight to his mind through his immediate presence. The concluding verse of the second Stabaka contains a prayer that he may become, even unto the end, a worshipper of Śiva, who is the source of all confidence. At the end of the third chapter he invites all to take refuge in the God even of the gods with the highest faith. In the concluding verse of the fourth Stabaka he confesses that Śiva, who is endowed with innate and unerring intuitive perception, is the authority that drives away all his doubts. The first of the concluding verses of the fifth chapter gives one the impression that Udayana wrote the whole work, but more especially the proofs of the last chapter, not simply with an eristic purpose as it might appear at first sight, but with a view to drawing the atheists to faith in Īśvara; for he prays here that Īśvara, who is full of compassion, may in his mercy draw towards him in the course of time the stony hearts of those who, despite the several arguments from reason and revelation brought forward to them, are still devoid of faith in him. The verse that follows reflects the author's own longing to be united with God, a longing expressed in words that recall those of St. Augustine: "... *quia fecisti nos ad te, et inquietum est cor nostrum donec requiescat in te*". Udayana pours out his heart in the following words: "Thou who art beautiful by nature, although our minds are, indeed, since long immersed in thee, O Source of bliss! still they are even today restless and unsatisfied. Hence, O Lord! hasten to show thy mercy, so that our minds being fixed solely on thee, we may not attain a hundred times the torments of

---

[35] H. JACOBI: Gottesidee p. 58.

[36] Cf. NKus 19, 3—4.

Yama (i. e. death)"[37]. The last verse of the Nyāyakusumāñjali breathes an air of that self-abandonment and confidence in God characteristic of mystics of all religions, seeking only his will and pleasure: "Thus, what does it matter whether this handful of flowers of logic (i. e. this work, Nyāyakusumāñjali) of radiant splendour makes the two feet, right and left, (of Īśvara) fragrant or not? But may the Teacher of the teacher of Indra be pleased with this offering (placed by me) at his footstool"[38].

These passages, it seems to me, bear ample testimony to the fact that Udayana was, besides being a great philosophical apologist of Hindu theism, also an ardent devotee and lover of Īśvara whose existence he wanted to vindicate in this work.

In forming an estimate of Udayana it is necessary to consider the opinions of other scholars regarding him.

There are scholars who maintain that the merit of combining the two schools of Nyāya and Vaiśeṣika "for the first time into a joint form" goes to Udayana[39]. Such a statement is open to misunderstanding. The fact that he is the first author of the school who has written commentaries on the basic works of both schools is not, in my opinion, a decisive argument that he is the first to combine the two systems, because firstly, though he is the first author whose works on both these schools have actually come down to us, we are not sure that he had no precursors in that line whose works have been lost to us now; secondly,—and this is important—the works of the earlier Nyāya commentators show that such a process of amalgamation of the two systems had been going on much earlier than in Udayana's time. Moreover, the two schools maintained some distinctive doctrines of their own to which they firmly clung even during the time of Udayana[40], that is, in case he really refers to the theories of Vaiśeṣikas of his own day.

Another observation made about Udayana concerns his attitude towards Vedānta. Some scholars maintain that he "shows leanings towards the Vedānta"[41], some speak of the "Vedāntic influence upon Udayana" and his "predilection towards Vedānta"[42], others claim that he "was inclined to

---

[37] NKus 576, 1—4:
asmākan tu nisargasundara cirāc ceto nimagnaṃ tvayī-
ty addhā'nandanidhe tathāpi taralaṃ nādyāpi santṛpyate /
tan nātha tvaritaṃ vidhehi karuṇāṃ yena tvadekāgratām
yāte cetasi nāpnuvāma śataśo yāmyāḥ punar yātanāḥ //

[38] Ibid. 576, 5—8:
ity eṣa nītikusumāñjalir ujjvalaśrīr
yad vāsayed api ca dakṣiṇavāmakau dvau /
no vā tataḥ kim amareśaguror gurus tu
prīto'stv anena padapīṭhasamarpitena //

[39] Gopinath Kaviraj: Gleanings p. 20; U. Mishra: HIP II, pp. 148—149.

[40] I have in mind here the Vaiśeṣika view of only two *pramāṇāni, pratyakṣam* and *anumānam*, while the Naiyāyikas accept, in addition, also *upamānam* and *śabdaḥ*. Cf. NKus 371, 5ff.; 388, 1ff.

[41] D. N. Shastri: Critique of Indian Realism, p. 116.

[42] D. C. Bhattacharya: HNNM, p. 45.

Advaitism"[43], while still others go to the extent of asserting that he was a "staunch believer of Advaita"[44]. It is, indeed, true that among the opponents the Vedāntins are less often mentioned or refuted in his works than the Mīmāṃsakas, Sāṃkhyins or Cārvākas. This is especially remarkable in the Nyāyakusumāñjali where only once the view of a Vedāntin, namely Bhāskara, is mentioned together with the views of some others concerning the factor that determines a new creation after dissolution[45]. That he did not enter into controversy with the Vedāntins on the Īśvara doctrine itself may be accounted for by the fact that these—even the Advaita Vedāntins—admit an Īśvara, though in a manner different from that taught in the Nyāya-Vaiśeṣika school. With regard to the alleged predilection of Udayana for Vedānta as shown in the last section of the Ātmatattvaviveka[46], the following observation may be made. While pointing out in that passage the gradual ascent in the path of the worship of the Supreme Soul, the author indicates the superior position of the Vedānta compared with the Pūrvamīmāṃsā, Cārvāka, Sāṃkhya etc., in as far as some Vedāntins teach Brahmā to be of the nature of pure, self-illuminating consciousness. But it is to be noted that in the concluding lines of this passage he exhorts his reader not to enter the city of liberation (*mokṣanagaram*) by these "side-gates" or "inferior entrances" (*apadvāram*), but, having avoided (*vihāya*) them, to enter by the "front-gate" or "main entrance" (*puradvāram*)[47], by which he, no doubt, means his own system. In conclusion, with regard to Udayana's attitude towards Vedānta, we may say with G. Kaviraj that, "though professedly a Naiyāyika, he had the highest regard for Vedānta in its most rigorous and unfalsified form"[48], but in no case can it be said that he was a staunch believer of Advaita.

Some scholars consider Udayana to be arrogant in his observations[49]. It is, indeed, true that he occasionally uses somewhat caustic, contemptuous or unfriendly expressions or remarks towards his opponents[50]. Such expressions

---

[43] Cf. Narendrachandra Vedantatirtha's Introduction in NKus$_1$ Part II, p. xxix.

[44] S. Subrahmanya Sastri: Introduction to his edition of the NSa of Bhāsarvajña with the commentaries Nyāyamuktāvalī of Aparārkadeva and Nyāyakalānidhi of Ānandānubhavācārya, Madras Government Oriental Series, No. 147, Madras 1961, p. 13.

[45] Cf. NKus 303, 12—13.

[46] ATV 448, 1—450, 11.

[47] Cf. ATV 451, 6—7.

[48] Gopinath Kaviraj: Gleanings pp. 21—22.

[49] D. N. Shastri (op. cit. p. 120) speaks of Udayana's "sense of arrogance"; D. C. Bhattacharya (HNNM, p. 15) refers to our author's "bantering style".

[50] A few examples of Udayana's unfriendly or sarcastic remarks to his opponents are: *yas tu nipuṇammanyo . . . pakṣayati sma . . .* (ATV 129, 5); *naivam uccair brūyāḥ, parair api kadācid evaṃ brūyeta* (ibid. 207, 3—4); *tiṣṭha vā matikardamam apahāya . . .* (ibid. 229, 12—13); Udayana calls the Buddhists *mandāḥ* (ibid. 372, 8). In NKus 297, 3 he calls his opponent *jaḍatama*. Cf. also ATV 175, 3—4; 238, 4; 263, 6; 393, 3; 405, 3; NKus 89, 1—2; 166, 2—3; 217, 7—8; 418, 6—8; 524, 3—5; Kir 287, 5—11. Note that the full import and force of these passages can be grasped only when one reads them in their context.

are found chiefly in his Ātmatattvaviveka and Nyāyakusumāñjali, both of which are treatises of controversy, written almost in the form of a dialogue between the author and the opponent or opponents in question. In such works one can easily understand, especially if one keeps in mind the acrimony with which the doctrines in dispute were attacked by the opponents, that the author was at times driven beyond the borders of forbearance and that he gave vent to his feelings of emotion in such expressions. Besides, when one considers the methods of Indian controversy as found in logical works, one may even consider it a part of the art of dialectics[51]. Hence, even though such expressions are met with in his works, still it would be incorrect, in my opinion, to accuse him of arrogance as though he alone were guilty of such a fault. Moreover, as even the scholars who speak of the arrogance of Udayana admit, such an attitude towards the opponents is found mostly in his earlier works, gradually diminishing with his maturer years.

Contrary to the opinion of most scholars, D. N. Shastri finds in the works of Udayana "a glimpse of the method of subtle argumentation without much substance" which, in his view, is the chief characteristic of Navya-Nyāya. "Like the writers of the Navya-Nyāya school, he lacks philosophical insight and originality, and, as in their case, words get the better of the sense"[52]. These statements regarding the characteristic of the Navya-Nyāya school and about Udayana as a thinker are, in my opinion, not only too harsh and unjust, but also influenced by the author's own conception of philosophy. When we compare Udayana's works with those of the other Indian philosophers who preceded him or were his contemporaries, there is no doubt that he takes his place among the great thinkers of India, both for his originality and deep philosophical insight.

Quite in accordance with the tradition of the Nyāya-Vaiśeṣikas Udayana was a Śaivite, and the Īśvara of whom he speaks in his works is Śiva. Although in the course of his discussions with the opponent he does not speak of Īśvara as Śiva, the concluding verses of the second und fourth Stabakas of the Nyāyakusumāñjali as well as the introductory verse of the Lakṣaṇāvalī where Śiva is mentioned reveal that he was a devout worshipper of that god[53].

---

[51] Cf. NM I, 162, 11: *āḥ kumate; ayi mūḍha* (ibid. 162, 17). Cf. Jayanta's caustic remark to the Mīmāṃsakas ibid. 214, 24—27; 216, 26; 216, 28—29; 373, 24 etc.; Śrīharṣa calls his opponent *paraṃ manda* (KhKhKh 279, 5—6).

[52] Critique of Indian Realism, p. 120.

[53] Cf. the introductory verse of LV: *praṇamya pārvatīnāthaṃ* . . ., U. Mishra (HIP II, pp. 155—156) maintains that "Udayana cannot be called a Śaiva alone or a Vaiṣṇava alone or even a Śākta alone", since all the Maithilīs—Udayana is said to have been a Maithilī—are at the same time Śākta, Śaiva and Vaiṣṇava. In my opinion, our only reliable source of knowing Udayana are his works and these do not give us enough evidence to characterise him as a Śākta or Vaiṣṇava, except perhaps in the sense of the general "inclusivistic" tendency of Hinduism according to which he would have worshipped Śakti and Viṣṇu as different forms or manifestations of Śiva.

The most important contribution of Udayana to the Īśvara doctrine lies especially in establishing the existence of Īśvara. He has not only refuted in detail the opponents' arguments for the non-existence of Īśvara, but has also brought forward, as we shall see, a series of proofs for his existence[54].

---

[54] Cf. pp. 77ff.

CHAPTER TWO

THE NYĀYAKUSUMĀÑJALI

1. GENRE AND STRUCTURE

The Nyāyakusumāñjali belongs to that genre of Indian philosophic literature known as Prakaraṇa which corresponds to the Western concept of a monograph. As it consists of memorial verses (*kārikā*) interspersed with prose explanations, it can be called a Miśraprakaraṇa.

There are on the whole seventy-three verses distributed unequally in five chapters or Stabakas (i. e. 'cluster of blossoms', 'bunch of flowers') as they are named, each containing respectively twenty, four, twenty-three, six and twenty verses. These verses form the core of the work, the prose passage that accompanies each being an elaborate explanation of it, often with long discussions with the opponents.

An analysis of the Nyāyakusumāñjali shows that Udayana has faithfully followed a plan in this work. After the opening verse which is a dedication of his work in the form of a garland consisting of flowers of logic—hence the name Nyāyakusumāñjali—at the feet of the Lord, he mentions in very clear terms the theme of the work, namely the Supreme Soul: "Here (= in this work) is being investigated that Supreme Soul whose worship the wise consider to be the path towards heaven and liberation"[55].

Then follows a short prose passage where Udayana brings forward a sort of *apologia pro opere suo.* Men of all religious sects and philosophical convictions, the Cārvākas themselves not excepted, says he, admit in some manner or other, under some name or other, a Supreme Being, so that his existence cannot even be doubted. In other words, the universal acceptance of a Supreme Being seems to make a treatise vindicating his existence a superfluous enterprise. Udayana prefers, therefore, to look upon his work more as an act of homage or worship of the Lord than as a philosophical disquisition that purports to establish the existence of Īśvara: "This logical investigation of the Lord, which partakes of the designation of reflection (and) which follows (the acceptance of) the Śruti, is made (by me) as an act of worship"[56]. For, observes he, although Īśvara has been abundantly spoken of in the Śrutis, Smṛtis, Itihāsas, Purāṇas etc., nevertheless that is not sufficient. He should also be made the object of reflection (*mananam*), so that one may convince

---

[55] NKus 11, 1—12, 1.
[56] Ibid. 19, 3—4.

oneself and penetrate deeply into the truth about the Lord who has been spoken of in the sacred scriptures, in accordance with the Smṛti passage that says: "It is (only) by ascertaining by means of the three ways of sacred scripture, inference and the delight of the exercise of meditation that one attains the supreme concentration"[57].

After these introductory lines Udayana brings forward five principal arguments of the opponents which are said to invalidate (*bādheta*) the existence of Īśvara: "With regard to this (= the existence of Īśvara) there are five erroneous opinions (which assert that there exists no Īśvara) on the ground that: 1) there is no other-worldly means (of attaining) a world beyond; 2) even otherwise (i. e. even without assuming an Īśvara) the performance of the means of (attaining) the world beyond is possible; 3) there are arguments that make known his non-existence; 4) even if (Īśvara) existed, he would not be a source of valid cognition; and 5) there are no arguments that can validly establish his (existence)"[58].

With the enumeration of these five principal objections of the opponents of the existence of Īśvara, Udayana indicates also the theme dealt with in each of the five chapters of his Nyāyakusumāñjali. This division warns us at the same time that we should not look there for a complete treatise on Nyāya-Vaiśeṣika Īśvara doctrine under its diverse aspects, but that it deals primarily and directly with the existence of Īśvara.

In spite of this clear indication of the arrangement of his Nyāyakusumāñjali some scholars have tried to explain the division of the work differently. They are of the opinion that the first Stabaka refutes the view of the Cārvākas, the second the view of the Mīmāṃsakas, the third that of the Buddhists, the fourth that of the Jains and the fifth the view of the Sāṃkhyins[59]. An analysis of the Nyāyakusumāñjali, however, reveals that such a classification is very misleading. It can be granted that all these schools were, in a greater or lesser degree, opponents of the Īśvara doctrine and that they have been either explicitly mentioned or implicitly intended and refuted in this work; but to say that a particular chapter is directed against a particular school of opponents is not correct. For instance, even though it might be said that the first and the second Stabakas are directed mainly against the Cārvākas and the Mīmāṃsakas

---

[57] Ibid. 20, 2—3. According to a principle generally accepted in Nyāya (Udayana himself refers to it in NP 59, 15: *sandigdhe nyāyaḥ pravartate*), logical proofs are to be brought forward only with regard to what is doubted. As the belief in Īśvara is said to be universal, perhaps Udayana brings forward this motive also in justification of his logical treatment of Īśvara.

[58] Ibid. 29, 1 continued on 40, 2.

[59] Candrakantadeva Sarma in his Sanskrit Introduction to the BI edition of the NKus maintained (ibid. pp. 4—6) this view which was later followed by several other scholars including probably H. Jacobi. (Cf. Gottesidee p. 63). The same view was held by Narendra C. Bhattacharya (cf. his English Introduction to his edition of the Kusumāñjalikārikā with the commentary of Rāmabhadra Sārvabhauma, p. 1 [= small Roman number 50]), U. Mishra (HIP II, pp. 180—187); Kishore Nath Jha (see his article: *nyāyakusumāñjalau prācīnācāryaprabhāvaḥ*, p. 1).

respectively, Udayana brings even in these chapters the views of other schools[60]. That Udayana did not intend each chapter to be the refutation of a particular school can be clearly seen from the third Stabaka where Udayana deals with and refutes the views of different philosophical schools, including the views of the classical Vaiśeṣikas who maintained that comparison (*upamānam*) and verbal testimony (*śabdaḥ*) were not distinct and independent means of valid cognition, but reducible to inference. Although there are scholars who maintain that the fourth chapter is directed against the Jains, an analysis of this chapter reveals no specific refutation of any Jaina doctrine; the Stabaka in question is mainly devoted to the refutation of the Mīmāṃsaka view of valid cognition as the cognition of what was earlier not cognized (*agṛhītagrāhitvam*) and to the establishment of the author's view of the nature of valid cognition as the experience of an object as it really is (*yathārthānubhavaḥ*), and some related problems. As a matter of fact, Udayana nowhere mentions the Jains in his discussions in the Nyāyakusumāñjali. The only time they are mentioned —under the name of Digambaras—is in the prose passage at the beginning, where men of different religious persuasions and philosophic schools are said to believe, under some name or other, in a Supreme Being[61]. Nor is it correct to maintain that the fifth Stabaka is directed against the Sāṃkhya school of opponents. It cannot be said to be directed more against the Sāṃkhyins than against the other deniers of Īśvara; for an analysis of this chapter shows that it is devoted to an explanation of the different proofs for the existence of Īśvara indicated by their logical reasons (*hetuḥ*) in its first verse. As we shall see later, of the two series of proofs, those of the first series are proposed to all opponents, while those of the second series are more specifically intended for the Mīmāṃsakas. Consequently we cannot place the fifth chapter on a par with the other four chapters, much less consider it as a refutation of the objections of a particular school, such as the Sāṃkhya, against the existence of Īśvara.

Hence, instead of maintaining that each chapter is intended as a refutation of a particular philosophic school, it is better to accept the division and arrangement of the Nyāyakusumāñjali as it has been indicated by Udayana himself in the five erroneous opinions or objections (*vipratipattiḥ*) set forth at the commencement of his work and to say that each chapter of the Nyāyakusumāñjali deals with and refutes one of the five erroneous opinions in the order in which they have been enunciated. Such a conception also explains the fact that in the same chapter views of different schools concerning the problem under discussion are mentioned and discussed[62].

The five Stabakas of the Nyāyakusumāñjali may be divided into two unequal parts. The first part consisting of the first four Stabakas and occupying the bulk of the work may be characterized as "negative" part, in the sense

---

[60] v. g. of the Sāṃkhyas. Cf. NKus 169, 3—179, 3; 303, 11—308, 4.

[61] Cf. NKus 17, 2.

[62] Udayana follows a similar procedure also in his ATV where, at the beginning of the work, he brings forward four erroneous views concerning the nature of the soul (cf. ATV 5, 1—2) each of which is then made the theme of the four respective chapters of that work.

that its main purport is to refute the objections of the different schools against the existence of Iśvara. Various such objections are discussed and refuted here and thus the ground is prepared for the fifth Stabaka. This last chapter can then be designated as the "positive" part in as far as the author aims at establishing the existence of Īśvara by positive proofs for his existence. Several such proofs have been brought forward in this chapter and defended against possible objections of the opponents.

Comparing the relative importance and merit of these two parts one can readily subscribe to the view of H. JACOBI: „Die Stärke von Udayana's Werk liegt nicht in seinem positiven letzten Teile, sondern in den vorhergehenden vier Teilen (oder Sträußen), in denen er die Ansichten der Atheisten, nämlich der Cārvākas, Mīmāṃsakas, Buddhisten, Jainas und Sāṃkhya's widerlegt und so den Boden vorbereitet, aus dem die Überzeugung von der Schöpfertätigkeit des Īśvara gewissermaßen von selbst hervorwächst"[63]. This observation should not, however, lead us to underestimate Udayana's positive contribution to the defence of the existence of Īśvara. For, as we shall see later, he brings forward not only those proofs that were formulated before him, but also some additional ones which, as far as we are able to judge from the available literature, were either his own or at least, in any case, not found in the literature that has come down to us from the period before him.

As we said earlier, the Nyāyakusumāñjali consists of seventy-three Kārikās or memorial verses[64] with prose explanations of them. The introductory and the concluding verses of the entire work as well as the concluding verses at the end of each chapter are not explained by the author; in fact, they do not require to be explained, as they are devotional verses of dedication or of worship. The other Kārikās enunciate in a very condensed form the arguments that he explains in the prose passage that follows. These are mostly so compact in form that they are often hardly intelligible without the prose explanation. Hence it is easily understandable why even a translation unaccompanied by a good commentary often fails to make the idea clear. In fact, for an easier and better understanding of these Kārikās, the best procedure seems to be not to delay long at the beginning in struggling to understand them, but

---

[63] H. JACOBI: Gottesidee p. 63.

[64] Some authors speak of 72 Kārikās of the NKus (v. g. E. B. COWELL: The Kusumánjali, p. X; M. WINTERNITZ: Geschichte der indischen Litteratur, Vol. III, p. 466). But comparing the seven editions of the Kārikās that were available to me for consultation, I find that four editions of the entire Nyāyakusumāñjaliprakaraṇam as well as the edition of the Kārikās with the commentary of Rāmabhadra Sārvabhauma number Kārikā 6 of the fifth Stabaka as a separate Kārikā, while the editions with the commentary of Haridāsa Bhaṭṭācārya have not marked it off as a separate Kārikā, but taken it as a part of the commentary to the preceding Kārikā. It is quite probable that the scribe of the manuscript on which the edition of E. B. COWELL is based forgot to indicate that verse as a separate Kārikā. That Haridāsa Bhaṭṭācārya himself considered this verse to be a separate Kārikā seems to be evident from the introduction of the sentence preceding this verse: *athavā kāryatvādikam anyathā vyākhyāyate*, which introduces a new series of proofs for Īśvara's existence.

to proceed with the prose passage and then come back to the Kārikā which was explained in the prose passage. It looks as though Udayana himself was aware of the fact that his Kārikās would not ordinarily be understood without an explanation; for after the fifth Kārikā of the third Stabaka, which is the only Kārikā for which Udayana gives no explanation at all, and which seems to be exceptional as regards clarity, he remarks that it requires no explanation as it is clear by itself[65]. Had not Udayana himself favoured us with a prose explanation of the Kārikās in the Nyāyakusumāñjali, it is doubtful whether we would ever have been able to guess exactly what the author had meant by them[66].

With a view to compare the lengths of the chapters of the Nyāyakusumāñjali—as the hitherto printed editions contain commentaries printed side by side with the text, at times going far beyond the commented text itself, so that it is not easy to form an accurate judgement about the length of Udayana's text from the number of pages of these editions—the present author took the trouble of counting the lines of each of the five Stabakas. The text used is the KSS edition. Only the text, including the dedicatory and concluding verses of the work as well as of each Stabaka, has been taken into account, but the introductory lines at the beginning of the Stabakas such as *śrīgaṇeśāya namaḥ. nyāyakusumāñjalau . . . stabakaḥ* as well as the concluding colophons such as *iti . . . stabakaḥ* have been left out of consideration. Incomplete lines are counted as one. Thus counted, the five Stabakas have the following numbers of lines:

Stabaka	No. of lines	Relative size
I	523	3rd longest
II	500	4th longest
III	748	2nd longest
IV	222	shortest
V	892	longest

Moreover, the proof based on *kāryatvam* in the first series of proofs has 167 lines in print, while that based on *pratyayaḥ* in the second series has 385. The latter proof occupies more than one-third of the total length of the fifth Stabaka and is more than one-and-a-half times the length of the entire fourth Stabaka.

---

[65] NKus 334, 1: *nigadavyākhyātam etat.*

[66] It would be incorrect to imagine that Udayana first composed only the Kārikās to which he later added a prose explanation in order to make them understandable. He must have rather planned the Kārikās as well as the prose explanation as a single whole. The Kārikās alone would have failed to bring out the context and the meaning of the arguments contained in them. Indeed they serve the purpose of formulating the main lines of arguments in a very concise form and helping the traditional students to keep in memory all the arguments in the form of verses.

2. Characteristics of Composition and Style

A few observations on some of the important characteristics of composition and style followed by Udayana in his Nyāyakusumāñjali are opportune here, as they will be helpful towards a better understanding and evaluation of this work.

We have already remarked that our author has indicated the general plan of his Nyāyakusumāñjali as a whole by the five erroneous opinions or objections set forth at the beginning of the work. This plan is worked out in the order in which it has been enunciated, although it does not prevent the author from bringing in, during the treatment of certain problems, an occasional excursus which, though related to the problem under discussion, may not be immediately or directly necessary in the context[67].

An analysis of the chapters of the Nyāyakusumāñjali shows that its author follows a clear plan also in each of them. The plan of the argumentation is sometimes indicated by him at the beginning of the discussion of each chapter, or of each problem within the chapter, by enunciating a series of alternative answers (*vikalpaḥ*) to the problem, so that a careful reader can easily make out where one point of the argument ends and another begins. The reader can verify at the close of the chapter that its treatment agrees perfectly with the alternatives proposed either at the beginning of the chapter or for each subsidiary problem within the chapter, as the case may be.

A striking feature of Udayana's argumentation, a feature that is not met with, at least to the same degree, in the works of the Nyāya-Vaiśeṣika authors before him, though it seems to have found great favour in the eyes of the later philosophic writers of eminence such as Śrīharṣa, Citsukha, Vallabha and Madhusūdanasarasvatī, is the series of alternatives at the beginning of his argumentation (*vikalpaḥ*) for interpreting a given statement or the decisive term in an argument, sometimes a few, at other times many. After that he takes up each of these alternatives in the given order and tries to show the opponent that the position taken by him is wrong, either because it leads to consequences that are logically unacceptable to the opponent himself or because it involves other logical fallacies. Examples of such argumentation are so numerous in the Nyāyakusumāñjali that they do not need to be specially indicated.

It is interesting to note that in his argumentation with the opponent Udayana not infrequently uses the very arguments or even the very expressions of his opponent in order to refute him. His controversy with the Prābhākaras where he argues that, in case the opponent advocates a distinct means of cognition (*pramāṇam*) in order to cognize similarity (*sādṛśyam*), he should for the same reason admit another distinct means of cognition in order to cognize dissimilarity (*vaidharmyam*)[68], or his refutation of the Mīmāṃsaka theory of cognized-

[67] For example, the excursus in NKus 366, 1—368, 5 on the question where the *aprayojakahetuḥ* is to be classified, or ibid. 319, 3—324, 3 as to why there is no simultaneous cognition of diverse objects and no cognition at all in deep sleep.
[68] Cf. NKus 375, 3—376, 4.

ness (*jñātatā*)[69] are two examples from many in which he uses the very arguments of the opponents to refute them. A verse of the third Stabaka where he answers the Prābhākaras by changing a single word of the original verse of Śālikanātha is an example of the use he makes of the very same expressions of the opponent to refute him.[70]

A careful reader of the Nyāyakusumāñjali cannot fail to be struck by the fact that Udayana proceeds progressively in his argumentation with the opponent. He argues in many cases step by step, showing at the same time the inconsistency or the falsity of the view of his opponent and finally establishes his own view as the only one logically acceptable. His argumentation with the advocates of the theory of all-pervasiveness (*vibhutvam*) of the Manas and the establishment of its atomic size (*aṇutvam*)[71], or his refutation of the *anvitābhidhāna*-theory of the Prābhākaras[72] may be mentioned as typical examples of such a procedure in argumentation.

In the Nyāyakusumāñjali we meet also with another, though less frequent and less important, feature of Udayana's method of argumentation, namely a chain of arguments by which the opponent is, as it were, pursued and forced to yield. His argumentation with those who stated that activity of body or speech is the sole means of knowing the existence of other souls is an instance in point[73]. Another example can be found in his argumentation where he shows his opponent that there is no necessary relation between cognition (*buddhiḥ*) and non-eternal effort (*anityaprayatnaḥ*) so that the former can be found even when the latter is absent[74].

Some features of Udayana's argumentation, which are interesting from the point of view of Indian logic, may be briefly mentioned here. Our author

---

[69] Compare, for example, NKus 465, 9—12 with ibid. 465, 12—16; ibid. 465, 17—467, 3 with 464, 14—465, 3: See also ibid. 215, 1—218, 1; 231, 3—232, 3; 193, 2—8; 469, 4—470, 3. When the opponent argues that the reasoning of Udayana contains a fallacy, our author answers by a sort of *retorqueo argumentum*, that the opponent's argument, too, is not free from the same fault. The principle behind such a way of argumentation may be found in a statement of Udayana in his Kir 314, 7—8: *yadi tūbhayoḥ samaḥ samādhir doṣo vā, na tarhi vayam eke paryanuyojyāḥ.*

[70] Cf. NKus 413, 1—4. The original verse in PrP 400, 12—13 ran as follows:
prāthamyād abhidhātṛtvāt tātparyāvagamād api /
padānām eva sā śaktir varam abhyupagamyatām //

Better known is the verse in ATV 186, 1—4:
śabdasya kācid api vastuni mānasiddhā
bādhāvidhivyavahṛtiḥ kim ihāsti no vā /
asty eva cet katham iyanti na dūṣaṇāni
nāsty eva cet svavacanapratirodhasiddhiḥ //

which is an answer to Jñānaśrīmitra (quoted by Udayana in NVTP 713, 12—15):
dharmasya kasyacid avastuni mānasiddhā
bādhāvidhir vyavahṛtiḥ kim ihāsti no vā /
kvāpy asti cet katham iyanti na dūṣaṇāni
nāsty eva cet svavacanapratirodhasiddhiḥ. //

[71] Cf. NKus 314, 3—323, 4.

[72] Ibid. 401, 1—404, 11.

[73] Ibid. 327, 1—7. Cf. also ibid. 504, 2—505, 7.

[74] Ibid. 497, 13—498, 8.

lays great stress on the importance and necessity of *tarkaḥ* or negative conditional argument. In his Nyāyakusumāñjali he observes that argumentations that are not supported by such *tarka*-arguments are not effective (*aprayojaka-*)[75]. A careful perusal of the Nyāyakusumāñjali shows that its author followed this principle very closely. For his formal arguments are in most cases followed by supporting or favourable negative conditional arguments (*anukūlatarkaḥ*) where he points out the undesirable consequences that would follow if the thesis he has proposed is not accepted[76]. The reason for emphasising the importance and necessity of *tarkaḥ* is that it serves as an efficient means to remove the doubts concerning the valid application of the reason (*hetuḥ*)[77]. A reason is invalidly applied, if it is found also in the dissimilar cases (*vipakṣe*); but the *tarka-* argument indicates the absence of the reason in the dissimilar cases by pointing out the undesirable consequences that would otherwise follow. In his argumentations we often come across passages where he either asks from the opponent, or himself proposes in support of his own thesis, an argument that would show the contradiction that arises, if the reason were also found in the dissimilar cases (*vipakṣe bādhakam*). Such an argument strengthens the necessary relation between the probans and the probandum (*sādhyam*), which is the most essential element in valid logical reasoning. In fact, he considers this establishment of the absence of the reason in the dissimilar cases to be the characteristic mark of the necessary relation[78]. Another feature of his argumentation is that he exposes and defends his own thesis (*pakṣaḥ*) in shorter or longer discussions with the opponent in question, showing that theses other than his own are unacceptable either because of the logical fallacies that invalidate them or because of the undesirable consequences that would follow from their acceptance, and then concludes his argumentation by formulating it in syllogistic form introduced by expressions like *tad ayaṃ prayogaḥ* or *atra prayogaḥ*. Though less numerous than in his other works, instances of this are found also in the Nyāyakusumāñjali.

Like his earlier work Ātmatattvaviveka, the Nyāyakusumāñjali, too, is a treatise of controversy written in such a manner that the reader can almost imagine himself to be present at an actual debate between Udayana and his opponent. Now, one of the difficulties in studying this work is that of tracing exactly the particular opponent with whom he is engaged in arguing or whose views he occasionally refers to. In a few cases he does mention the school of thinkers against whom his arguments are directed. In most cases, one who is well acquainted with the works of the different Indian philosophical thinkers

---

[75] Ibid. 351, 2: *yatrānukūlatarko nāsti so 'prayojakaḥ*.

[76] Cf. ATV 317, 2ff.; 369, 4ff.; NKus 456, 1—3; Kir 103, 6—8; 138, 14—17. In NKus 500, 1—5 Udayana rejects the *pratikūlatarkāḥ* of the opponents as *tarkābhāsāḥ* and brings forward an *anukūlatarkaḥ* which is said to be a *bhūṣaṇam* for the proof of Īśvara. See also Kir 193, 7—8.

[77] In Kir 301, 16—17 we read: *tarkaś ca sarvaśaṅkānirākaraṇapaṭīyan virājate*. In ATV 235, 1 Udayana describes *tarkaḥ* as *vyāptibalam ālambya aniṣṭaprasaṅgarūpaḥ*.

[78] Cf. NKus 365, 9.

is able to surmise without great difficulty who the other partner in the controversy is. In some cases, however, it is not possible to trace the other partner, or at least the particular author Udayana has in view, especially since the works of some philosophers prior to him have been lost to us. This difficulty is all the greater due to his terse way of referring to the views or statements of the opponent. In the controversial works such as those of Jñānaśrī and Ratnakīrti, to mention two authors from the period of Udayana himself, we frequently come across entire passages quoted, in most cases *verbatim*, often with the name of their author or of the work from where they are taken. Udayana seems to have followed a different method. He refers very rarely to authors by name[79], and quotes scarcely, if at all, from texts except the Sūtra-texts or the Śruti- or Smṛti works, which, too, are less frequently quoted than in most of the other authors. In his controversies he refers to the doctrines of others mostly in the form of mere indications, sometimes by a single word, rather than by a complete statement[80]. He uses words sparingly specially when referring to the views of the opponents. Sometimes he mentions only the probans (*hetuḥ*) and the example (*dṛṣṭāntaḥ*) without the thesis (*pratijñā*)[81], at other times only the probans[82]. The result is that the reader himself has to re-construct completely the original argument and find out for himself whose view is being referred to.

It is no wonder, then, that ancient commentators as well as modern scholars seem to be unanimous in their verdict that the Nyāyakusumāñjali is not an easy work. Varadarāja says in his commentary (Bodhanī) on the Nyāyakusumāñjali: "One who is not accustomed to the impenetrable path of Udayana stumbles at every step. It is for the sake of such a person that this Kusumāñjalibodhanī is written (lit. victorious)"[83]. Vardhamāna says in his commentary (Prakāśa), that the Nyāyakusumāñjali is "very difficult" (*ativiṣama-*)[84]. Those modern scholars who have attempted a study of this work are almost unanimous in echoing the views of Varadarāja and Vardha-

---

[79] In fact, the authors outside his school whom Udayana mentions by name are very few in number. Such are: Patāñjali (Kir 266, 8), Dignāga (NVTP 11, 4; 651, 4; NP 18, 1; 55, 3), Jñānaśrī (ATV 119, 1; NVTP 713, 11), Jaimini (NVTP 321, 9), Prabhākara (NVTP 413, 8), Bhāskara (NKus 303, 13), Jinendra (ATV 430, 6), Jagadindu (ATV 430, 6), Kīrti [= Dharmakīrti] (ATV 431, 6; NVTP 651, 4; 668, 3), Prajñākara (ATV 431, 6; under the name of Vārttikālaṅkāra: NVTP 730, 9; Kir 146, 21), Subhūti (ATV 432, 6), Śauṇḍika (ATV 432, 4).

[80] Some instances from the NKus alone, cf. 72, 1—2; 81, 1; 118, 2—3; 200, 3; 256, 1; 269, 6.

[81] E. g. NKus 269, 6: *etena śravaṇatvāt śabdatvavad ity api parāstam.*

[82] E. g. NKus 464, 12: *etena kṣaṇikatvād iti nirastam.* 486, 7: *etena tadvyāpakarahitatvād iti . . . asiddhatvaṃ veditavyam.* See also 72, 1—2.

[83] Cf. NKus 2, 3—4:

audayane pathi gahane videśikaḥ pratipadaṃ skhalati lokaḥ /
tasya kṛte kṛtir eṣā kusumāñjalibodhanī jayati //

The same author calls the first Stabaka of the NKus "impenetrable" (*gahana-*). See NKus 208, 17.

[84] Cf. the concluding verse of NKusPr: . . . *tasyātmajo 'tiviṣamaṃ kusumāñjaliṃ taṃ prakāśayat . . .*

māna. Thus E. B. COWELL who, as a pioneer in the study of Udayana, translated into English the verses of the Nyāyakusumāñjali—the explanation in prose by Udayana himself was unknown when he wrote—remarked in his Preface that "as the author's (= Udayana's) aim was to pack his arguments into the smallest possible compass, the book is of course unintelligible without a commentary"[85]. The discovery of the complete text of the Nyāyakusumāñjali with the prose commentary, no doubt, facilitated the understanding of the Kārikās; nevertheless the text remained difficult to grasp. The reason for the difficulty in the understanding of this work has been aptly expressed by H. JACOBI as follows: „Der Kusumānjali ist ein sehr schweres Buch. Um es vollständig zu verstehen, muß der Leser nicht nur gründlich mit allen Finessen der indischen Dialektik vertraut sein, sondern auch den Standpunkt aller philosophischen Schulen und überhaupt möglichen Standpunkte für die Beurteilung jeder auftauchenden Frage mit allen Konsequenzen immer klar im Bewußtsein haben, um die oft nur durch ein Wort, einen technischen Ausdruck angedeutete Absicht des Verfassers richtig zu erfassen. Das wird aber meistens nur einem einheimischen Gelehrten, dem die ununterbrochene Tradition zur Seite steht, möglich sein. Solch' ein dialektisches Kunstwerk muß dem kompetenten zeitgenössischen Gelehrten einen ganz eigenartigen intellektuellen Genuß geboten haben, für den uns das Verständnis abgeht"[86].

There are also other features of Udayana's style that may be mentioned here. Frequently he uses synonyms even in the case of technical philosophical terms. Then there is his usage of apt maxims and similes, examples of which can be traced also in the Nyāyakusumāñjali[87]. Occasionally Udayana formulates his arguments with special rhetorical force, as for example when he argues that if syllables, which make up words, were not eternal, words themselves would be less eternal and the Veda which consists of word-groups would be much less eternal[88]. Another interesting, though less frequent, feature of his works is the use of alliteration usually rare in philosophical works[89].

---

[85] E. B. COWELL: The Kusumáñjali, p. X.

[86] H. JACOBI: Gottesidee p. 58—59. Similarly Swami RAVI TIRTHA wrote: "The text [of the Nyāyakusumāñjali] is a very difficult one ... Even to a good Sanskrit scholar the text is a hard nut to crack" (The Nyāyakusumāñjali of Udayanācārya, ... p. xiv. Cf. also p. vii). SATKARI MOOKERJEE (in his Foreword to the ASS edition of the NKus, Part I, p. xii) and GOPINATH KAVIRAJ (in his Foreword to the KSS edition of the NKus, p. 1 and PWSBS, Vol. II, p. 160) also speak of the difficulty in studying the text of the NKus.

[87] Some examples: *so 'yam ubhayataḥpāśā rajjuḥ* (NKus 337, 2; NVTP 648, 5; LV 18, 16—17); *vṛścikabhiyā palāyamānasya āśīviṣamukhe nipātaḥ* (NKus 301, 1); *tathā ca ghaṭṭakuṭyāṃ prabhātaḥ* (NKus 423, 9); *tad etat vikrītagavīrakṣaṇam* (ATV 210, 4); *tad etadāyātaṃ pradīpāntareṇa pradīpaṃ nirvāpya timirāpādanam* (ATV 285, 5—6); *palāyamānam api gale pāśena vadhvākṛṣyānayet* (Kir 145, 10—11).

[88] NKus 280, 3—5: *yadā ca varṇā eva na nityās tadā kaiva kathā puruṣavivakṣādhīnānupūrvyādiviśiṣṭavarṇasamūharūpāṇāṃ* (wrongly printed ... *sagūharūpāṇāṃ*) *padānāṃ, kuṭastarāñ ca tatsamūharacanāviśeṣasvabhāvasya vākyasya, kuṭastamāṃ tatsamūhasya vedasya*. A similar rhetorical formulation can be found also in the ATV 69, 1—4.

[89] NKus 292, 7—9: *kupitakapikapolāntargatodumbaramaśakasamūhavat, davadahanadahyamānadārūdaravighūrṇamānaghuṇasaṅghātavat, pralayapavanollāsanī-*

It may be pointed out in this connection that there are several passages of the Nyāyakusumāñjali which recur either exactly in the same formulation or with slight unimportant modifications in the Kiraṇāvalī[90]. This repetition can be easily accounted for by the fact that the same problem or theme has been spoken of in both these works, although in a different context.

The Nyāyakusumāñjali occupies a place of prime importance in the Nyāya-Vaiśeṣika literature; for it is the most elaborate and most fundamental work of the school on the Īśvara doctrine. It rightly deserves the name of the classic of Indian philosophic theism. E. B. COWELL considered the work to be "as much inferior to the tenth book of Plato's Laws or the twelfth of Aristotle's Metaphysics, as Hindu philosophy itself is to that of Greece"; nevertheless he added that "it cannot be uninteresting to trace the brave efforts of a Hindu thinker, far away from the circle of Christianity, who, perplexed by the doubts or open disbelief taught in many of the systems current in his day, endeavoured, however vainly, to build for his countrymen the first truth of Theology on a firm logical foundation.

'. . . . . *Audacia certe*
Laus erit in magnis et voluisse sat est'."[91]

More than a century has gone by since COWELL wrote the above lines and the Western knowledge of Hindu philosophy and religion has increased and its attitude towards them considerably modified. When COWELL wrote the above lines he was unaware of the fact that he had before him only a very small portion of Udayana's own work[92], namely the Kārikās. His knowledge of Udayana was mainly through a late commentator, Haridāsa Bhaṭṭācārya, whose commentary is considerably shorter in size and inferior in quality than the prose explanations of Udayana himself. Consequently he was not in a position to make an adequate study of Udayana or sufficiently appreciate his contribution. Although no exhaustive studies of the Kusumāñjali have appeared even to this day, we have the complete text of the work with several valuable commentaries of authors earlier than Haridāsa Bhaṭṭācārya. Had COWELL the opportunity of studying this work, as we now have, I believe he would have modified his statement about the value of the Nyāyakusumāñjali.

---

yaurvānalanipātipotasāṃyātrikasārthavad veti. Also ATV 223, 9—11; Kir 232, 15. I am grateful to Prof. GONDA for drawing my attention to this point.

[90] For example: NKus 379, 3—380, 5 = Kir 322, 10—23; NKus 380, 8—381, 6 = Kir 322, 24—323, 9; NKus 388, 1—390, 5 = Kir 309, 18—310, 12; NKus 391, 1—392, 2 = Kir 310, 13—24; NKus 430, 2—431, 2 = Kir 328, 17—329, 2. This list is not complete.

[91] The Kusumánjali, p. v.

[92] He had, indeed, correctly guessed that Udayana's original work must have contained a prose "commentary" to his verses. Cf. The Kusumánjali, pp. x—xi.

3. Analysis of the Nyāyakusumāñjali*

STABAKA I

2, 1—40, 2	INTRODUCTORY PART
2, 1—6, 2	Dedicatory verse.
11, 1—12, 1	The theme dealt with in this book, namely the Supreme Soul (*paramātmā*).
14, 1—20, 4	Reason for the logical discussion on Īśvara: Despite the fact that Īśvara is acknowledged by all philosophical schools and religious sects under some name or other, this study which is to be designated as reflection (*mananam*) is made as an act of worship (*upāsanā*) that comes after the listening to the scriptures (*śravaṇam*).
29, 1—40, 2	The five objections against the existence of Īśvara are: 1) There is no supra-mundane (*alaukika-*) means of attaining the other world (*paralokaḥ*). 2) The performance of the religious rites etc. which are the means of attaining the other world would be possible even without assuming an Īśvara. 3) There are means of valid cognition that make known the non-existence of Īśvara. 4) Even if Īśvara does exist, he is not a source of valid cognition. 5) There are no arguments to establish the existence of Īśvara. [The answers to these five main objections form the contents of the five respective chapters of the NKus].
	REFUTATION OF THE FIRST OBJECTION
41, 1—44, 1	Kārikā mentioning five arguments for the existence of a supra-mundane means for attaining the other world. There is a supra-mundane cause (called Apūrvam) because: I. This world (*saṃsāraḥ*) is dependent (*sāpekṣa-*) on causes. II. The stream of causes is beginningless. III. There is diversity (*vaicitryam*) of effects. IV. There is universal practice (*viśvavṛttiḥ*) of sacrificial rites etc. V. The experience (of pleasure and pain) is confined to each individual soul. [The discussion of these five arguments forms the subject-matter of the first Stabaka].

* The edition referred to is the KSS edition of 1957. The first number refers to the page, the second to the line on that page.

45, 1—60, 2 I. THIS WORLD IS DEPENDENT ON CAUSES

45, 1—2 If this world were not dependent, it would either be or not be, but would not be occasional (*kadācit*).

49, 1—60, 2 Refutation of the view that this world comes into being *akasmāt*. Udayana mentions five alternative ways in which the term *akasmāt* may be understood, namely in the sense of *kāraṇaniṣedhaḥ*, *bhavanapratiṣedhaḥ*, *svātmahetukatvam*, *nirupākhyahetukatvam* and *svabhāvaniyatatvam*, and argues that in none of these senses the world can be said to be *akasmāt*. The view of the Svabhāvavādin that the origination of the world at a particular time is determined by its proper nature is refuted in greater detail than the others (52, 3—60, 2). Since there is a determined limit of time in which it comes into being, one must admit its dependence upon causes for its origination.

60, 3—91, 2 II. THE STREAM OF CAUSES IS BEGINNINGLESS:

60, 3—67, 3 The opponent argues that, even granting the dependence on causes to be established by an effect's having a limit (*avadhiḥ*), nevertheless, as one of the limits cannot be perceived in the case of the world, its dependence on causes cannot be established. This is rejected on the ground that the uninterrupted stream of causes is beginningless (*anādi-*).

67, 3—73, 3 The determination of causal relation is with regard to the class (*jātiḥ*), and not with regard to the individual (*vyaktiḥ*), and there is a law that from a specific class of causes there arises a specific class of effects.

81, 1—91, 2 The causal relation with regard to a class indicated by exclusion (*apohaḥ*) from what does not belong to that class, as postulated by the Buddhists, is rejected.

91, 3—96, 2 III. THERE IS DIVERSITY OF EFFECTS:

91, 3—96, 2 Refutation of the view that there is no diversity of causes, but that there is only one (*eka-*) cause (91, 3—94, 1) or many causes of one single class (*ekajātīya-*) (94, 2—95, 4). The diversity of effects necessarily requires diversity of co-operating causes (*sahakārī*).

96, 3—166, 3 IV. THERE IS UNIVERSAL PRACTICE OF SACRIFICIAL RITES ETC.:

96, 3—101, 2 Refutation of the view that the diversity of effects can be explained solely by the co-operating causes that are visible.

The universal practice of sacrifices (such as the Jyotiṣṭoma) and other pious works (such as building temples, tanks etc.), often at the cost of great effort and money, in order to obtain merit for attaining the other world would not be explicable on such an assumption. Motives of profit, esteem, pleasure etc. cannot explain the universality of such practices.

101, 3—103, 1 Almsgiving, study of the Veda etc. cannot themselves be the diverse causes that explain the diversity of the world; for these last but a moment, while the desired fruit is attained only at a later time. Hence there must be some supra-sensible quality that exists after and beyond these actions, and this quality is the Apūrvam.

103, 2—166, 3 Discussion with the Śaktivādin on the nature of this Apūrvam and refutation of the view that this quality is nothing but a supra-sensible attribute of the material elements (*atīndriyaḥ bhūtadharmaḥ*).

103, 2—125, 1 a) The supra-sensible quality produced by sacrifices etc. is not an innate potency (*sahajaśaktiḥ*) of the material elements.

103, 2—119, 3 Refutation of the view that the quality produced by sacrifice etc. is nothing but a supra-sensible attribute of the material elements themselves, like the qualities of heaviness etc. The opponent had argued: the burning of the hand when, unaccompanied by Mantras that counteract burning, it is brought into contact with fire, cannot be accounted for by the non-existence of counteracting agents such as the Mantra, since non-existence, being a non-entity, cannot be a cause; and consequently one has to conclude to a supra-sensible quality in the fire that is conducive to burning which, when unimpaired, produces the effect, but when hindered or removed by means of counteracting agents, does not produce the effect of burning. Udayana shows that non-existence (*abhāvaḥ*) is also a cause and that obstruction of the effect consists, not in the suppression or removal of some invisible potency, but in the incompleteness (*vikalatvam*) of the causal complex (*sāmagrī*).

119, 4—125, 1 Discussion on the nature of the obstruction of the effect: Refutation of the view of some Ekadeśins that obstruction of the effect consists in nothing but the non-origination of the effect (*kāryānutpādaḥ*) (119, 4—120, 4). The theory of innate potency (*śaktiḥ*) as brought forward by the Śaktivādins cannot satisfactorily explain the fact of obstruction of the effect.

125, 2—166, 3 b) The supra-sensible quality produced by sacrifices etc. is not an acquired potency (*ādheyaśaktiḥ*) of the material elements:

125, 2—138, 4 The opponent argues that, like the perfection produced by the sprinkling of water on grain etc., the supra-sensible quality produced by sacrifice etc. also is an acquired potency of the material elements themselves. Udayana establishes that, just as it is the soul (of the sacrificer) that is perfected by the oblations in the fire accompanied by the Mantras, and not the fire nor the gods, so also it is the soul (of the person who sprinkles) that is perfected by the ritual sprinkling of water on the grain etc., and not the grain etc. Just as the clouds, though themselves not the substratum of the perfection or quality produced by the Kārīrī sacrifice, become capable of producing rain through contact with the person (= soul) who is the substratum of the quality produced by that sacrifice , so also grain etc., when in contact with persons (= souls) who are the substratum of the quality produced by the action of sprinkling etc. become capable of producing the effect. The use of those grains etc. another time is because of certain Vedic prescriptions.

140, 1—144, 5 Refutation of an inferential argument that it is the grain etc. that are perfected by the sprinkling with water etc., and not the soul. Udayana concludes that particular effects are produced by the particular arrangement of atoms that possess qualities effected by heat (*pākajaviśeṣaḥ*).

144, 6—146, 4 In the case of the elements, water, fire and air, which cannot have the qualities effected by heat, the qualities of visibility (*udbhavatvam*), non-visibility (*anudbhavatvam*), liquidity (*dravatvam*), hardness (*kaṭhinatvam*) etc. are produced by the conjunction of different causes. Atoms produce particular substances only when assisted by special Adṛṣṭam, and the difference of products arises from the difference of substances.

146, 4—147, 3 In the case of images (*pratimā*) etc., it is only because the deity in question has been made present in them through the ceremony of consecration (*pratiṣṭhā*) that worship of them produces merit, while irreverence towards them produces demerit in a person.

147, 3—4 The power of water, sprout etc., which have been sanctified by Mantras, to remove poison, sickness etc. is also explained in the same manner.

148, 1—149, 6 Udayana gives three explanations for the validity of the ordeal of being weighed in balance, etc. His own view is that such an ordeal is valid because the deities presiding over merit etc. that are made to be present there reveal, in accordance with the actions of the accused, his innocence or guilt.

150, 1—166, 3 The Naiyāyikas too admit potency (*śaktiḥ*), but only in the sense of causality (*kāraṇatvam*).

167, 1—206, 2 V. Experience (of Pleasure and Pain) is Confined to each Individual Soul:

167, 1—169, 2 That it is the soul itself, and not the elements (constituting the body), that is perfected, is determined by the fact that the souls, though omnipresent by their nature, have determined experience of pleasure and pain in a particular body with senses proper to it.

169, 3 For the same reason is the Sāṃkhya view of experience rejected.

169, 4—174, 7 A short exposition of the Sāṃkhya view of Puruṣa according to which merit, demerit etc. (= Apūrvam) are dispositions of the Buddhi, the Puruṣa itself being eternally immutable and inactive.

174, 7—179, 3 Refutation of the Sāṃkhya view of Puruṣa as eternally immutable.

180, 1—182, 1 Against the Cārvākas who maintain that the soul, which is the experiencer, is nothing else than the elements which, becoming sentient, have been modified in the form of the body, Udayana establishes the existence of eternal, omnipresent souls, distinct from the material elements (= body); for otherwise recollection of past experiences would not be possible.

182, 2—198, 5 The Cārvāka view that there is no need of postulating an eternal, permanent soul, since recollection of past experiences can be explained solely by the causality of the material elements that produce momentary recollections in a particular order, so as to give the impression of a continuity, is rejected by Udayana because the theory of momentariness (*kṣaṇikatvam*) of reality is not acceptable; for there is neither perception (*pratyakṣam*) nor inference (*anumānam*) to prove it.

198, 6—200, 2 The view of the Cārvāka that there is at least doubt (*sandehaḥ*) of momentariness as sufficient proof for his theory, is rejected by Udayana since, on account of the undeniability of the recollection of the past experiences, there can be no legitimate doubt as to the permanence of reality.

200, 3—200, 7 Since universal doubt is self-contradictory, the Cārvāka statement that it is unauthoritative to speak of valid cognition is rejected.

201, 1—202, 8 The objection of the Cārvāka that the notion of causality, whether it is considered as belonging to the nature of a being or as conditioned by an adjunct, is incompatible with permanence of reality, and consequently momentariness of reality has to be accepted, is rejected.

202, 9—206, 2 The objection that, even if reality is permanent, causality is incompatible with an eternal and omnipresent (*vibhu-*) soul, since with regard to such realities no non-concomitance (*vyatirekaḥ*) can be established, is rejected.

208, 1—4 Concluding verse of the Stabaka.

STABAKA II

Refutation of the Second Objection

209, 4—6 The reality of Apūrvam being established, it follows that, as people like us cannot perceive the means for producing it, there must be a supra-mundane, omniscient perceiver of the same (and this perceiver is Īśvara).

210, 1—2 The opponent argues that the transmission of Dharma (*dharmasaṃpradāyaḥ*) or religious duties which are the means of producing Apūrvam is possible without an Īśvara:
a) through the Veda that is eternal and devoid of faults (Cfr. 211, 1—305, 6);
b) through persons who have obtained omniscience through Yoga and religious rites (*karma*) (Cfr. 306, 1—308, 4).

210, 3—4 Kārikā enunciating the answer of Udayana that the transmission of Dharma or religious duties is possible in neither way. For:
I. Validity of cognition is not intrinsic (*svataḥ*), but extrinsic (*parataḥ*).
II. There are creations and dissolutions of the universe.
III. There can be no confidence in the transmission of Dharma by a person other than Īśvara.
IV. There is no other way of explaining the transmission of Dharma except through Īśvara.
[The explanation of these four themes forms the content of the second Stabaka]

211, 1—280, 5 I. Validity of Cognition is not Intrinsic, but Extrinsic:

211, 1—220, 2 A) Refutation of the theory of intrinsic validity of cognition:
211, 1—214, 3 Valid cognition is dependent upon a cause other than the cause of cognition.

215, 1—218, 1 Valid cognition derived from verbal testimony (*śābdī pramā*) cannot be said to have its validity from the mere absence of faults of the person that gives testimony, such as desire to deceive others, etc., but rather from the good qualities (of correct knowledge, truthfulness etc.) in him.

218, 2—220, 2 Rejects the view of the Mīmāṃsakas that, since the Veda is devoid of a person as author (*apauruṣeya-*), it is the very absence of faults in the speaker (*vaktṛdoṣābhāvaḥ*) that is the cause of the validity of the Veda, and not the good qualities of the speaker, and that consequently it is the absence of faults, and not the good qualities, that causes the validity of cognition.

220, 3—233, 3 B) Establishment of the extrinsic validity of cognition:

220, 3—230, 1 Validity is extrinsically cognised since one has doubts about validity until one knows it from repeated practice. If validity were intrinsically cognised, there would be no doubt about it.

230, 2—233, 3 Rejects the opponent's view that the theory of extrinsic validity would lead to an infinite regress (*anavasthā*).

233, 4—234, 1 When the opponent argues that, even granting validity to be extrinsic, nevertheless, being eternal, the Vedas are independent of an author or cause, and they are valid because they are accepted by the large multitude of people (*mahājanaparigrahaḥ*), Udayana answers that both the assumptions of the opponent are unproved (*asiddha-*). For:
a) The Veda cannot be eternal.
b) The acceptance of the Veda by the large multitude of people cannot be the cause of the validity of the Veda.

234, 1—302, 6 a) The Veda cannot be eternal:

234, 1—235, 2 The very syllables (*varṇaḥ*) are not eternal. The non-permanence of sound is grasped through direct perception (*pratyakṣam*).

235, 3—257, 8 Excursus on the manner of perceiving the destruction of sound: Refutation of the view of some Ekadeśins that the destruction (or posterior non-existence) of sound (*śabda-pradhvaṃsaḥ*) is not perceived by the senses, but is inferred. The anterior non-existence (*prāgabhāvaḥ*) of sound is also known through direct perception of the senses.

259, 1 Proof for the non-eternity of sound: "Sound is non-eternal, because it has the property of being produced, like a pot."

259, 1—272, 10 The above proof is free from logical fallacies; for:
1) Its Hetu is not *bādhita-* (259, 1—264, 1).
2) Its Hetu has no *satpratipakṣatvam* (265, 1—269, 8).

3) Its Hetu has neither *virodhaḥ* nor *vyabhicāraḥ* (270, 1).
4) Its Hetu is not *asiddha-*. There is neither *svarūpāsiddhiḥ* (270, 1—12) nor *vyāpyatvāsiddhiḥ* (271, 1—272, 10).
Hence the necessary relation between 'sound' and 'non-eternity' is established.

273, 1—2 The theory of non-permanence of sound does not go against the convention of a fixed (or permanent) meaning for a word.

274, 1—278, 4 Excursus: What is the object of the word (*padārthaḥ*)? Is it the class (*jātiḥ*) or the individual (*vyaktiḥ*)? Rejection of the Mīmāṃsaka view that what is designated by the word is the class and that the individual is cognised through 'inclusion' (*ākṣepaḥ*). Excursus on the nature of *ākṣepaḥ* (274, 2—278, 4). *ākṣepaḥ* is neither inference (*anumānam*) (274, 1—275, 3), nor implication (*arthāpattiḥ*) (275, 3—276, 2), nor is it inclusion of the particular (*viśeṣaparyavasānam*) (277, 1—278, 4).

279, 1—280, 5 Conclusion of the explanation of the non-eternity of the Veda from the non-eternity of the sound: If the syllables are not eternal, neither the words composed of them nor the sentences formed from such words, and much less the Veda which consists of such sentences can be eternal.

280, 6—7 The opponent's attempt to defend the eternity of the Veda by interpreting eternity in the sense of an uninterrupted series is rejected, because on account of the cycles of creations and dissolutions, such an uninterrupted series cannot be given.

280, 6—305, 6 II. There are Creations and Dissolutions of the Universe:

280, 8—10 Five arguments of the opponents to show that there are no creations and dissolutions:
1) There is a law that day and night are preceded by day and night.
2) The simultaneous cessation of all functions is impossible, since deeds mature at different times.
3) The ascertainment of caste etc. would be impossible.
4) The convention (regarding the meaning of words) being unknowable by perception, there would be cessation of all verbal communications.
5) The traditions of making pot etc. would cease to be.

281, 1—286, 9 Udayana's answer to these five objections:
Kārikā formulating the answers in brief (281, 2—3).
Answer to argument 1): (281, 4—283, 2)

Answer to argument 2): (283, 3—285, 5)
Answer to argument 3): (285, 6—286, 4)
Answer to argument 4): (286, 5—8)
Answer to argument 5): (286, 8—9).

286, 10—291, 2 Proofs for creation and dissolution.

291, 2—292, 9 Rejection of the (Mīmāṃsaka) view that creation and dissolution consists only in the origination and destruction (*avāpodvāpaḥ*) of the parts without there being a creation or dissolution of the whole. Udayana states that there will be destruction of the entire universe down to its ultimate atoms.

292, 10—293, 15 (Not only inference but) also observation leads us to the fact of total dissolution; for we observe in the universe a gradual deterioration in birth, performance of sanctifying rites, study of the Veda etc.

293, 15—299, 8 Rejection of the view that, since there are only as many Vedic texts as are now available, there is no deterioration in the study of the Veda. Udayana argues that some of the Vedic texts have been lost through deterioration in Vedic studies; for the Vedic texts (or passages) on which some religious observances are based, are no more to be found.

299, 9—300, 5 Refutation of the view that there is no dissappearance of the Vedic branches (*śākhocchedaḥ*) since those Vedic branches, which are said to have now disappeared, are really to be found in some other place.

300, 6—8 Udayana concludes: On account of the daily gradual diminution of the physical and mental powers of man, the study of Veda also diminishes accordingly. That it still continues to some extent is due to its universal acceptance.

300, 9—301, 4 Answer to the objection that there is no disappearance of the Vedic branches, since otherwise there will be no certainty as to the manner of performing even a single rite; for, the details found in the works of different Vedic branches are necessary, argues the opponent, for the correct performance of rites.

301, 4—302, 6 The process of dissolution and creation goes on like the current of the Sarasvatī river.

302, 7—305, 6 b) The acceptance of the Veda by the large multitude of people cannot be the cause of the validity of the Veda (Cfr. 233, 4—234, 1):

302, 7—8 Explanation of the term "acceptance by the large multitude of people" (*mahājanaparigrahaḥ*).

302, 9—303, 10 The acceptance of the Vedic prescriptions by the large multitude of people is not possible without a cause; but there are no visible causes for it. Udayana mentions here a series of possible visible causes none of which can be applied to the acceptance of the Veda, though they are applicable to the acceptance of the scriptures of the Buddhists etc.

303, 11—305, 4 Excursus: Different theories as to the particular factor that causes creation after a dissolution. Udayana rejects the views of the Sāṃkhyins, of the Vedāntin Bhāskara and of the Buddhists, and defends his own view that it is the particular time (*kālaviśeṣaḥ*).

305, 4—6 Since there is interruption of the Veda at the time of the dissolution, the acceptance by the large multitude cannot be admitted as the source of the validity of the Veda. Moreover, such an acceptance does not cause (*na kāraka-*) validity, but rather reveals or makes it known (*jñāpaka-*).

306, 1—308, 4 III. There can be no Confidence in the Transmission of Dharma by a Person other than Īśvara:

306, 1—3 The opponent (Sāṃkhyin) argues that, since Kapila etc. who have acquired omniscience through Yoga and religious rites are enough to explain the transmission of the Veda, there is no need of an Īśvara as the teacher of the Veda.

306, 3—308, 4 The answer of Udayana:

a) Even if Kapila etc. possess the power of intuition (*bhāvanā*), still it does not produce genuine immediate vision (*sākṣātkāraḥ*), and hence people will not have confidence (or certainty) in a Veda of which Kapila etc. would be the original authors (306, 4—5).

b) Nor can it be admitted that the teaching of Kapila etc. can produce confidence (or certainty) in us on account of its agreement with what is known through other means of cognition such as Āgama (306, 5—8).

c) There can be no intuition with regard to what has not been earlier perceived (306, 8—9).

d) Nor can Kapila etc. know that Yoga and religious rites are the means to what is salutary, except through the Veda (306, 9—307, 5).

e) Nor can it be admitted that there can be confidence in the teachings of Kapila etc. as authoritative from the fact that there is general agreement of the teachings of these sages (307, 5—308, 4).

308, 5—11 IV. There is no other Way of Explaining the Transmission of Dharma Except through Īśvara:

308, 5—11 The theory (of the Mīmāṃsakas) that the transmission of the religious duties can be explained by the fact that, at the time of the new creation, teachers of different social classes (*varṇaḥ*) coming from some other planet teach men on earth the different religious duties, is not acceptable; for such a passage or travel from one planet to another is not possible.

309, 1—4 Concluding verse of the Stabaka.

STABAKA III

Refutation of the Third Objection

[Taking one by one the different means of valid cognition admitted by the opponents, Udayana shows in this Stabaka that none of them can disprove the existence of Īśvara].

311, 4—371, 4 Direct Perception and Inference cannot Disprove the Existence of Īśvara:

311, 4—312, 2 The opponent argues that both direct perception (*pratyakṣam*) and inference (*anumānam*) disprove the existence of Īśvara; for:

a) Were he existent, he would have been perceived, but he is not perceived.

b) Inference also shows that he does not exist, since the pervading factors such as the purpose of gaining something for oneself, etc. (*svārthādi*) that are concomitant with an agent (*kartā*) are not found in him.

312, 3—5 Kārikā enunciating the answer of Udayana:

ad a) With regard to the existence of an object that is not perceptible one cannot bring forward an objection based on its non-perception.

ad b) An inference for the non-existence of Īśvara based on the non-perception of the pervading factors is invalid, since there is the fallacy of *āśrayāsiddhiḥ*.

[Udayana now deals with direct perception and inference separately.]

312, 6—326, 8 I. Direct Perception (Pratyakṣam) cannot Disprove the Existence of Īśvara:

312, 6—313, 1 Non-perception of an object cannot be the basis for the negation of the existence of that object; for our soul (*ātmā*), though perceptible, is not actually perceived at the time of deep sleep, and yet it is not non-existent at that time.

313, 1—324, 3 Excursus 1:

Why is the soul, though perceptible, not actually perceived at the time of deep sleep? The soul is perceived only as the subject or substratum of special qualities such as cognition, desire etc. But as there is no contact of the senses with the Manas at the time of deep sleep, there is no cognition, and consequently the soul is not perceived at that time (313, 1—314, 2).

Refutation of the theory of those (= Mīmāṃsakas) who maintain that the Manas is omnipresent (*vibhu-*), and establishment of its atomic (*aṇu-*) size (314, 3—323, 4).

When the Manas is not in contact with the external senses, the soul is not the substratum of cognition etc., and so the soul is not perceived at the time of deep sleep (323, 5—324, 3).

324, 4—325, 5 Excursus 2:

Why is it that one cannot perceive the soul of another person? Because the Manas and the senses which a soul acquires by virtue of its own Adṛṣṭam belong only to that soul.

325, 6—326, 8 Rejection of an objection (*pratibandhi*-argument) that, if non-perception is not a valid reason for concluding to the non-existence of Īśvara, then the non-perception of the hare's horns also cannot be a valid reason for establishing their non-existence.

327, 1—334, 1 II. Inference (Anumānam) cannot Disprove the Existence of Īśvara:

327, 1—327, 6 An objection that the Supreme Soul is cognisable only by the activities of body and speech and that the absence of such activities in Īśvara leads one to conclude to his non-existence is rejected.

327, 7—328, 4 Udayana concludes that every effect has a cause conformable to it.

328, 5—329, 6 The argument that the existence of Īśvara is to be denied since the pervading factors (such as the body, the purpose of gaining something for oneself, etc.) that pervade the agent cannot be found in him, is rejected by Udayana because this argument has the defect of *āśrayāsiddhiḥ*; for the opponent does not admit the existence of Īśvara nor his omniscience. And a substratum (*āśrayaḥ*) that is accepted on account of a fallacy (*ābhāsapratipanna-*) cannot be a real substratum nor can it be an object of denial.

329, 6—331, 3 Excursus:

How can hare's horns be denied? They are denied on the ground that, though horns on the head of a hare would have been perceivable, they are not at all perceived. And the statement "There are no hare's horns" means only that there is absence of horns in the subject called "hare".

332, 1—333, 5 An argument that there is no fallacy of *āśrayāsiddhiḥ* (Cfr. 328, 7) since souls exist and omniscience and creative activity are denied to them, is rejected.

333, 6—334, 1 Another argument that there is no fallacy of *āśrayāsiddhiḥ*, since Īśvara is accepted by the Naiyāyikas and the common people, is rejected.

[Here follows a section that cannot easily be classified either under direct perception or under inference. It is a long excursus dealing with the different theories of determining the absence of an adjunct (*upādhiḥ*) in inference. It begins with direct perception and passes over to inference: 334, 2—371, 4.]

[Direct perception cannot disprove the existence of Īśvara 334, 2—336, 8]:

334, 2—336, 2 Refutation of the Cārvāka argument that whatever is not perceived, does not exist, and that, since Īśvara is not perceived, he does not exist.

336, 3—7 Some views of the Cārvākas that are to be rejected on the same grounds.

336, 8 The Mīmāṃsaka is to be placated and threatened.

[Udayana now passes on to the discussion of the manner of determining the necessary relation (*pratibandhaḥ*) necessary for a valid inference 336, 9—371, 4]:

336, 9—337, 2 Cārvāka's objection: If one does not admit the denial of what is invisible on the ground of its non-perception, then the denial of invisible adjuncts (*anupalabhyopādhiḥ*) would not be possible; and thus the necessary relation which is the seed of inference will not be established.

337, 3—338, 7 a) Ekadeśin's answer to the Cārvāka: Even if there is no exclusion of adjuncts, still the necessary relation can be established by ascertaining the four or five forms of the Hetu on the sole basis of the perception of the Hetu in the homogeneous cases (*sapakṣaḥ*) and its non-perception in the heterogeneous cases (*vipakṣaḥ*).

339, 1—3 Cārvāka objects to the answer of the Ekadeśin: How can one know in that case that a certain Hetu deviates from the Sādhya and another Hetu does not, since there is no special factor for determining it?

339, 3—8 Cārvāka rejects the Ekadeśin's view that there is the nature (*svabhāvaḥ*) to determine the deviation or otherwise of the Hetu.

340, 1—2 Ekadeśin brings forward an inference by which the absence of adjunct can be established: "When a thing has, at no time and by no means of cognition, been perceived to possess a quality [in the case in question, an adjunct], it does not possess it".

340, 2—4 Cārvāka rejects the validity of this argument since, being itself an inference, it presupposes absence of any adjunct, and thus it is subject to the fault of infinite regress.

340, 5—341, 3 b) The answer of the Buddhist: The necessary relation can be established by applying the laws of identity (*tādātmyam*) and 'origination from it' (*tadutpattiḥ*).

341, 3—5 Cārvāka's answer to the Buddhist: In this way one of the grounds of non-deviation of the Hetu will not be established. Moreover, how is it that there is no deviation in the case of identity and 'origination from it'?

341, 6—365, 12 c) Udayana's reply:

1. To the Cārvāka (341, 6—365, 6):

i) Inference is to be admitted, since the very doubt of deviation presupposes it (341, 6—342, 6)

ii) The doubt of deviation can be got rid of by applying Tarka-argument (342, 7—343, 4).

iii) There is no infinite regress in the application of Tarka, since contradiction acts as a limit to doubt (345, 1—347, 2).
iv) There is no supra-sensible adjunct (*atīndriyopādhiḥ*), for ascertaining the absence of which a means of cognition is to be sought. There is merely a doubt whether the necessary relation is effected by the presence of another factor, and this doubt can be dispelled by applying Tarka (348, 1—351, 1).

v) The Hetu lacking a favourable Tarka (*anukūlatarkaḥ*) to support it is an ineffective Hetu (*aprayojakahetuḥ*). An ineffective Hetu is of two kinds: a Hetu of which there is doubt whether it has an adjunct, and a Hetu of which there is certainty that there is an adjunct (353, 2—3). Excursus on *upādhiḥ* (351, 4—365, 6).

2. To the Buddhist (365, 7—12):
It is Tarka that is the means of ascertaining the necessary relation between the Hetu and the Sādhya even on the basis of identity and 'origination from it'.

366, 1—371, 4 Excursus: Under which of the Hetvābhāsa-s is the *aprayojakahetuḥ* to be classified? Udayana holds that it is to be classified under *asiddhahetuḥ*.

371, 5—386, 3 III. Comparison (Upamānam) cannot Disprove the Existence of Īśvara:

371, 5—373, 7 The view of some (= Vaiśeṣikas) that comparison (*upamānam*) cannot be suspected of being a means of disproving the existence of Īśvara, since in their view, even counting non-existence (*abhāvaḥ*), there are only seven categories of reality, and similarity (*sādṛśyam*) which is said to be the proper object of comparison is not one of them.

374, 1—375, 2 The view of some others (= Bhāṭṭa-Mīmāṃsakas) who, identifying similarity with the generality (*sāmānyam*) accepted by the Vaiśeṣikas, argue that comparison has a proper object, namely generality. And the cognition, "This object before me is similar to that object [seen by me elsewhere]" is not produced by the senses nor by mere recollection (*smaraṇam*), and hence it is produced by a distinct means of cognition called comparison.

375, 2—376, 7 The answer of the Vaiśeṣikas to the Bhāṭṭas: If a separate means of cognition called comparison is necessary for cognising similarity, then for the same reason another distinct means of cognition — thus, for the Bhāṭṭas, a seventh means of cognition — will have to be admitted by the Bhāṭṭas for cognising dissimilarity. If, however, they claim that dissimilarity is cognised through the means of cognition called implication (*arthāpattiḥ*), they should equally admit that similarity, too, can be cognised through implication without having to postulate a separate means of cognition called comparison.

The answer of Udayana (377, 1—386, 3):

A) Udayana establishes that comparison is a means of valid cognition distinct from the others (377, 1—386, 2):

377, 1—378, 3 Comparison has for its object the relation of a name with the object named (*saṃjñāsaṃjñisambandhaḥ*), a relation that cannot be grasped by direct perception (*pratyakṣam*) or by verbal testimony (*śabdaḥ*) alone.

378, 4—7 The view of some that the relation of the name to the object named can be grasped either by verbal testimony alone or through inference.

378, 7—381, 6 Udayana rejects the view that it is verbal testimony that is the means for cognising the relation of the name to the object named.

381, 7—382, 3 Udayana rejects the argument of the opponents that it is inference that is the means for determining the relation of the name with the object named. Their argument was:

"The word *gavayaḥ* is expressive of [the animal called] gavaya, because cultured people apply it to that [animal] without its having a function [to express] any other [object], just like word 'cow' [applied] with regard to a cow". Udayana answers that this argument is vitiated by the fallacy of *asiddhatvam*.

382, 4—385, 4 The opponent argues that the statement, "That which is similar to a cow is a thing [called] gavaya" intends to express pervasion (*vyāptiḥ*) and that the hearer, having known the relation makes the inference: "This [animal before me] is a gavaya, because it has similarity to the cow, like an object known through the statement of similarity". Consequently it is inference that is the means of cognising the relation of a name to the object named. Udayana rejects this argument.

386, 1—2 [Having thus established the independent status of comparison,] Udayana defines it as the application of the meaning of a sentence, in which is mentioned a word whose established meaning is not known, to an object.

B) Though comparison is a distinct means of valid cognition, it cannot disprove the existence of Īśvara:

386, 2—3 Udayana gives the reason why comparison cannot disprove the existence of Īśvara: it is because Īśvara does not fall under the proper object of comparison which is the relation of a name to the object named on the basis of similarity.

388, 1—417, 6 VERBAL TESTIMONY (ŚABDAḤ) CANNOT DISPROVE THE EXISTENCE OF ĪŚVARA:

388, 1—398, 7 A) Verbal testimony is an independent means of valid cognition:

388, 1—390, 5 Vaiśeṣikas etc. maintain that verbal testimony cannot be a means of valid cognition that can disprove the existence of Īśvara, since it is not different from inference. They bring forward two arguments to show that verbal testimony can be reduced to inference:

1) "These word-meanings have mutual association, because they are reminded of by means of words that have syntactic expectancy (*ākāṅkṣā*) etc., like the meaning of the words 'Bring the cow'".

2) "These words presuppose the cognition of the association of the meanings that have been recalled to mind, because when there is syntactic expectancy etc., they cause recollection of it, like the words 'Bring the cow'".

390, 6—398, 7 The answer of Udayana:
a) Kārikā enunciating Udayana's answer (390, 7—8).
b) Rejection of argument 1) above (391, 1—392, 8).
c) Rejection of argument 2) above, after a detailed analysis of the nature of *ākāṅkṣā* (392, 9—398, 7). Udayana defines *ākāṅkṣā* as *jijñāsāṃ prati yogyatā* (398, 5).

401, 1—414, 2 Excursus: Refutation of the Anvitābhidhāna theory:

401, 1—404, 11 Refutation of the view of the Prābhākaras who accept Vedic testimony as an independent means of valid cognition on the ground that, the Veda being without an author, there is no possibility of an inference of the cognition of its author, but reduce the secular verbal testimony to inference, since with regard to it an inference of the cognition of the speaker is possible. Udayana argues that the Prābhākara view will logically lead to the Veda being a mere reiteration of what is already known.

405, 1—414, 2 Refutation of the theory of Anvitābhidhāna and the establishment of the Abhihitānvaya-theory.

415, 1—417, 6 B) Though verbal testimony is an independent means of valid cognition, it does not disprove the existence of Īśvara:

415, 1—5 The opponent argues that the Vedic texts themselves disprove the existence of Īśvara, since there are passages in them that deny Īśvara to be omniscient and creator of the universe.

415, 5—417, 6 Udayana's reply:
a) If the Vedic pasages where the non-existence of an omniscient creator is spoken of are not the words of a trustworthy person, they are not valid means of cognition. A person who gives trustworthy testimony concerning things that are supra-sensible must necessarily be omniscient.
b) The argument that Īśvara does not exist, because there are passages in the sacred scriptures that deny his existence, is vitiated by the defect of uncertainty (*anaikāntikatvam*); for there are other passages in the sacred scriptures, more numerous than those which deny his existence, that proclaim Īśvara to be the creator of the universe.
c) The scriptural passages which are said to teach the inactivity of the spirit are to be understood in a different sense, namely that the spirit is free from all impure attributes.

417, 7—426, 2 V. Implication (Arthāpattiḥ) cannot Disprove the Existence of Īśvara:

417, 7—418, 8 A) Implication (*arthāpattiḥ*) does not disprove the existence of Īśvara:

417, 7—9 The opponent argues: If Īśvara existed, he would not have instructed men through the Veda; for it cannot be admitted that he is unable to make men perform sacrifices etc. without his teaching them. Hence the very fact of instruction which is incompatible with Īśvara implies his non-existence.

417, 9—418, 8 Udayana refutes this argument and establishes that the reverse is true, namely that instruction, far from implying the non-existence of Īśvara, implies it as cause of the instruction.

419, 1—426, 2 B) Implication is not a means of cognition distinct from inference:

419, 1—422, 2 Implication is not distinct from inference, because in popular speech (*loke*) one does not mention it as a separate means of cognition, and because it cannot be any other means of cognition than inference. Udayana shows that in the example (of implication) "Caitra, though alive, is not at home", the conclusion "therefore he exists elsewhere" is nothing but the result of an inference.

422, 3—425, 3 Refutation of the argument that implication and inference are not identical since the former produces absence of contradiction between two cognitions that are apparently in contradiction with each other, while the latter is not at all so. Udayana shows that the process by which the advocate of implication reconciles two cognitions that are apparently in contradiction with each other is identical with the process of establishing the logical pervasion (*vyāptiḥ*), and that hence implication is nothing but inference.

425, 3—426, 1 Refutation of the view that implication postulated by the Mīmāṃsakas is identical with the inference called *kevala-vyatirekī* admitted by the Naiyāyikas.

426, 1—2 Conclusion: implication is a synonym (*paryāyaḥ*) for inference or a name for a particular type of it, like *pūrvavat*, *śeṣavat* and *sāmānyatodṛṣṭam*.

427, 1—448, 10 VI. Non-Perception (Anupalabdhiḥ) cannot Disprove the Existence of Īśvara:

[Udayana reminds his readers on 427, 1 that he has already shown (see section on direct perception: 311, 4—336, 7) that non-perception cannot disprove the existence of Īśvara since he does not belong to the domain of perceptible objects. He devotes this section therefore only to showing that non-perception is not a means of cognition distinct from direct perception (*pratyakṣam*). He brings forward eight arguments to establish that absence or non-existence (*abhāvaḥ*) of an object is grasped by means of the senses (therefore through direct perception or *pratyakṣam*), and not through another means of cognition called non-perception (*anupalabdhiḥ*), as the Mīmāṃsakas maintain, and that consequently the means of cognition called non-perception is not distinct from direct perception.]

427, 3—4 Kārikā mentioning the first four arguments to prove that the senses are the means for cognising non-existence.

427, 5—430, 1 Argument 1: Because non-existence of a thing is directly cognised (*sākṣātkāritvam*).

430, 1—437, 4 Argument 2: Because the cognition of the non-existence of a thing is produced immediately through the operation of a sense that is not exhausted in any other object.

437, 5—440, 8 Argument 3: Because the cognition of the non-existence of an object takes place without the cognition of its instrument.

440, 9—441, 5 Argument 4: Because the Manas can produce cognition of external objects only in dependence upon a means of cognition that has the nature of existence, and not through the assistance of mere non-existence.

441, 6—8 Kārikā mentioning four more arguments to show that it is the senses that are the means of cognising non-existence.

442, 1—4 Argument 5: That means of cognition which cognises the existence of an object must also be that which cognises its non-existence. The senses being the means of cognising the existence of a thing must also be the means of cognising its non-existence.

442, 5—443, 3 Argument 6: Because the operation of cognising non-existence is not interrupted by the cognition of the subject of that non-existence. In other words, even though the senses are employed in grasping the subject of non-existence, still there is no interruption of the activity of cognising the non-existence itself of that subject.

443, 4—11 Argument 7: That on account of the defect of which there arises erroneous cognition (*viparyayaḥ*) of the non-existence of an existent thing is the instrument for cognising non-existence. And it is due to the defect of the senses that there arises erroneous cognition of the non-existence of an existent thing.

444, 1—445, 2 Argument 8: If the determinate cognition of the non-existence of a thing (v. g. "Here on the ground there is no pot") is not grasped by the instrumentality of the senses, the Mīmāṃsakas will have to postulate a seventh means of valid cognition; for, if the senses are said to be exhausted in grasping only the subject, then non-perception would, in the same manner, be exhausted in cognising only the quality, and thus non-perception will not be the means for cognising non-existence.

445, 3—446, 2 The opponent proposes four arguments to prove that non-perception is a distinct means of cognition which has for its object the quality of non-existence in a subject:

1) The cognition of non-existence ("Here on the ground there is no pot") is a qualified cognition. Being an effect of a cognition of qualification, the qualified cognition presupposes an anterior cognition of the qualification (namely, non-existence) through non-perception. The capacity of the senses to cognise the qualified subject cannot be extended also to the cognition of the qualification. Otherwise the sense of sight which produces the cognition "Sandal-wood is fragrant" would be able to grasp fragrance in general.

2) The determinate cognition of non-existence cannot be produced by the senses, since they can produce determinate cognitions only with regard to the objects which have been perceived (*ālocitaḥ*) by them.

3) Cognition through the senses presupposes conjunction of the sense with the object cognised. But none of the kinds of conjunctions admitted by the opponent (= Nyāya-Vaiśeṣika) can be applied to the conjunction of a sense with non-existence.

4) Even the opponent has necessarily to admit non-perception, since there is cognition of non-existence.

446, 2—448, 10 Udayana rejects these arguments and establishes that non-perception is not a separate means of cognition and that the non-existence of a thing is cognised by direct perception.

449, 1—4 The concluding verse of the Stabaka.

STABAKA IV

Refutation of the Fourth Objection

[The major portion of this Stabaka is devoted to the refutation of the Mīmāṃsaka theory that valid cognition must be of an object not previously cognised. Udayana then shows that the cognition of Īśvara cannot be said to be invalid even according to the definition of valid cognition given by the opponents. The validity of his cognition being thus established, he can be a source of valid cognition to us through the communication of the Veda.]

450, 4—474, 10 I. DISCUSSION ON THE VALIDITY AND NATURE OF COGNITION:

450, 4—458, 3 A) Refutation of the view that valid cognition (*pramā*) must be a cognition of what has not been previously cognised (*anadhigatārthajñānam* or *agṛhītagrāhitvam*):

450, 4—5 The objection that, even if Īśvara exists, still his cognition would not be valid, since it would lack the characteristic note of valid cognition, namely "not being previously cognised".

450, 6—452, 3 Udayana's answer: The definition of valid cognition as the cognition of what has not been previously cognised has the defects of:

1) a pervasion that is too wide (*ativyāptiḥ*); for such a definition would be applicable also to erroneous cognitions.

2) a pervasion that is too narrow (*avyāptiḥ*: literally 'non-pervasion'); for it would not be applicable to continuous cognitions (*dhārāvāhikabuddhiḥ*).

452, 3—455, 6 Discussion on the validity of continuous cognitions:

452, 3—453, 6 Refutation of the view that even in the case of continuous cognitions there is the characteristic note of "not being previously cognised", effected by the adjunct of time (*kālaḥ*).

454, 1—455, 6 The opponent proposes cognisedness (*jñātatā*) as the factor that confers on the different moments of the continuous cognition the characteristic of "not having been previously cognised". Udayana answers:

1) Cognisedness will be refuted (see 459, 2—462, 8).

2) If there were cognisedness to confer on the posterior moment of the continuous cognition the characteristic of "not having been previously cognised", then, for the same reason, remembrance, too, would turn out to be valid cognition.

455, 6—458, 3 Discussion on the validity of remembrance (*smṛtiḥ*).

B) The definition of valid cognition as brought forward by the Mīmāṃsakas does not affect the validity of Īśvara's cognition:

458, 4—459, 2 Udayana argues that, even if "not having been previously cognised" were an essential characteristic of valid cognition, still Īśvara's cognition cannot be considered as invalid (*apramā*), since (being one and without successive moments,) it does not have the nature of a cognition of what is previously cognised (*gṛhītagrāhitvam*).

459, 2—463, 5 C) Refutation of cognisedness (*jñātatā*):

[The Bhāṭṭa-Mīmāṃsakas bring forward some arguments to establish cognisedness, and Udayana refutes them.]

459, 3—5	Argument 1: If there were no cognisedness, the cognition of one object would not be distinguishable from that of another object.
459, 6—460, 8	Udayana's refutation of this argument.
460, 9	Argument 2: One concludes to cognisedness because of the pervasion (*vyāptiḥ*) that every activity should produce something in the object.
460, 9—461, 7	Udayana's refutation of this argument.
461, 8—10	Argument 3: Cognisedness is established by experience (*anubhavasiddha-*); for, when we say in a general manner, "This object is known" and in a more specific manner, "This object is directly perceived", we ascribe to the object itself some qualification.
461, 10—462, 8	Udayana's refutation of this argument.
462, 9—463, 1	The objection that a thing cannot be an object since it is not the substratum of fruit, is rejected. [Probably the opponent argued for cognisedness: "A thing is the substratum of the fruit produced by the activity of cognition, because it is called the object of cognition".]
463, 2—3	Argument 4: Cognisedness is established from the fact that cognition, being supra-sensible (*atīndriya-*), is inferred from it.
463, 4—5	Udayana rejects this argument since it implies reciprocal dependence, and because cognition is not supra-sensible.
463, 5—474, 10	D) Refutation of the view that cognition is supra-sensible (*atīndriya-*):
	[The Bhāṭṭa-Mīmāṃsakas bring forward some arguments to prove that cognition is supra-sensible and Udayana refutes them:]
463, 5—6	Argument 1: Cognition is supra-sensible, because it cannot be perceived by the senses.
463, 6—464, 10	Refutation of this argument: It is vitiated by logical fallacies. Moreover, the fact that there is indifference towards objects of cognition during the time of deep sleep shows that at other times cognition is perceptible.
464, 11	Argument 2: (referred to only by the Hetu): Cognition is supra-sensible, because it lasts only for a moment (*kṣaṇikatvāt*).
464, 11—13	Rejection of this argument as invalid, since its Hetu is vitiated by faults.
464, 14—465, 3	The opponent (= Mahāvratīya) argues for the momentary nature of cognition.
465, 4—469, 3	Refutation of his argument.

469, 4—6 Argument 3: If cognition were perceptual, there would be no passing over to the object.

469, 7—470, 3 Refutation of this argument.

470, 4—471, 1 Argument 4: Cognition is supra-sensible, because it cannot be apprehended either by conceptual (*savikalpaka-*) cognition or solely by non-conceptual (*nirvikalpaka-*) cognition.

471, 1—473, 1 Refutation of this argument.

473, 2—4 Argument 5: Cognition is supra-sensible, since otherwise its determination by supra-sensible (imperceptible) objects such as the atoms would be inexplicable.

473, 4—474, 9 Udayana's answer to this argument.

474, 9—10 Conclusion of the discussion on the perceptual nature of cognition: The argument for the perceptibility of cognition is perception itself.

475, 1—477, 11 II. Vindication of the Validity of the Cognition of Īśvara:

475, 1—2 The opponent argues:
1) Īśvara's cognition is not valid cognition (*pramā*) since, being eternal, it has not the nature of being a fruit (of a means of valid cognition) (*aphalatvāt*).
2) His cognition is not a means of valid cognition (*pramāṇam*) since it does not cause (*akārakatvāt*) valid cognition.
3) Hence its substratum is not a subject of valid cognition (*pramātā*).

475, 2—476, 7 Udayana's answer:
ad 1): Valid cognition consists in the correct experience of the object, regardless of the consideration whether it is eternal or non-eternal. Moreover, the argument has the fallacy of *āśrayāsiddhiḥ* or *bādhaḥ*.
ad 2): It is conceded that the cognition of Īśvara is not an instrument of valid cognition, since it has no causal relation to his cognition.
ad 3): The fact that Īśvara is the subject of valid cognition consists in this alone that valid cognition inheres in him.

476, 8—9 Objection: Means of valid cognition (*pramāṇam*) is so called because by means of it an object is validly cognised, and a "valid cogniser" (*pramātā*) is so called becauses he cognises validly. Thus these two words *pramāṇam* and *pramātā* are expressions for something that causes. How can they, then, mean something that does not cause in the case of Īśvara and his cognition?

476, 9—12 Answer: The signification of the terms *pramāṇam* and *pramātā* as cause is only from the point of view of derivation as given by the grammarians.

476, 12—477, 1 Objection: In that case you go against the teaching of your own system; for, you will have to admit a fifth means of valid cognition (namely Īśvara's cognition), since it does not have as instrument the senses nor mark nor verbal testimony, and hence cannot be classed under any of the four means of valid cognition admitted by you.

477, 1—2 Answer: On account of Īśvara's being connected with a valid cognition that is immediate, it is included under direct perception (*pratyakṣam*).

477, 3—7 Objection: The cognition of Īśvara cannot be valid, since it is erroneous when it has for its object errors of people like us. On the other hand, if it does not apprehend the wrong cognitions of people like us, then the instructions he gives us for the avoidance of those errors will have a non-omniscient cause (*asarvajñapūrvakatvam*).

477, 7—11 Answer: Even though error is invalid cognition, still the cognition that has it for its object and shows that it is invalid, is itself not erroneous.

478, 1—4 The concluding verse of the Stabaka.

STABAKA V

Refutation of the Fifth Objection

[Udayana brings forward in this Stabaka a number of proofs to establish the existence of Īśvara.]

479, 5—6 Objection that there are no proofs for the existence of Īśvara.

479, 6—8 Answer: Kārikā where Udayana mentions, in the form of Hetu-s, the proofs dealt with in this Stabaka.
[Udayana gives two series of proofs based on a double interpretation of the Hetu-s mentioned in the Kārikā.]

479, 9—519, 3 A) The First Series of Proofs:

[In this first series of proofs Īśvara is established as the creator, sustainer and destroyer of the universe, the instructor of the living beings and the author of the Veda.]

479, 9—503, 11 Proof 1: *kāryatvāt*:
[Īśvara's existence is established from the fact that the earth etc., being effects, presuppose a cause that produces them.]

479, 9	Formulation of the proof: Earth etc. presuppose a maker, because they are effects. [Udayana now establishes the validity of this proof by showing that it is free from logical fallacies.]
485, 1—2	Kārikā stating that the proof is free from logical fallacies.
485, 3—492, 2	Refutation of the view that the maker of earth etc. must be bodied.
492, 3—493, 6	Refutation of the objection that the Hetu *kāryatvam* is inconclusive because of doubt concerning the *vyatireki*.
493, 7—494, 2	The opponent attacks the Sādhya and argues that the proof has *satpratipakṣatvam*.
494, 3—9	The opponent attacks the example (*dṛṣṭāntaḥ*) and argues that the proof has *siddhasādhanatvam*.
494, 10—12	The opponent attacks the Hetu on the ground that it is conditioned (*upādhimat*).
494, 13—496, 6	Answer to the objection of *satpratipakṣatvam*.
496, 7—497, 12	Answer to the objection of *siddhasādhanatvam*.
497, 13—499, 9	Answer to the objection that the Hetu is conditioned.
500, 1—5	A favourable Tarka argument in support of the first proof.
500, 6—502, 7	Objection of the opponent (= Buddhist) that the causal relation can be determined only between two visible things and that consequently causality can be ascribed only to a bodied agent, is refuted.
502, 8—13	Refutation of an objection that, if Īśvara is independent of other causes for producing the universe, there would be creation at all times; if, on the other hand, he is dependent upon other causes, he is not Īśvara.
503, 1—11	Scriptural passages (with commentary) in confirmation of the first proof.
503, 12—505, 20	Proof 2: *āyojanāt*: [Īśvara's existence is proved from the necessity of a conscious agent to impel the atoms to combine themselves and form the universe.]
503, 12—505, 8	The proof is formulated and shown to be free from logical fallacies.
505, 9—20	Scriptural texts (with commentary) in confirmation of this proof.
506, 1—17	Proof 3: *dhṛteḥ*: [Īśvara's existence is established from the necessity of a supporting agent of the universe preventing it from falling down.]
506, 1—10	The proof is formulated and objections to it are answered.

506, 10—17	Scriptural texts (with commentary) in confirmation of this proof.
507, 1—7	Proof 4: *saṃharaṇāt*: [Īśvara's existence is inferred from the necessity of a being endowed with the quality of effort (*prayatnaḥ*) in order to cause the dissolution of the universe into its ultimate components.]
507, 1—2	Formulation of the proof.
507, 2—7	Confirmation through scriptural passages.
507, 8—508, 20	Proof 5: *padāt*: [Īśvara's existence is established from the fact that at the time of the new creation an instructor is required to teach the living beings the different usages.]
507, 8—508, 5	Formulation of the proof.
508, 6—11	Refutation of the view that usages (*vyavahāraḥ*), being beginningless, do not require to be taught by somebody.
508, 12—14	Refutation of the view that Īśvara cannot be the teacher of usages to the living beings, since he is not bodied. Udayana admits that Īśvara does take up a body from time to time when the nature of the effect to be produced necessarily requires it.
508, 14—20	Confirmation of the proof through scriptural passages.
509, 1—6	Proof 6: *pratyayāt*: [The existence of Īśvara is proved from the authoritativeness of the Vedic tradition.]
509, 1—6	Formulation of the proof and its explanation.
509, 7—510, 5	Proof 7: *śruteḥ*: [Īśvara's existence is proved from the fact that the Vedic nature (*vedatvam*) of the Veda requires an omniscient author.]
509, 7—8	Formulation of the proof.
510, 1—5	Explanation of the nature of Veda (*vedatvam*).
511, 1—514, 4	Proof 8: *anvayataḥ* (= *vākyāt* of 479, 8): [Īśvara's existence is established from the fact that the Vedic sentences require a person as author.]
511, 1	Formulation of the proof.
511, 2—512, 3	Rejection of the objection [of the Mīmāṃsakas] that, as the author of the Veda is not remembered, there is no such author.
512, 4—513, 2	Rejection of a *satpratipakṣa*-argument that the Veda has no person as author.

513, 3—8	Rejection of the view that the Veda has no author (*vaktā*: literally 'speaker'), since in the absence of senses, external as well as internal, such a person would not have knowledge of supra-sensible realities.
513, 9—514, 4	Rejection of the objection that the Hetu of the proof (namely, *vākyatvāt*) is *aprayojaka-*.
514, 5—519, 3	Proof 9: *saṃkhyāviśeṣāt*: [Īśvara's existence is inferred from the necessity of a relating cognition (*apekṣābuddhiḥ*), at the time of the origin of the universe, in order to produce the plural number which in turn causes magnitude in the triads].
514, 5—517, 1	Udayana establishes that the cause of magnitude in the triads is the plural number (*anekasaṃkhyā*).
517, 1—518, 3	Udayana establishes the existence of Īśvara as the subject of the relating cognition that produces this plural number.
518, 3—519, 3	Refutation of the view that the relating cognition of beings like us or Adṛṣṭam can explain the magnitude of the created universe.
519, 4—573, 6	B) The Second Series of Proofs: [In this second series of proofs Īśvara is established as the author of the Veda.]
519, 4—522, 9	Proof 1: *kāryatvāt*: [Īśvara's existence is argued from the fact that the intention or purport (*tātparyam*) that is expressed in some Vedic sentences implies an author.]
520, 2—521, 15	*kāryatvam* is here taken in the sense of *tātparyam*. In an excursus on the exact meaning of *param* contained in the word *tātparyam*, Udayana argues that it means neither *sādhyam*, nor *pratipādyam*, nor *prayojanam*, but *uddeśyam*.
521, 16—18	Application of *tātparyam* to the Veda: Since the Arthavāda passages in the Veda express the intention or purport (*uddeśyam*) of a person, such an eminent person is inferred.
521, 19—522, 3	Formulation of the proof in syllogistic form.
522, 4—9	Tarka argument in confirmation.
522, 10—523, 6	Proofs 2, 3 and 4: *āyojanāt, dhṛtyādeḥ*: [Proofs 3 and 4 are not introduced by Udayana in his customary manner with the mentioning of the Hetu. In these proofs Īśvara's existence is argued from the fact that the explanation of the Veda that is indispensable for understanding its meaning requires a person who perceives the totality of the Veda.]
522, 10—15	*āyojanam* means here *vyākhyānam* (= explanation). Formulation of the proof based on this interpretation.

522, 16—523, 6	(According to commentators) the proofs based on *dhṛtyādeḥ*.
523, 7—525, 7	Proof 5: *padāt*: [Īśvara's existence is proved from certain words in the Veda which are applied by the wise only to the maker of the universe.]
523, 7—524, 14	Proof based on words such as *praṇavaḥ*, *īśvaraḥ* and *iśānaḥ* found in the Veda.
524, 15—24	Proof based on the words in the first person found in the Veda.
525, 1—7	Proof based on relative pronouns as well as particles found in the Veda.
525, 8—568, 10	Proof 6: *pratyayāt*: [Īśvara's existence is established from the fact that the verbal suffix of optatives found in the Vedic injunctions expresses the will of a person.]
525, 8—11	*pratyayaḥ* means here the verbal suffix of the optative (*vidhipratyayaḥ* or *liṅ*). Since optative suffixes express the will of a person, Īśvara is inferred as the author of the Vedic injunctions.
525, 12—15	Activity (with regard to religious duties) is the product of injunctions (*vidhiḥ*). [Here follows a long excursus on the nature of the *vidhiḥ* (525, 16—567, 15). Only the main outlines of this section are mentioned below.]
525, 16—526, 4	Vidhi is: 1) either the attribute of the agent (*kartṛdharmaḥ*), 2) or of the action (*karmadharmaḥ*), 3) or of the instrument (*karaṇadharmaḥ*), 4) or of the enjoining person (*niyoktṛdharmaḥ*).
526, 5—544, 3	Vidhi is not the attribute of the agent,
544, 4—554, 17	nor of the action,
555, 1—567, 2	nor of the instrument.
567, 2—15	But Vidhi is the attribute of the enjoining person and expresses the will of that person that, in order to gain a certain desirable object, some action is to be performed (in the case of positive injunctions or Vidhi properly so called), or that, in order to avoid a certain undesirable object, one should abstain from some action (in the case of negative injunctions or *niṣedhaḥ*).
568, 1—10	This principle is applied to the Veda, the injunctions of which are the expression of the will of Īśvara.
568, 11—570, 11	Proof 7: *śruteḥ*: [Īśvara's existence is inferred from the fact that in all the

Vedic branches he is spoken of under some name or other as worthy of worship.]

568, 11—569, 4 There are no Vedic branches where Īśvara is not spoken of under some name or other, and they are to be understood in the primary sense of the words (*mukhyārthatayā*).

569, 5—570, 11 Refutation of the argument that the Vedic passages, where Īśvara is spoken of, are not valid, as they are mere statements of facts (*siddhārthatayā*).

571, 1—3 Proof 8: *vākyāt*:
[Īśvara's existence is inferred from the fact that the association of word-meanings in the Vedic sentences implies a cogniser of that association.]

571, 1—3 *vākyatvam* here means *saṃsargabhedapratipādakatvam*. Formulation of the proof.

572, 1—573, 6 Proof 9: *saṃkhyāviśeṣāt*:
[Īśvara's existence is established from the verbal forms in the first person found in the Veda as well as from the names of the Vedic branches.]

572, 1—3 Kārikā mentioning the proofs.

572, 4—6 Proof based on the number expressed by the verbal forms in the first person found in the Veda.

572, 7—13 Proof based on the names of the Vedic branches such as Kāṭhaka, Kālāpaka etc.

572, 14—573, 6 Refutation of other explanations of the names of the abovementioned Vedic branches.

573, 7—576, 8 C) CONCLUDING REMARKS:

573, 7 Īśvara has been known through scriptures and through inference (as shown in the fifth Stabaka). By some people he is also directly perceived (*sākṣād api dṛśyate*).

573, 8—574, 17 The objection that the causal complex for directly perceiving Īśvara is absent, is rejected by Udayana; for the Yogins who have experience of such direct vision of Īśvara possess intuitive power (*bhāvanā*) which is assisted by merit (*dharmaḥ*).

574, 18—21 A confirming argument (*vipakṣe bādhakam*) to show that Īśvara is knowable by direct perception (*sākṣātkāritvam*).

574, 22—575, 14 Mention of several scriptural and other passages where Īśvara and worship of him are spoken of.

575, 15—576, 8 The concluding verses where Udayana prays Īśvara to draw, through his mercy and in his own time, towards himself the hard-hearted deniers of his. He then places once again this work at the feet of Śiva.

PART TWO

UDAYANA'S DOCTRINE OF ĪŚVARA

Chapter One

PROOFS FOR THE EXISTENCE OF ĪŚVARA

The author of the Nyāyakusumāñjali seems to have taken upon himself as his special task the vindication of the existence of Īśvara against the attacks of the non-theistic opponents. An important feature of the Īśvara doctrine as found in his works is, as we observed earlier, that it deals primarily—one would almost say, exclusively—with the existence of Īśvara leaving the other aspects almost untouched, or in any case relegated to a subordinate place. If ever some aspects of the Īśvara doctrine other than his existence are mentioned or spoken of, such as his omniscience or other qualities, they are brought in only in as far as they have a bearing on the central theme of the existence of Īśvara.

Such an emphasis on the existence of Īśvara with an apparent disregard for or neglect of the other aspects of the Īśvara doctrine such as his nature or attributes was not without an important ground. In the earlier period of the Nyāya-Vaiśeṣika theism, that is to say, up to about the seventh century A. D., the controversy around Īśvara had a different outlook. While commenting on the Nyāyasūtras IV, 1, 19—21, the Nyāya commentators gave an exposition, however brief, of the different aspects of the Īśvara doctrine such as his existence, his nature, his attributes or qualities and the motives of his activity[93]. With regard to the existence of Īśvara, various arguments were thought out so that there were a series of proofs based on different logical reasons (*hetuḥ*). The opponents of the Īśvara doctrine, on their part, based their objections on certain facts of human life such as the presence of inequality or pain that would go against the theists' assumption of an equitable and compassionate Īśvara[94], or on the inconsistencies or contradictions arising from his nature or attributes as taught by the defenders of theism[95]. But there came a decisive

---

[93] Cf. the commentaries of Pakṣilasvāmin and Uddyotakara on NSu IV, 1, 19—21. Praśastapāda (6th century Vaiśeṣika author) also, treats of the different aspects of the Īśvara doctrine. Cf. G. Chemparathy: The Īśvara doctrine of Praśastapāda, pp. 65—87.

[94] Cf. YD 71, 12—22; ŚV (Saṃbandhākṣepaparihāraḥ) verse 49; BCA IX, verses 119—126 (pp. 253, 28—261, 5).

[95] Among the inconsistencies or antinomies brought forward by the opponents are the following: How could Īśvara be the creator of the universe, if he has no body? How can the eternity of Īśvara's desire (*icchā*) and effort (*prayatnaḥ*) be reconciled with the fact of creation and dissolution of the universe that take place in succession? How can the effort of Īśvara be dependent upon his cognition, if this effort is eternal? What purpose is there for an absolutely self-sufficient Īśvara in creating the universe since he has nothing to gain from it for himself? If he

turn in the development of the Īśvara doctrine from the time of that great Buddhist thinker and dialectician of the seventh century A. D., Dharmakīrti, who is, in the words of T. VETTER, „der wohl neben Dignāga einflußreichste buddhistische Denker der nachklassischen Periode der indischen Philosophie"[96]. In his Pramāṇavārttika he initiated a new approach to the problem of Īśvara and a new method of attacking the Nyāya-Vaiśeṣika Īśvara doctrine. Leaving aside the other aspects of the Īśvara doctrine he centred his offensives against the Nyāya-Vaiśeṣika proofs for the existence of Īśvara, and this, too, from the aspect of their logical validity. Such a change of approach was quite in line with the developments in Indian logic inaugurated by Dignāga and continued and perfected by himself. He argued that the proofs advanced by the Nyāya-Vaiśeṣika theists to establish the existence of Īśvara were vitiated by logical fallacies and that consequently they were incorrect or invalid. He even went further and called in question the very possibility of establishing the existence of Īśvara by arguments, since in his view the very conception of an eternal cause, as the Nyāya-Vaiśeṣika theists assume Īśvara to be, implies a contradiction[97].

Since the opponents of the Īśvara doctrine now launched their attacks principally on the existence of Īśvara and this, too, with special emphasis on the logical aspects of the proofs themselves, the champions of Nyāya-Vaiśeṣika theism, too, found themselves compelled to effect a corresponding shift in their treatment of the subject by making the existence of Īśvara the central theme of their own defence and, as their opponents did, with an emphasis on the logical aspect. Such a change of perspective of the Īśvara doctrine is clearly seen when the passages in the Nyāya-Vaiśeṣika works dealing with this theme before and after Dharmakīrti are compared.

The Buddhists were among the bitterest opponents of Nyāya-Vaiśeṣika theism and they carried on their opposition to the Īśvara doctrine now after the model of the author of the Pramāṇavārttika[98]. Perhaps the greatest

---

creates the universe for the sake of others, why should there be pain in the world? Such problems can be found in the pages of the earlier Nyāya-Vaiśeṣika works that defend theism or in the works of the non-theistic schools. Cf., for example, the excursus on Īśvara in NV 949, 2ff.; ŚV (Saṃbandhākṣepaparihāraḥ) verses 43ff. Udayana himself refers to such problems in ATV 379, 3ff.; 408, 1ff.; NKus 500, 6ff.; 502, 8ff.; Kir 101, 15—19. Cf. also G. CHEMPARATHY: The Testimony of the Yuktidīpikā concerning the Īśvara doctrine of the Pāśupatas and Vaiśeṣikas, p. 137ff.; also: Two early Buddhist refutations of the existence of Īśvara as the creator of the universe, pp. 87—88 and 95—96.

[96] T. VETTER: Erkenntnisprobleme bei Dharmakīrti, p. 5.

[97] Cf. PV Chapter II, verses 10—29 (pp. 35, 17—50, 16); also: G. OBERHAMMER: Zum Problem des Gottesbeweises in der indischen Philosophie, pp. 10ff.

[98] Cf. Īśvaraparīkṣā in the TS of Śāntarakṣita with the commentary TSP of Kamalaśīla (TS 51, 1—74, 10). Mention may be made here also of a less known Buddhist work against the Īśvara doctrine, the Īśvarabhaṅgasiddhi by a certain Śubhagupta who, according to E. FRAUWALLNER (Landmarks in the history of Indian Logic, p. 147), lived ca. 720—780 A. D. and whose Tibetan name Dge-bsruṅs has been wrongly translated as Kalyāṇarakṣita (E. FRAUWALLNER: Zu den buddhistischen Texten in der Zeit Khri-sroṅ-lde-btsan's, pp. 98—99).

Buddhist thinker after Dharmakīrti who made a thoroughgoing and systematic attack on the Nyāya-Vaiśeṣika Īśvara doctrine in an independent treatise was Jñānaśrī, most probably a senior contemporary of Udayana. His lengthy treatise in three parts against the existence of Īśvara[99] can be said to be the most systematic attack on the Īśvara doctrine brought forward by any opponent of theism after Dharmakīrti. He, too, had made the existence of Īśvara the central theme of his attack.

Under such circumstances it is quite understandable that in his Nyāyakusumāñjali which was intended to be a counter-attack on the arguments of the opponents as well as a thorough vindication of the existence of Īśvara, Udayana focussed his attention on this particular aspect of the doctrine which was most at stake, leaving the other aspects either untouched or completely in the background. Just as it might be said that the greatest Buddhist attack on the Īśvara doctrine after Dharmakīrti came from the pen of Jñānaśrī, we might also say that the most thorough and the most elaborate refutation of the arguments of the opponents as well as the most systematic Nyāya-Vaiśeṣika vindication of all times of the existence of Īśvara came from the pen of Udayana.

But the Nyāya-Vaiśeṣika theism had to face strong opposition not only from non-Hindu thinkers such as the Buddhists, but also from some orthodox followers of Hinduism and its schools of thought. The Mīmāṃsaka school of philosophy which, despite its adherence to the fold of Hinduism and its claims to give the authentic interpretation of the sacred Scriptures of Hinduism, was, paradoxical though it may seem, "the most atheistic of the philosophical systems of Brahmanical India"[100]. Although the Mīmāṃsakas accept a number of deities to whom the prescribed offerings are made, these deities do not occupy the place of a supreme God or fulfil any of the functions that are usually ascribed to him. In any case, in the course of time these deities were reduced to such a shadowy existence that the later Mīmāṃsakas denied any existence to them beyond the Mantras and explained the passages wherein these deities are mentioned to be mere Arthavādas or praises of sacrifices[101]. Moreover, they, too, had begun to oppose the Nyāya-Vaiśeṣika theism as the Buddhists had done. Kumārila who was probably a contemporary of Dharmakīrti[102] had subjected the Nyāya-Vaiśeṣika doctrine of Īśvara as the omniscient creator of the universe and as the author of the Veda to a scathing criticism[103].

---

[99] The three parts of this treatise are respectively a *pūrvapakṣaḥ* containing the arguments brought forward for the existence of Īśvara by the Nyāya-Vaiśeṣikas, a short *uttarapakṣaḥ* refuting these arguments, and lastly an extensive refutation of the doctrine of Īśvara in the form of an elaborate commentary on the seven verses in which Dharmakīrti had summed up his arguments against the proofs of the theists. Cf. JMN pp. 233—316.

[100] Cf. L. Renou: Religions of Ancient India, p. 43. Also P. Tuxen: Religions of India, p. 103.

[101] Cf. A. B. Keith: The Karma Mīmāṃsā, pp. 77—78.

[102] According to E. Frauwallner (Geschichte II, p. 24), Kumārila lived in the first half of the seventh century A. D.

[103] Cf. chiefly his ŚV, Sambandhākṣepaparihāraḥ, especially verses 43—82.

In his refutation of the opponents of theism, Udayana seems to have been, in a sense, more severe towards the Mīmāṃsakas than towards any other non-theistic school. In any case, he has devoted a large portion of his Nyāyakusumāñjali to discuss their objections against the Īśvara doctrine and to refute them. Almost the entire second Stabaka is devoted to the refutation of the Mīmāṃsaka view of eternity of the Vedas independent of an Īśvara. Similarly the fourth Stabaka refutes the Mīmāṃsaka view of valid cognition in order to establish the validity of cognition of Īśvara. Finally, the second series of proofs for the existence of Īśvara in the fifth Stabaka are, as we shall see, specially intended for the Mīmāṃsakas in order to show them that the very Veda, which they accept as infallible and the authentic interpreters of which they claim to be, presupposes the existence of Īśvara as its author.

The other opponents of theism belonging to the Hindu systems of thought were the Cārvākas and the Sāṃkhyins. The little that we know of the former is from the fragments of their works quoted by their adversaries[104]. Although they are refuted by Udayana as opponents of theism, most probably they had no influence on Indian thought at the time we are concerned with. The Sāṃkhyins, on the other hand, had developed a more philosophic system that exerted a deeper and broader influence on Indian thought. During the time of Udayana, they were not so influential as they had once been. Moreover, some of them had already accepted the Īśvara doctrine and thus separated themselves from the orthodox school.

The following study of the Īśvara doctrine is based on the materials found in the hitherto published works of Udayana. In fact all his major works supply some material on the Īśvara doctrine. Thus while smaller parts of his Nyāyavārttikatātparyapariśuddhi and Kiraṇāvalī as well as a larger portion of the Ātmatattvaviveka deal with Īśvara, the entire Nyāyakusumāñjali is devoted, as we have remarked earlier, to the vindication of the existence of Īśvara.

This study of the Īśvara doctrine is arranged as follows. After a brief exposition of the proofs for the existence of Īśvara as advanced by Udayana we shall make a few observations regarding the relation of this Īśvara to the created universe. This relation will be considered under two main aspects, namely as the creator of the universe and as the teacher of the living beings. The question as to whether he has also some other roles such as Christianity ascribes to God will be briefly touched upon. After that the motives of Īśvara in his dealings with the created universe will be examined. Then follows a study on the nature of Īśvara as it is understood in the context of the Nyāya-Vaiśeṣika philosophy. This is followed by an inquiry into the attributes or qualities of Īśvara. Of these attributes, the cognition of Īśvara is the most important and the one on which we are better informed than on the others, and consequently it will be treated at some length. Though the material on the other attributes of Īśvara is rather scanty, an attempt will be made to

---

[104] As an exception the Tattvopaplavasiṃha of Jayarāśi Bhaṭṭa can be mentioned.

gather all the data on this subject found scattered in his works, so that we can have as complete a picture of Udayana's Īśvara as possible. A brief consideration of his personal contribution to the Nyāya-Vaiśeṣika Īśvara doctrine brings our study to a close.

The most important contribution of Udayana to the Nyāya-Vaiśeṣika theism is the vindication of the existence of Īśvara against the objections of the opponents. This he did not only by answering the objections of the non-theists but also by bringing forward a series of positive proofs. In the present study we shall mention the important ideas of Udayana regarding the existence of Īśvara without, however, going into all the details. We shall take note of those points of discussions with the opponents which either shed light on or are necessary for the understanding of the proofs; but much of the discussions that deal with the purely logical aspect of the proofs will be left out of consideration, as these do not enrich the substance of the proofs themselves, and, moreover, require on the part of the reader an acquaintance with all the intricacies of Indian logic. As the Nyāyakusumāñjali deals especially with this aspect of the Īśvara doctrine we shall base our study mainly on it, mentioning, however, parallel or complementary ideas from his other works, wherever it is thought necessary or useful.

Before we pass on to the positive proofs of Udayana in the fifth Stabaka, it is important for us to inquire whether there are not ideas or even arguments in the first four Stabakas that contribute, at least indirectly, to establish the existence of Īśvara. The introductory prose passage of the Nyāyakusumāñjali presents, in my opinion, a proof for the existence of Īśvara, that we might term in our modern terminology a historic or ethnological proof. In this passage the author poses the question whether it is possible at all to doubt the existence of Īśvara, since everyone recognizes him under some name or other: "Here (in the consideration of the Supreme Soul) whom all worship (under some name or other), no matter whichever of the (four) objects of existence (*puruṣārthaḥ*) they strive after,—the followers of the Upaniṣads (= Vedāntins) as one having a nature that is pure and conscious (*śuddhabuddhasvabhāvaḥ*); the followers of Kapila (= Sāṃkhyins) as the primeval omniscient 'perfect one'; the followers of Patañjali (= Yogins) as (a special Puruṣa) who, untouched by the 'afflictions' (*kleśaḥ*), actions (*karma*), fruition (*vipākaḥ*) and impressions (*āśayaḥ*), having assumed control (*adhiṣṭhāya*) over a body of manifestation (*nirmāṇakāyaḥ*), reveals the traditions (of Veda and usages) (*sampradāyaḥ*) and favours (the living beings to attain the fruits of their actions such as heaven and liberation); the Great Pāśupatas as one who cannot be defiled even by (the observances of) what is opposed to the Veda and the ordinary practices and as one who is independent (of the Karma of the living beings in his activities); the Śaivites as Śiva; the Vaiṣṇavites as Puruṣottama; those versed in the Puraṇās as the (paternal) grandfather (*pitāmahaḥ*); those versed in sacrifices as the Sacrificial Person (*yajñapuruṣaḥ*); the Saugatas (= Buddhists) as the Omniscient; the Digambaras (= 'the sky-clad' Jains) as one free from obstruction (*nirāvaraṇaḥ*); the Mīmāṃsakas as one who is enjoined (in the Vedas) as deserving worship; the Cārvākas as one established according to the secular usage [of the term] (*lokavyavahārasiddha-*); the Naiyāyikas as one endowed with all (those attributes) that have been ascribed (to him); in short, whom even the artisans (recognize and worship) as the Viśvakarman (= "all-Creator")—(when there is such a universal recognition of the Supreme Soul) how can there be doubt with regard to (the existence of) that adorable (*bhagavān*) Bhava (= Śiva) whose majesty has in this manner been at all times recognized (*āsaṃsāraṃ prasiddhānubhāve*) like caste (*jātiḥ*), (Brahmanic) clan (*gotram*), list of ancestors (*pravaraḥ*), branch (*caraṇaḥ*) (i. e. school of Veda), family duties (*kuladharmaḥ*) etc.? What is there to be established?"[105]

Interesting in this passage is that Udayana names here almost all groups of persons of the India of his time as they would be classified according to their adherence to philosophical schools or religious sects. In other words, Udayana seems to suggest that the entire Hindu, Buddhist and Jain population of India believes in the existence of a Supreme Being, even if that Being may be known by different names, and that consequently the existence of a Supreme Being cannot be called into question. It is true that Udayana himself does not make this fact the basis of an argument for the existence of Īśvara. As a matter of fact, he could not make such a widespread belief in a Supreme Being an argument to prove to his opponents the existence of Īśvara, since these opponents, especially the Cārvākas, the Buddhists, the Mīmāṃsakas, the Sāṃkhyins and the Jains, did not admit the existence of an Īśvara such as the Nyāya-Vaiśeṣikas taught. He could, at the most, have argued that even his opponents believed in some manner in a Being like Īśvara; but that would not have proved the existence of a Supreme Being as Udayana wanted to establish.

Though the first four Stabakas are essentially refutations of the objections of the adversaries, they contribute, however indirectly, to the establishment of the existence of Īśvara, either in so far as the objections of the opponents are answered or in so far as they contain ideas that are closely connected with the proofs that are formulated in the last Stabaka. Hence a few brief observations on these "indirect proofs" may be made here.

In the first Stabaka Udayana discusses mainly with the Cārvākas who had denied the reality of an other-worldly invisible fruit of actions called Adṛṣṭam (or Apūrvam) that conditions the future mode of existence of the soul. In establishing the existence of such an Adṛṣṭam that inheres in the soul which is shown to be distinct from the body, the author of the Nyāyakusumāñjali

[105] NKus 14, 1—19, 2: *iha yady api yaṃ kam api puruṣārtham arthayamānāḥ śuddhabuddhasvabhāva ity aupaniṣadāḥ, ādividvān siddha iti kāpilāḥ, kleśakarmavipākāśayair aparāmṛṣṭo nirmāṇakāyam adhiṣṭhāya sampradāyapradyotako 'nugrāhakaś ceti pātañjalāḥ, lokavedaviruddhair api nirlepaḥ svatantraś ceti mahāpāśupatāḥ, śiva iti śaivāḥ, puruṣottama iti vaiṣṇavāḥ, pitāmaha iti paurāṇikāḥ, yajñapuruṣa iti yājñikāḥ, sarvajña iti saugatāḥ, nirāvaraṇa iti digambarāḥ, upāsyatvena deśita iti mīmāṃsakāḥ, lokavyavahārasiddha iti cārvākāḥ, yāvaduktopapanna iti naiyāyikāḥ, kiṃ bahunā, kāravo 'pi yaṃ viśvakarmety upāsate, tasminn evaṃ jātigotrapravaracaraṇakuladharmādivad āsaṃsāraṃ prasiddhānubhāve bhagavati bhave sandeha eva kutaḥ? kiṃ nirūpaṇīyam?*

has prepared the basis for an argument for the existence of Īśvara. For, being unconscious (*acetana-*) like the other causes of the universe, this Adṛṣṭam cannot direct its own operation, but needs to be guided by a conscious agent who could be none other than Īśvara. Although Udayana does not draw this conclusion at the end of the first Stabaka—it was meant only to establish the existence of an other-wordly means that determines the next life—he includes this argument in the second proof dealt with in the fifth Stabaka.

On the other hand, it is interesting to note that Udayana seems to have related the proof for the existence of Adṛṣṭam to the second Stabaka; for in the opening lines of this Stabaka he argues that, the existence of an other-worldly cause as the Adṛṣṭam being established, there should necessarily be some means that produce it, and that, as such means are not perceptible to beings like us, one should assume the existence of an extraordinary person (*lokottara-*) who is able to perceive all things (*sarvānubhāvī*) including those that are imperceptible to ordinary persons. The means that produce the invisible fruit are the performances of rituals and sacrifices such as the Agniṣṭoma prescribed in the Veda. In the course of the second Stabaka Udayana establishes that, on account of the non-eternal nature of words and sentences and because of the periodic recurrence of dissolutions and creations, the theory of the eternity of Veda (*vedanityatvam*) is unacceptable, and that, as no person other than Īśvara can be the instructor of the living beings at the beginning of a new creation, he should be accepted as the author of the Veda. Even though there is no formulation of the proof for the existence of Īśvara here at the end of the Stabaka, the discussions in this chapter find their formal expression in some proofs of the fifth Stabaka.

The third Stabaka makes a very substantial contribution to the establishment of the existence of Īśvara in that it shows that none of the means of cognition (*pramāṇam*) admitted by the opponents, namely direct perception (*pratyakṣam*), inference (*anumānam*), comparison (*upamānam*), verbal testimony (*śabdaḥ*), implication (*arthāpattiḥ*) or non-perception (*anupalabdhiḥ*), can disprove it. In these six means of valid cognition Udayana has summed up all the means of valid cognition that were accepted at his time by the different philosophical schools[106]. He concedes that Īśvara is not perceived; but he argues at the same time that perception (*pratyakṣam*) and non-perception (*anupalabdhiḥ*) are possible only with regard to objects that can be perceived (*yogya-*), and consequently they cannot serve as means of cognition of the existence or non-existence of Īśvara who is imperceptible (*ayogya-*) to the senses[107]. With regard to inference (*anumānam*) the author establishes that the necessary relation between effect (*kāryam*) and agent (*kartā*) can be

---

[106] Other means of valid cogniton such as *ceṣṭā*, *sambhavaḥ*, *aitihyaḥ* etc. had already long been given up as *pramāṇa*-s. Cf. YD 33, 9f.; PDhS 319, 1—2; 326, 1—330, 1.

[107] When Udayana speaks in a later portion of his NKus (573, 7) of the direct perception of Īśvara, he does not mean an ordinary perception, but an extraordinary kind of perception produced by special causes as *dharmaviśeṣaḥ*.

determined beyond all doubt and that in such a case inference from a visible effect to an invisible cause is not only possible, but also valid. The application of this principle to the existence of Īśvara itself is postponed to the last Stabaka. His main interest here is to refute the view that inference disproves the existence of Īśvara. He argues that the inferential arguments advanced by the opponents to prove the non-existence of Īśvara are vitiated by logical fallacies and therefore invalid. Although comparison (*upamānam*) is a distinct means of valid cognition, it cannot serve as a means to prove or disprove the existence of Īśvara, since its formal object is only the relation of a name to the object named (*saṃjñāsaṃjñisaṃbandhamātram*) on the basis of similarity (*sādṛśyam*), and not existence or non-existence. As regards verbal testimony (*śabdaḥ*) he shows that the Vedas not only do not deny the existence of Īśvara, as the opponents claim, but also contain passages, more numerous than those that are alleged to deny him, which proclaim him as the omniscient creator of the universe. The Vedic passages which the opponents bring forward as suggesting the non-existence of Īśvara as omniscient creator of the universe need to be differently interpreted. Implication (*arthāpattiḥ*) and non-perception (*anupalabdhiḥ*) are not distinct from inference and perception. Moreover, the argument from implication brought forward by the opponents to prove the non-existence of Īśvara, rather argues precisely for the contrary; for the fact of Vedic instruction, far from suggesting the non-existence of Īśvara, as the opponents claim, necessarily implies it.

Although the third Stabaka does not intend to prove positively the existence of Īśvara, nevertheless, as M. Hiriyanna points out, the demonstration that none of the means of cognition, recognized as such by the opponents, can be adduced to show Īśvara's non-existence, has undoubtedly some weight with those who make much of the opposite fact that the existence of Īśvara can never be proved[108].

The fourth Stabaka contributes to the proof of the existence of Īśvara in as far as it shows the untenability of the view that, even if an Īśvara existed, he would not be a source of valid cognition for the human beings through his teaching of the Veda, as his own cognition would be devoid of the characteristic qualities of validity. Udayana shows that the opponent's conception of valid cognition is incorrect and that valid cognition is possible in Īśvara.

The first four Stabakas thus contribute to the proofs for the existence of Īśvara in their own way. Some of the ideas found in them are worked out and formulated as proofs in the last Stabaka. In any case, these Stabakas can be said to be a preparation for the proofs themselves in as far as they prepare the ground for them by showing the opponents that their own arguments against the existence of Īśvara are devoid of any validity. The ground being thus prepared, Udayana can now pass on to the direct proofs for the existence of Īśvara limiting himself hereafter to those objections of the opponents that directly concern his proofs. This he does in the last Stabaka

---

[108] Outlines of Indian Philosophy, p. 243.

of the Nyāyakusumāñjali which, except for the concluding passages, deals with the proofs for the existence of Īśvara.

Udayana's proofs for the existence of Īśvara can be found in the Ātmatattvaviveka, Kiraṇāvalī and, more especially, in the Nyāyakusumāñjali[109]. The proofs found in the first two of these works are very few. As they recur in a different formulation in the Nyāyakusumāñjali they will be briefly spoken of in our treatment of the proofs as found in it.

The opening lines of the fifth Stabaka contain an interesting general remark. In answer to the objection that all that has been said about Īśvara would be true, if there were proofs to establish his existence, but that such proofs are not to be found, he remarks: "It is not the fault of the post (*sthāṇuḥ*) that the blind man (*andhaḥ*) does not see it"[110]. When we take into account that the words *sthāṇuḥ* as well as *andhaḥ* are used here as *mots à double entente*, we see that this statement is somewhat of a reproach in disguise to the opponent, reminding him that it is not the fault of Śiva—*sthāṇuḥ* is also the name of Śiva who is supposed to remain as motionless as the trunk of a tree during his meditations[111]—that his deniers are blind to his existence. With this remark he passes on to enumerate the reasons by means of which his existence can be cognized.

In the first verse of the fifth Stabaka Udayana mentions a number of arguments for proving the existence of Īśvara: "An omniscient (and) immutable (Īśvara) can be established from effect, combination, from support etc., from human usages, from authoritativeness, from the sacred scriptures, from sentence and from special number"[112].

Even though the implications of some of the logical reasons (*hetuḥ*) of these arguments may not be clear at first sight, the probandum (*sādhyam*), namely an omniscient and immutable Īśvara and a series of reasons for establishing the probandum are enunciated in clear terms. In the pages that follow, while exposing each of these arguments, Udayana formulates most of them in the usual syllogistic form with the thesis (*pratijñā*), the reason and, in some cases, also example (*dṛṣṭāntaḥ*).

There is another important observation to be made concerning the arguments mentioned in this verse. The entire fifth Stabaka is devoted to an exposition of these arguments in the order in which they are mentioned here through their logical reasons (*hetuḥ*). These logical reasons are interpreted in two different ways, a procedure that is possible thanks to the multiple significative power of Sanskrit words. Udayana can thereby offer two series of different proofs, each of the logical reasons being interpreted in two—or in some cases, more—significations. The translation of the verse given above

---

109 Probably also in the NVTP to NSu IV, 1, 19—21.

110 NKus 479, 6: *na hy eṣa sthāṇor aparādho yad enam andho na paśyati.*

111 Cf. J. Gonda: Viṣṇuism and Śivaism, p. 14.

112 NKus 479, 7—8:
kāryāyojanadhṛtyādeḥ padāt pratyayataḥ śruteḥ /
vākyāt saṃkhyāviśeṣāc ca sādhyo viśvavid avyayaḥ //

corresponds to the first interpretation of these logical reasons; their second interpretation will be indicated later on when the second series of proofs will be considered. We shall at first study the first series of proofs in the order in which Udayana deals with them, following his exposition as closely as possible.

1. The First Series of Proofs

Proof 1: (*kāryatvāt* = because of [its] being an effect).

1. The proof *par excellence* brought forward by the Nyāya-Vaiśeṣikas for the existence of Īśvara is based on the fact that the created universe has the nature of an effect. Udayana, too, gives it priority and formulates it briefly as follows:

"Earth etc. have a maker as their cause;
because they have the nature of effect"[113].

In this short syllogism with only the thesis (*pratijñā*) and the logical reason (*hetuḥ*), the subject of the thesis, namely "earth etc." stands for all things that have "the nature of effect" (*kāryatvam*), in other words, are produced. Excluded from it are all realities that are not effects such as the atoms of the four elements: earth, water, fire and wind, the souls and other eternal substances like Ether (*ākāśaḥ*), Time (*kālaḥ*), Space (*dik*) and Manas and other eternal realities. What is to be proved (*sādhyam*) is a maker (*kartā*) who is the cause of earth etc. With the term 'maker' is meant an agent that employs or directs the class of causes that are known to be able to produce the effect[114]. The "maker" that is postulated here as the cause of "earth etc." is not just any agent, but one that can adequately account for the existence of the effect in question. Although this maker is not explicitly said to be the Īśvara, Udayana shows in the long exposition of the proof that the "maker" in question cannot but be eternal and omniscient and hence is none other than Īśvara. The 'nature of an effect' (or: 'being produced') (*kāryatvam*) consists therein that a reality which was earlier non-existent comes into existence (*kāryatvam abhūtvā bhāvitvam*), explains Udayana[115]. It presupposes in the reality that has newly come into existence a relation of posteriority with regard to another anterior reality which is termed its cause[116].

It is quite understandable that Udayana devotes to this proof more space and attention than he did to the other proofs[117]. For not only is it the classic proof of the school for establishing the existence of Īśvara, but it is also the one that was the main target of attack of the opponents, as is testified by the literature on Īśvara on the side of both the Nyāya-Vaiśeṣikas and their oppo-

---

[113] Ib d. 469, 9: *kṣityādi kartṛpūrvakam, kāryatvāt.*

[114] Cf. Kir 104, 11—12: *paridṛṣṭasāmarthyakārakacakraprayoktuḥ kartṛśabda-vācyatvāt.*

[115] Kir 29, 14.

[116] Cf. NVTP 669, 3—4: *tasmāt pūrvakālabhāvaniyamaḥ kāraṇatvam paścādbhā-vitāniyamaḥ kāryatvam.* See also NKus 51, 3; NP 43, 8—9; NVTP 586, 7—8.

[117] In fact, with the exception of the proof from *pratyayaḥ* in the second series of proofs, it is the one that Udayana deals with at the greatest length.

nents. Following the custom of the writers of the period, after formulating his proof, Udayana shows that it is free from all logical fallacies that would make it invalid. We shall not enter into the details of his discussion with the opponent because that would take us into the intricacies of Indian logic with its list of fallacies. Suffice it to say here that Udayana establishes that there is a necessary relation (*pratibandhaḥ*) between an effect and its cause, that the maker of the earth etc. cannot be possessed of a body (*śarīravat*) as the human agents are, but that, being endowed with eternal cognition (*jñānam*) and effort (*prayatnaḥ*), he produces the earth etc. solely by his effort without requiring a body.

Udayana brings forward this proof also in his Ātmatattvaviveka and the Kiraṇāvalī in a modified formulation. In the first-named work he formulates a proof to establish the existence of a maker of the universe as follows:

> "That with regard to which there is dispute whether it has a maker,
> has indeed a maker;
> because it has the nature of effect"[118].

In order to understand the thesis (*pratijñā*) of this syllogism one should keep in mind the context in which it appears. It is in the context of establishing the validity (*prāmāṇyam*) of the sacred scriptures that the theme of Īśvara is spoken of in the Ātmatattvaviveka. In answer to Udayana who affirmed the validity of the sacred scriptures on the ground of their being taught by a trustworthy person (*āptoktatvāt*), the opponent (a Buddhist) asserts that such a trustworthy teacher of the sacred scriptures is not established (*asiddha-*). To that Udayana's answer is that a maker of the universe is established by inference, and he formulates the syllogism which we have translated above. Udayana will later on show the opponent that this maker of the universe is also the instructor of the sacred scriptures, but we shall not enter into it now as it does not concern our present purpose. Although the subject of the thesis in this proof has a different formulation from that of the proof which we studied in the Nyāyakusumāñjali, the idea is the very same. "That with regard to which there is dispute whether it has a maker" is nothing else than the "earth etc." of the syllogism in the Nyāyakusumāñjali and this was evident to the philosophers of the time even without explicit specification. As in the case of the proof in the Nyāyakusumāñjali, here, too, after formulating his argument, Udayana vindicates it against the possible attacks of the opponents.

In an excursus on Īśvara at the end of his commentary on Praśastapāda's account of the dissolution and creation of the universe, which is exclusively devoted to the existence of Īśvara, Udayana brings forward the following proof:

> "That which has origination independent of a body, has for (its)
> cause an intelligent being;
> because it has the nature of that which has a cause.

[118] ATV 377, 6—7: *vivādādhyāsitakartṛkaṃ hi sakartṛkaṃ kāryatvāt iti.*

That which has a cause has an intelligent being as cause, like a chariot.
And so is this (which has origination independent of a body).
Hence (this, too,) has an intelligent being as (its) cause"[119].

Here, too, Udayana goes on to show that his argument is free from all logical fallacies, but what is more interesting to us is the syllogism itself. First of all we notice here a full five-membered syllogism in contrast to the previous two proofs where the last three members were left out to be completed, if necessary, by the reader. The first two members, the thesis and the logical reason have here quite a different formulation. The subject of the thesis "that which has origination independent of a body" (*śarīrānapekṣotpattikam*) might, at first sight, appear unclear, and Udayana himself has not given us an explanation for his usage of this expression here. But when one recalls the various formulations[120] given to this proof by previous Nyāya-Vaiśeṣikas, one can conclude that what is meant by it are those things at whose origination no bodied person as cause is perceived. Such are, for instance, the mountains, trees etc. But the expression of Udayana applies in particular to the origination of the universe at the beginning of a new creation when there is no bodied agent at all. The logical reason "because it has the nature of that which has a cause" (*kāraṇavattvāt*) is, as far as the meaning is concerned, identical with the logical reason mentioned in the proofs of the Nyāyakusumāñjali and the Ātmatattvaviveka, namely "because it has the nature of effect" (*kāryatvāt*); for that which has a cause is nothing else than an effect. Thus, despite the difference in formulation, the three proofs which we have cited are identical in content.

If we now glance back at the three formulations of the proof, we see that the maker who is established as the cause of the created universe is expressed by the general term of "maker" (*kartā*) or "intelligent being" (*buddhimat*). But not any maker nor any intelligent being can be the cause of the universe. Hence it is that in the discussions following the formulation of the proof, Udayana shows this maker or intelligent being to be eternal (*nitya-*) and omniscient (*sarvajña-*). We know from the history of the Īśvara doctrine of the Nyāya-Vaiśeṣikas the following: having established, on the basis of pervasion (*vyāptiḥ*) between what is to be proved (*sādhyam*) and the logical reason (*hetuḥ*), a maker in general (*kartṛsāmānyam*), that is to say, a maker without further specification of the qualities he should possess, the theists had further argued for a special maker (*kartṛviśeṣaḥ*), a maker endowed with special qualities, especially eternal cognition. There were different ways of inferring this special maker, and some Nyāya-Vaiśeṣikas admitted more than one way

---

[119] Kir 97, 10—12: *śarīrānapekṣotpattikaṃ buddhimatpūrvakaṃ kāraṇavattvāt. yat kāraṇavat tad buddhimatpūrvakaṃ, yathā rathaḥ. tathā caitat, tasmād buddhimatpūrvakaṃ.*

[120] We may mention also another formulation of the same proof found in the LV 14, 14—15: *aṅkurādikaṃ sakartṛkaṃ kāryatvāt ghaṭavad iti tatsiddhiḥ.* "Sprout etc. have an agent, because they have the nature of effect (or: 'being produced'), like the pot; thus is his (existence) established". Here, again, there is no difference in the fundamental idea of the proof.

of doing so[121]. The argument that found the greatest favour with them was the fact that the nature of effect (*kāryatvam*) is an attribute of the subject of the thesis (*pakṣadharmatā*). Udayana, too, accepts this method of determining the special maker of the universe. In answer to the enquiry of the opponent how a special maker of the universe can be established, the author of the Kiraṇāvalī remarks: "When the prescribed method of (establishing) what is to be proved in general is undertaken on the strength of the relation of the logical reason in general, there is inclusion of the particular that is unknown on the strength of its (= logical reason) being the attribute of the subject that co-operates with it"[122]. Applying this principle to our concrete case in question it means that, after a "maker in general" (*kartṛsāmānyam*) for "earth etc." has been established from their nature of effect, on the strength of the pervasion that should exist between the probans and the probandum, one concludes by a further process to a special maker (*kartṛviśeṣaḥ*), that is to say, a maker endowed with eternal omniscience, on the strength of the probans being an attribute of the subject of the thesis. It is only if the maker of earth etc. is eternally omniscient, that the attribute (*dharmaḥ*) of effect (*kāryatvam*) can belong to the earth etc. which are the subject (*pakṣaḥ*) of the thesis; it is only an eternally omniscient agent that can be the cause of the earth etc., since otherwise it will not come into existence at all.

As we mentioned earlier Udayana attaches great importance to negative conditional argument (*tarkaḥ*) which he adduces in most cases of proofs in confirmation of his argument. Such a *tarka*-argument is found also for this proof which in the Kiraṇāvalī reads as follows: "If the effect comes into being without (its) maker, it would be able to come into being even without the

---

[121] When we speak here of a *kartṛviśeṣaḥ* or 'special maker', we mean a maker who is endowed with eternal omniscience. The other specific qualities of such a maker are rooted in this basic quality. The omniscience of Īśvara has been established by Nyāya-Vaiśeṣikas by means of different arguments. Some of them (v. g. Praśastapāda, Triolocana and Udayana himself as shown below pp. 166ff.) prove it from the fact that he knows all the causes of the universe. (Cf. TSP 55, 19—26; G. CHEMPARATHY: The Īśvara doctrine of Praśastapāda, pp. 77ff.; JMN 239, 15—25). Others argued for his omniscience from the fact that he has cognition of all the cognisables (Cf. G. CHEMPARATHY: Two little-known fragments from early Vaiśeṣika literature on the omniscience of Īśvara, 125ff.). Some others (v. g. Vācaspati, Vittoka, Udayana) proved it on the basis of *pakṣadharmatā* (Cf. NVTT 954, 11—18; JMN 241, 1—19; JMN 242, 1—3). Some admitted an *argumentum per exclusionem* (*pariśeṣyānumānam*) to prove the omniscience of Īśvara which consists in excluding a non-omniscient agent as the maker of the universe (v. g. Vācaspati in NVTT 956, 24—957, 15). Jayanta mentions, besides these, also other methods of establishing the *kartṛviśeṣaḥ* of the universe (NM I, 183, 12—184, 20). Cf. also G. OBERHAMMER: Der Svābhāvika-sambandha, ein geschichtlicher Beitrag zur Nyāya-Logik, pp. 150ff.

[122] Kir 103, 13—104, 1: *sādhanasāmānyasambandhabalena sādhyasāmānyavidhāv upakrānte tatsahakāripakṣadharmatābalenāpratīte viśeṣe paryavasānāt.* See also ibid. 98, 9—11 and 104, 16—17; NKus 485, 10—11; NVTP 752, 3—754, 7. Cf. p. 169.

other causes, and thus it would be deprived of (its) very nature of effect"[123]. In this argument Udayana emphasises the necessary relation (*pratibandhaḥ*) that exists between the effect and the cause; "for the effect implies (its) agent as cause in order that it may come into existence"[124]. The necessary relation between the effect and the cause being thus established, it follows logically that from the 'nature of effect' (*kāryatvam*) found in the created universe[125], an adequate agent, namely Īśvara, can be legitimately and validly inferred.

Moreover, Udayana confirms the purely philosophical reasoning by citing scriptural passages, both Śruti and Smṛti, that convey the same idea.
a) Śruti: "Having eyes on all sides and having mouth on all sides, having hands on all sides and feet on all sides, the one God, creating heaven and earth, wields with his hands and wings" (ṚV. X, 81, 3, Śvet Up. III, 3).
b) Smṛti: "I am the source of all things. Everything originates from me" (Bh. Gītā X, 8a).

Udayana further states that the passages in the sacred scriptures where Brahmā etc. are said to be the creators are to be interpreted as referring to Īśvara[126].

Proof 2: (*āyojanāt* = because of combination).

Closely related to the first proof is the second which is formulated as follows:

> "(An omniscient and unchangeable Īśvara can be inferred) also from "combination' (of the atoms etc.) . . . For the atoms etc. operate only when they are combined together by a conscious being;
> because (they are) unconscious;
> like an axe etc."[127].

---

[123] Kir 103, 6—8: *yadi kāryaṃ kartāram atipatet tatkāraṇāntaram apy atipatet, tathā ca kāryatvād eva hīyata iti* . . . In NKus 500, 3—5 Udayana expresses the same idea as follows: *kārakavyāpāravigame hi kāryānutpattiprasaṅgaḥ. cetanācetanavyāpārayor hetuphalabhāvāvadhāraṇāt kāraṇāntarābhāve iva kartrabhāve kāryānutpattiprasaṅgaḥ, kartur api kāraṇatvāt.* "In the absence of the activity of a cause, there would be non-origination of the effect. Since the activity of a conscious [agent] and that of unconscious [causes] have been determined to be in the relation of cause and effect, when the [conscious] agent is absent, there follows non-origination of the effect in the same way as when any other causes are absent; for the agent, too, has the nature of a cause [of that effect]"). See also NKus 502, 3—4: . . . *yadi kartāram atipatya kāryaṃ syāt svabhāvam evātipated iti kāryavilopaprasaṅga iti.*

[124] Kir 4, 10—11: *kāryaṃ hi hetunā vinātmānam anāpnuvad hetumattayā kartāram ākṣipati.*

[125] The Nyāya-Vaiśeṣikas have argued for the *kāryatvam* of earth, mountains etc., among other reasons, from the fact that these are made of parts (*sāvayavatvam*). Udayana himself follows this view in Kir 97, 13—15.

[126] NKus 503, 11. Cf. also Kir 90, 18—19 and 96, 17—18 where it is said that *īśvara eva kāryavaśād brahmādiśarīram upādatte.*

[127] NKus 503, 15: *paramāṇvādayo hi cetanāyojitāḥ pravarttante acetanatvād vāsyādivat.*

This proof is based on the necessity of a conscious agent to direct, at the time of creation, the activity of the different causes that go into the production of the created universe. During the period that follows the complete dissolution of the universe, the composite substances remain in the form of atoms while the souls subsist without the body. The individual atoms have to be brought together in order that the non-living universe may come into being. In the same manner the souls should be brought into union with the bodies so that the universe of living beings may arise. But neither the atoms by themselves nor the souls by themselves can initiate or guide the movement (*karma*) that results in creation, as they are unconscious (*acetana-*). It should be kept in mind that, in the view of the Nyāya-Vaiśeṣikas, the soul is devoid of any actual consciousness or conscious activity when it is not united with a body; it is like any other component material of the universe with this difference that it contains in itself the potentiality for conscious operations from the moment it is united with the body. Even the other causes that are admitted to play a causal role are not able, by themselves alone or in combination, to explain the orignation of the universe. Two causes that are said to co-operate in all origination are Space (*dik*) and Time (*kālaḥ*)[128]; but, though eternal, these, too, cannot initiate the activity of creation since they are unconscious. The cause that has a very important role to play in the origination of the universe are the merits (*dharmaḥ*) and demerits (*adharmaḥ*) of the living beings, often designated in Nyāya-Vaiśeṣika works by the term Adṛṣṭam (unseen [power]). In fact, in the early Vaiśeṣika the Adṛṣṭam served as the factor that explained facts for which no explanation through visible causes could be found[129]. Even the first movements of the atoms that start the activity leading to the origination of the universe were, in the early school, ascribed to it[130]. But in course of time it was realized that, being unconscious, the Adṛṣṭam, too, could not adequately explain the origination of the universe. Hence, given the fact of the created universe, one should infer the existence of a cause which, even at the time of the beginning of creation, must be endowed with consciousness (*cetanatvam*) and which brings the causes together by setting them in motion. Such a cause is the Īśvara.

If such a conscious cause were not admitted, then it would follow that, the adequate cause being absent, the origination of the effect would be impossible, since it is accepted that the unconscious causes can operate in the production of an effect only when they are directed by a conscious agent[131].

In this connection it may be remarked that in an earlier passage of the Nyāyakusumāñjali Udayana states that at the beginning of a *kalpaḥ*—in other words, at the beginning of a new creation—the atoms are joined together

---

[128] Cf. Kir 38, 16—19 and 278, 5. . . . *dikkālāv īśvaraś ceti sādhāraṇāni nimittāni.* The universal causality of Space and Time is explained by the fact that every effect is produced in a particular place and at a particular time.

[129] Cf. VSu V, 1, 15; V, 2, 2—4; V, 2, 8; V, 2, 14; V, 2, 19. Cf. also NKus 148, 1—149, 6.

[130] Cf. VSu V, 2, 14. See also NKus 146, 2—4.

[131] Cf. NKus 503, 16—504, 1.

solely by the agency of Adṛṣṭam (*adṛṣṭād eva kevalāt)*[132]. This need not be interpreted as a contradiction of the basic idea of the above proof. The silence of Udayana on the role of Īśvara in this activity can be explained by the fact that the context in which the statement in question was made not only did not call for it, but also because a mention of Īśvara or his role would have been inappropriate there. For Udayana was discussing there with the Cārvākas in order to establish the existence of the invisible reality called Adṛṣṭam which they had denied[133].

In confirmation of his proof Udayana quotes some scriptural passages:

"When that god is awake, then this universe moves on; when he sleeps peacefully, then everything falls asleep (i. e. is devoid of any motion)"[134] (Manu I, 52).

"The living being is ignorant (*ajña-*); it is not master over its own happiness and pain. Directed by Īśvara, it will go to heaven or hell" (Mbh 3. 31. 27).

"It is under my guidance that the prime matter produces the movable and immovable beings (= this universe)" (Bh. Gītā IX, 10a).

"I cause the heat, I hold back as well as send forth rain" (Bh. Gītā IX, 19a).

Proof 3: (*dhṛteḥ* = because of support).

"The universe beginning with the earth and ending with Brahmā's Egg[135] is guided, directly or indirectly, by the effort of a supporting agent;
because, although it possesses weight, it has the property of not falling down;
like the body of a bird (flying) in the sky and like a substance that is attached to it"[136].

The argument does not require much explanation. The expression "the universe beginning with the earth and ending with Brahmā's Egg" (*kṣityādibrahmāṇḍaparyantaṃ jagat*) designates the totality of creation with all the worlds. In the example, the body of the flying bird is directly (*sākṣāt*) supported by the activity of the bird, while the substance (v. g. a prey) that it holds with its claws is indirectly (*paraṃparayā*) supported by it.

In this proof Udayana establishes the existence of Īśvara from the fact that the universe which possesses weight and which is believed to be suspended in endless space requires an agent to support or maintain it in firm position.

---

132 Cf. NKus 142, 3—5. .... (*kalpādau*) *vibhaktānām adṛṣṭād eva kevalān mithaḥ saṃsargaḥ* ...

133 Cf. Śaṅkaramiśra's commentary on this passage in NKusAm 71, 12—13.

134 Udayana explains the 'wakefulness' and 'sleep' of Īśvara as the presence and absence respectively of the co-operating causes. Cf. NKus 505, 16.

135 The term "Brahmā's Egg" (*brahmāṇḍaḥ*) designates the innumerable number of worlds. Cf. W. Kirfel: Kosmographie der Inder, pp. 4* and 55f.

136 NKus 506, 1—3: *kṣityādibrahmāṇḍaparyantaṃ hi jagat sākṣāt paramparayā vā vidhārakaprayatnādhiṣṭhitaṃ, gurutve saty apatanadharmakatvād viyati vihaṅgamaśarīravat tatsaṃyuktadravyavac ca.*

Every object that has weight tends to fall downwards, and with 'support' or 'maintenance' (*dhṛtiḥ*) is meant, as he explains elsewhere, 'the not falling down of a substance that has weight'[137]. The universe is conceived of as being supported by an agent, since it does not fall downwards from its position. Thus Īśvara is established in this proof as the supporter or the maintainer of the universe.

In this connection Udayana rejects the view of an opponent that the Adṛṣṭam alone is enough to explain the maintenance of the universe. He argues that the Adṛṣṭam is only a partial cause and that, even when it is present, an agent who supports it through his effort (*prayatnaḥ*) is necessarily to be admitted, since it has been established through the methods of concomitance (*anvayaḥ*) and non-concomitance (*vyatirekaḥ*) that preservation depends upon an agent that possesses effort (*prayatnavat*).

Udayana cites also scriptural passages to confirm this argument:

"O Gārgī, indeed, heaven and earth stand firm, supported by the command (*praśāsanam*) of this Imperishable One" (BĀUp. III, 8, 9).

"But the other is the highest Spirit, who has been declared the Supreme Self, (namely) the unchangeable Īśvara, who, permeating (*āviśya*: lit. 'entering') the three worlds, supports (them)" (Bh. Gītā XV, 17).

In his short commentary on these scriptural passages Udayana explains the activity of the supporting agent as an operation effected by means of effort (*prayatnaḥ*). Thus he interprets the expression *praśāsanam* which we translated above by the word "command" as "embodied effort" (*daṇḍabhūtaḥ prayatnaḥ*)[138], and *āveśa* or "permeation" through which the Supreme Self "supports" the triple world, as "the conjunction with a being that has cognition, desire and effort" (*jñānacikīrṣāprayatnavataḥ saṃyogaḥ*)[139]. Although in the first verse only two worlds, heaven and earth, and in the second only three worlds, are mentioned, they stand for all the worlds[140].

Furthermore, Udayana observes that the scriptural passages where Indra, Agni, Yama etc. are said to be the supporters or guardians of the worlds (*lokapālaḥ*)[141] are to be explained as referring to Īśvara. Similarly

---

[137] Kir 85, 16—17: *guruṇo dravyasyāpatanaṃ dhṛtiḥ*.

[138] Cf. NKus 506, 11.

[139] Ibid. 506, 15.

[140] In the Hindu cosmography there are different enumerations of worlds (*bhuvanam*). In some accounts only two—heaven and earth—, more often three —heaven, earth and the atmosphere—, worlds are mentioned. There is another list of seven worlds (Bhūr, Bhuvas, Svar, Mahar, Janas, Tapas, Satya) found in early literature. Praśastapāda admitted seven worlds (Cf. G. CHEMPARATHY: The Īśvara doctrine of Praśastapāda, p. 85), while Śaṅkaramiśra (in his NKusAm 344, 14—15) speaks of eleven worlds. Udayana speaks of the triple world (*trailokyam*: see ATV 123, 4—5) as well as of fourteen worlds (ATV 427, 1: *dvisaptabhaumabhuvanaprāsāda* . . .). He speaks of heaven (*dyauḥ*) as the designation for the seven upper worlds and earth (*bhūmiḥ*) for the lower seven (NKus 503, 9—10).

[141] Cf. NKus 506, 3—4. The Lokapāla-s are held to be the guardian deities of the four cardinal and the four intermediary points of the world. For a list of the eight Lokapāla-s cf. MONIER WILLIAMS: Sanskrit—English Dictionary, New edition 1964 p. 906, col. 3; W. KIRFEL: Die Kosmographie der Inder, p. 95.

scriptural passages as "All this is nothing but the Self" (Ch. Up. VII, 25, 2) are based on the fact that the Īśvara "permeates" all things[142].

In the same manner the passages in the scriptures where the tortoise (*kūrmaḥ*) etc. are said to have supported the earth are also to be interpreted in the sense that it is Īśvara himself who, taking the form of the tortoise etc., supported the earth[143].

Proof 4: (*saṃharaṇāt* = from dissolution).

It is to be noted that this proof has not been explicitly mentioned by Udayana among his proofs—or more correctly, among the logical reasons (*hetuḥ*) of his proofs—enumerated in the first Kārikā of the fifth Stabaka. It has, however, been meant by the "etc." (*ādi-*) in the expression *dhṛtyādeḥ* ("from support etc."), as the author of the commentary called Prakāśa informs us[144]. That Udayana himself meant this "etc." to be interpreted as "dissolution" (*saṃharaṇam*) is clear from the fact that, immediately after explaining the proof based on support (*dhṛtiḥ*), he passes on to the proof based on dissolution in the same manner as he did with the other proofs.

> "Indeed also from the dissolution (of the universe can the existence of Īśvara be inferred. For:)
> The universe beginning with Brahmā's Egg and ending with the dyads[145] is to be destroyed by a being possessed of effort;
> because it is destructible;
> like the cloth that is being torn"[146].

That there are periodical dissolutions (*pralayaḥ*) of the universe is admitted by all schools of Indian thought, excepting the Mīmāṃsakas, who conceive of dissolution in a sense different from that of the other schools[147]. The existence of the Īśvara is inferred on the ground that, just like the origination as well as the maintenance of the created universe, its dissolution, too, depends ultimately upon the effort (*prayatnaḥ*) of an agent. The Purāṇic accounts describing dissolution relate that, when the fixed period of the existence of the universe comes to an end, there arises in Īśvara the desire

---

According to the interpretation given by Saṅkaramiśra (NKusAm 344, 6—7), Īśvara permeates the bodies of the Lokapāla-s, and consequently it is Īśvara himself that protects and supports all the worlds.

[142] Cf. NKus 506, 4—5.

[143] Ibid. 506, 16—17. We may mention here also the mythological conceptions according to which Viṣṇu in the form of the serpent Śeṣa or Ananta carries the worlds on his head.

[144] Cf. NKus 507, 14.

[145] A 'dyad' is a compound arising from the combination of two atoms (*paramāṇuḥ*). Cf. p. 104f.

[146] NKus 507, 1—2: *saṃharaṇāt khalv api. brahmāṇḍādidvyaṇukaparyantaṃ jagat prayatnavadvināśyaṃ vināśyatvāt pāṭyamānapaṭavat.*

[147] The Mīmāṃsakas admit a partial dissolution consisting in the destruction of things as they daily take place, but they deny that there is a total simultaneous dissolution of all things. Cf. ṚP 144, 9—12. Udayana distinguishes his conception of destruction from that of the Mīmāṃsakas. Cf. Kir 217, 14—16.

to dissolve the universe, as a result of which there follows a process by which it becomes reduced to the primary or ultimate constituents out of which it had originated.

Udayana confirms his argument by scriptural passages:

"This (God), completely pervading all beings by (his) forms, makes them wander about for ever like a wheel through (the three states of) birth, growth and destruction" (Manu XII, 124)[148].

"O Son of Kuntī! all beings go into my nature at the end of a Kalpa; at the beginning of the (next) Kalpa I send them forth again" (Bh. Gītā IX, 7).

Moreover, observes our author, the passages in the sacred scriptures dealing with the destructive activity of Rudra are to be explained as referring to Īśvara; for it is Iśvara himself who, in his aspect (*aṃśaḥ*: literally 'portion') of Rudra, causes the dissolution of the universe[149].

Proof 5: (*padāt* = from human usages).

The existence of Īśvara can be inferred also from *padam*, a word for which it is difficult to find an English equivalent. Udayana himself explains its meaning as 'the usage of the elders' (*vṛddhavyavahāraḥ*)[150] which includes the usage of words, the practice of the different professional arts and all other usages of the daily life of man.

The author of the Nyāyakusumāñjali formulates the proof based on the usages as follows:

> "That skilfulness of a weaver etc. in making cloth etc., and the usage of words by adult men[151] as well as the usage of the letters (of the alphabet) in their order by children—all this rests upon (the teaching of) a person that is independent (of another that teaches him these things);
>
> because they have the nature of usage,
>
> like the skilfulness in effecting (completely) new (kinds of) pots made by very clever artisans; like the words 'Caitra', 'Maitra' etc.; like the letters (of the alphabet) on the (palm-)leaf; and like the order in the instruction of the letters given by Pāṇini"[152].

---

[148] Note that this verse, as it is found in the Manusmṛti, has a reading slightly different from Udayana's:
eṣa sarvāṇi bhūtāni pañcabhir vyāpya mūrtibhiḥ /
janmavṛddhikṣayair nityaṃ saṃsārayati cakravat //
Another reading of this verse is found in Bhāsarvajña's NBhu 461, 1—2.

[149] Cf. Śvet Up 3, 2 where Rudra is said to create, maintain and dissolve all the worlds. Śiva [= Rudra] is "famous for his preponderantly destructive energy" (J. Gonda: Viṣṇuism and Śivaism, p. 13).

[150] Cf. NKus 508, 1.

[151] Udayana uses the term *vyaktavācaḥ* which literally means 'those whose (usage of) speech is clear'. The adults who have complete command of language are meant here.

[152] NKus 508, 2—5: *yad etat paṭādinirmāṇanaipuṇyaṃ kuvindādīnāṃ vāgvyavahāraś ca vyaktavācāṃ lipitatkramavyavahāraś ca bālānāṃ sa sarvaḥ svatantrapuru-*

In this proof Udayana establishes the existence of Īśvara as the instructor of the first living beings at the time of the new creation. As these beings are at that moment absolutely ignorant of the different human usages (*padam* or *vyavahāraḥ*), they have to be instructed by someone who knows these usages already, without himself having to be instructed by another. Such an instructor who is eternally existent and omniscient is Īśvara.

The validity of this proof rests on two main presuppositions. First of all, it presupposes that there are periodical dissolutions (*pralayaḥ*) and creations (*sargaḥ*) of the universe. In the second Stabaka of his Nyāyakusumāñjali —and earlier in his Ātmatattvaviveka—Udayana has established, that at the end of a certain period, the whole universe will be dissolved into its component parts and that, after another period of rest of equal length, it will be created again, this process of dissolution and creation going on in an endless series[153]. Secondly, this proof presupposes that, at the beginning of creation, the newly created living beings have no knowledge of the human usages we spoke of above. The souls that are separated from the body during the long period of dissolution have, in the view of the Nyāya-Vaiśeṣikas, completely forgotten the usages they had learned in their earlier existences and they are not able to recollect them when they are united again with a body. The Nyāya-Vaiśeṣikas do not believe that the newly created living beings are able, by themselves and their own efforts, to learn the initial usages of words and traditional arts; hence they have to be instructed in them by another person. Thus from the necessity of a teacher of human usages, Udayana argues for the existence of an Īśvara.

There are several problems connected with the conception of Īśvara as the instructor of the living beings. One of the most important problems is how, being devoid of a body, he is able to fulfil this function. Udayana's explanations of the manner in which Īśvara teaches the living beings will be mentioned later when we consider this aspect of his relation to the universe[154].

ṣaviśrānto, vyavahāratvāt, nipuṇataraśilpinirmitāpūrvaghaṭaghaṭanānaipuṇyavat, caitramaitrādipadavat, patrākṣaravat, pāṇinīyavarṇanirdeśakramavac ceti.

The examples in this proof are taken from every day life in the traditional village. 'Caitra, Maitra etc.' refer to proper names. Palm-leaves were used (and are used even now in villages) for teaching children the letters of the alphabet; the master writes the letters of the alphabet on the dried palm-leaf with a pointed metal cylinder. When a coloured juice or powder is rubbed over the leaf, the letters shine out clearly. The young pupil, squatted on the ground, with very fine sand spread out before him, daily practises writing the letters of the alphabet on the sand, looking at the palm-leaf model. The instruction in the order of the letters as given in the beginning of Pāṇini's grammatical work is an absolute condition for studying his grammar.

[153] Cf. NKus 280, 6—305, 6; ATV 422, 7—427, 3 (*passim*); Kir 93, 10—11. Since the Mīmāṃsakas do not admit complete dissolution of the universe at one single time, they maintain that there is no interruption of the beginningless usages of the elders and that consequently there is no need to postulate an Īśvara as the teacher of such usages at the beginning of each new creation. Cf. Bṛh 143, 2; PrP 309, 8—11; ṚP 144, 9—12.

[154] Cf. pp. 152ff.

Suffice it here to observe that, although he does not admit Īśvara to possess a body like the embodied souls, he maintains that Īśvara takes up a body from time to time when certain effects to be produced or functions to be fulfilled absolutely require it. Although he does not explicitly apply this principle to the instructing functions of Īśvara, there is no doubt that he conceived of him as taking a temporary body for that purpose.

In confirmation of his proof Udayana brings forward scriptural passages: "I am the father, the mother, the ordainer, the grandsire of this universe" (Bh. Gītā IX, 17a).

"If ever I do not engage myself unwearied in action, O Son of Pṛthā, men shall follow my path completely. If I do not perform action, these worlds will fall into ruin" (Bh. Gītā III, 23—24a).

With the first passage Udayana wants to show that Īśvara, being the father, mother, the ordainer and the grandsire of the universe, fulfils the functions, directly or indirectly, not only of generating and protecting, but also of instructing the creatures in the usage of words and other usages of everyday practical life. The second passage would mean in our context that, unless God tirelessly engages himself in the action of supporting the universe and of teaching the living beings the different daily human usages, life in the world would be impossible.

Moreover, Udayana adds that the passages of the Yajurveda such as "Reverence to potters, the artisans" etc. (Vājasaneyī Saṃhitā XVI, 27) are to be interpreted as referring to Īśvara. In other words, it is Īśvara himself who, taking the body of potters, artisans etc., has taught the living beings the art of making pots and other things necessary for daily life[155].

Proof 6: (*pratyayāt* = from authoritativeness)

Udayana explains at first what he means by the term *pratyayaḥ*. "Here with the word *pratyayaḥ* is expressed the authoritativeness as regards certainty"[156]. What he means by this is, as can be gleaned from his later explanation, the authoritativeness on account of which the great multitude of people accept the Vedic scriptures in all confidence.

The proof is formulated as follows:

"This Āgama-tradition presupposes qualities in the cause;
because it has the nature of a means of valid cognition;
like direct perception etc."[157].

This argument is based on the fact that the sacred scriptures (*āgamaḥ*) which are handed down from generation to generation are accepted with absolute certainty by the large majority of people (*mahājanaparigrahaḥ*)[158]

[155] Cf. NKus 508, 20 and NKusPr 508, 31—32.

[156] NKus 509, 1: *pratyayaśabdenātra samāśvāsaviṣayaprāmāṇyam ucyate.*

[157] Ibid. 509, 2: *āgamasaṃpradāyo 'yaṃ kāraṇaguṇapūrvakaḥ pramāṇatvāt, pratyakṣādivat.*

[158] Although the term *mahājanaḥ* may mean 'great people' or 'great number of people', Udayana uses this term in this context in the latter sense. Cf. ATV 416, 7—417, 1; 418, 1; Kir 316, 1—2.

as a means of valid cognition. Although such an acceptance is not the cause of the validity (*prāmāṇyakāraka-*) of the scriptures, it does reveal it (*prāmāṇyajñāpaka-*)[159]. The reason for such an acceptance with firm trust cannot be intrinsic validity (*svataḥprāmāṇyam*), as the Mīmāṃsakas claim, but rather certain qualities in the cause that produce it. The most important quality that produces absolute certainty of authoritativeness of the sacred scriptures is that its author is omniscient. A non-omniscient author cannot have knowledge of *dharmaḥ* and *adharmaḥ* except through the scriptures, and hence he does not possess the quality that produces certainty in the minds of the people as regards validity. Hence an omniscient author of the scriptures should be assumed, and that is Īśvara.

Proof 7: (*śruteḥ* = from sacred scriptures).

"(Īśvara can be inferred) also from the sacred scriptures; for:
The Vedas are composed by an omniscient person;
because they have the nature of Veda;
But that which is not composed by an omniscient person is not a Veda;
like other (ordinary secular) statements"[160].

In order to understand this proof, we must know what Udayana means by 'the nature of Veda' (*vedatvam*). According to him this term expresses "the nature of statements that have been accepted by the large mass of people, while no other basis (for their acceptance) is perceivable"[161]. Udayana excludes some bases for the acceptance of the Vedas as authoritative by the large mass of people. Thus, the perception of people like us cannot be the basis of such acceptance, since we do not have perception of the invisible objects spoken of in the Vedas. Nor can error or desire for deceiving others be the reason for such acceptance, since it is impossible to assume that the great majority of the people are victims of error or of deception especially in a matter of such great consequence. Uninterrupted tradition (*paramparā*) alone cannot be the basis for such an acceptance; for it is necessarily interrupted at the time of the great dissolution (*mahāpralayaḥ*). Thus none of these reasons can account for the acceptance of the Vedas by the great multitude, and scriptures based on them are therefore devoid of "the nature of Veda" (*vedatvam*). Moreover, by such a definition of the nature of Veda the scriptures of other religious groups such as Buddhists or Jains are excluded from the Veda, since they lack the property of being accepted by the large mass of people (*mahājanaparigrahaḥ*). The qualifying clause "while no other basis is perceivable" (*anupalabhyamānamūlāntaratve sati*) also serves to exclude from the

---

159 Cf. NKus 305, 5—6; ATV 433, 1—2.

160 NKus 509, 7—8: *śruteḥ khalv api. tathā hi sarvajñapraṇītā vedāḥ, vedatvāt. yat punar na sarvajñapraṇītaṃ, nāsau vedo, yathetaravākyam.*

161 Ibid. 510, 1—3: *nanu kim idaṃ vedatvaṃ nāma? . . . anupalabhyamānamūlāntaratve sati mahājanaparigṛhītavākyatvasya tattvāt.*

Veda the works called Smṛtis which, though counted among the sacred scriptures of Hinduism, are considered to be of inferior authoritativeness. They are, besides, not only based on the Vedas but also derive their validity from them. "The nature of Veda" (*vedatvam*) thus expresses that property of the Veda which accounts for its general acceptance by the large mass of people and at the same time distinguishes it from all other scriptures, sacred or secular.

Such a property of the Vedas necessarily implies an omniscient author who has immediate perception of all that is spoken of in them[162]. This author is Īśvara.

In this context a passage in Kiraṇāvalī which bears close resemblance to the argument we have just considered may be mentioned. The primary aim of Udayana in this passage is not to prove the existence of Īśvara as the author of the sacred scriptures, but to show that the Vedas are uttered or communicated by a trustworthy person (*āptaḥ*):

"The Vedas have been uttered by a trustworthy person;
because they have been accepted by the great multitude of people;
But that which has not been uttered by a trustworthy person is not accepted by the great multitude of people;
like the statement of the man in the street"[163].

In this argument Udayana makes the fact of the acceptance of the Vedas by the large mass of people the reason for inferring that they have a trustworthy author. That this author is none other than Īśvara is clear from the author's explanations[164].

Proof 8: (*anvayataḥ* = from the connection [of words in a sentence]).

Udayana introduces this proof, as he does the others, by mentioning the logical reason (*hetuḥ*); but, while hitherto he used for enunciating the *hetu*-s the same terms as he mentioned in the introductory verse of the fifth Stabaka, he uses here the term *anvayataḥ* instead of the term *vākyāt*. That the author uses the term here in an identical sense is clear from his formulation of the proof in which the term *vākyatvam* is used as the *hetuḥ*:

"The sentences of the Veda are (composed) by a person;
because they have the nature of a sentence;
like the sentences (composed) by people like us"[165].

The argument hardly requires any comment, and Udayana himself does not give any explanation. Though it is addressed to any disbeliever in Īśvara, it has a special significance for the Mīmāṃsakas who, while admitting the

---

[162] Cf. ATV 421, 2—4: *tasmād evaṃrūpo 'pi mahājanaparigraho vedānām eveti so 'yam īdṛśo mahājanaparigraho vedasyāsarvajñatvapūrvakatve 'saṃbhavan sarvajñapūrvakatvena vyāpyate.*

[163] Kir 315, 17—19: *āptoktā vedāḥ, mahājanaparigṛhītatvāt, yat punar nāptoktaṃ na tat mahājanaparigṛhītaṃ, yathā rathyāpuruṣavākyam.* See also ATV 377, 4—5.

[164] Cf. Kir 315, 11—14; ATV 436, 1—4.

[165] NKus 511, 1: *vedavākyāni pauruṣeyāṇi vākyatvād, asmadādivākyavat.*

fact of Vedic sentences, deny to them an author. Although we do not know which of the Nyāya-Vaiśeṣikas was the first to formulate a proof for the existence of Īśvara from the fact that the Vedic sentences require an author, it is well known that, even much earlier than Udayana, it had raised objections from the side of the Mīmāṃsaka school, as can be found in the works of Kumārila, Prabhākara, Sālikanātha, Pārthasārathi etc.[166]. After the formulation of the proof, Udayana mentions most of these objections and offers answers to them.

The most important objection of the Mīmāṃsakas to this proof is that, to put it in terms of Indian logic, an author of the Veda is not proved (*asiddha-*). For, they argue, though such an author deserves to be remembered, he is, in fact, not remembered. If there were an author of the Veda, he would necessarily have been remembered as such by the successive generations of teachers, just as the Buddha is remembered today as the author of the sayings ascribed to him[167]. Udayana rejects this objection as unproved (*asiddha-*)[168] and quotes some scriptural passages wherein the Vedas are said to have a person as author: "And thereafter (i. e. after dissolution) the Vedas issued forth from his (four) mouths. And this Śruti is produced in each Manvantara differently" (quotation not identified). "I am the author of the Vedānta (i. e. Upaniṣads, which form part of the Veda) and the knower of the Veda" (Bh. Gītā XV, 15b). "From that Yajña (i. e. name of a form of Viṣṇu) which was completely offered were produced the Ṛks and the Sāmans" (RV. X, 90, 9).

The Mīmāṃsakas maintain that such alleged references to an author of the Veda are mere Arthavādas[169], namely passages that are meant only to eulogize the performance of an injunction. The author of the Nyāyakusumāñjali answers that such an interpretation is incorrect, since the remembrance of the author does not belong to the domain of injunctions (*vidhiḥ*), and consequently it cannot be taken as Arthavāda. Or, on the same principle, one would have equally to concede that, although Kālidāsa is remembered to be the author of Kumārasaṃbhava, Raghuvaṃśa etc., these works, too, have no author. If the opponents, however, admit that Kumārasaṃbhava etc. are composed by a person, then their logical reason "because the author is not remembered" (*asmaryamāṇakartṛkatvam*) for arguing that the Vedas have no author, is affected by the logical fallacy of uncertainty (*anaikāntikatvam*); for they accept the remembrance of the author of Kumārasaṃbhava etc. as having a meaning for itself, while they reduce the remembrance of the author of the Veda to be mere Arthavādas[170]. In his Kiraṇāvalī our author further points out that the non-remembrance of the author (*asmaryamāṇakartṛkatvam*) is even favourable to his view. "For from the very fact that there is no very clear remembrance is proved that there is an author. And never (has been

[166] Cf. ŚV 845, 7—8 (= Vākyādhikaraṇam, verse 1); Bṛh 283, 10ff.; ṚP 283, 25ff.; ŚD 468, 1ff.

[167] Cf. PrP 310, 4; ŚD 468, 5—470, 3.

[168] Cf. NKus 511, 2ff.

[169] Cf. ŚV 949, 3—4: . . . *vede 'pi tat[= kartṛ]smṛtir yā tu sā 'rthavādanibandhanā.*

[170] NKus 512, 1—3. Also Kir 316, 23ff. where the same ideas recur.

established) the absence of an author (or maker) merely on the ground of absence of very clear remembrance; if, on the other hand, it were so (i. e. if from absence of very clear remembrance of the author, the absence of the author were inferred), then it would follow that there is no author in the case of sentences with 'and so on' (*ity ādi*) and (abandoned) wells over-grown with plants"[171]. Although we do not now remember who, long long ago, dug the well, now unused and over-grown with wild plants, no one concludes from it that it came into being without a person (or persons) who dug it.

Udayana now mentions a second objection that there is an argument to prove the opposite thesis (*satpratipakṣaḥ*), namely that the Vedas have no author. With the usual economy of words he mentions only the logical reason of the argument, but formulated in full, it reads as follows:

"The Vedas are not (composed) by a person;
because they have for their object what does not belong to the domain of a means of valid cognition other (than verbal testimony);
That which is not so, is not thus (= That which is composed by a person has for object what belongs to the domain of a means of valid cognition other than verbal testimony);
like the statements of Manu etc."[172].

This argument is based on the presupposition that the author of a statement should have a direct perception of that on which he makes the statement, and not merely a cognition through verbal testimony of others. Udayana rejects this argument on the ground of two logical fallacies: it is unproved (*asiddha-*) with regard to the author; for Īśvara, the author of the Veda, has direct cognition of what is stated in it. It has, secondly, the defect of uncertainty (*anaikāntikatvam*) when applied to persons other than the author. Thus, for example, when someone, his face beaming with smile at the recollection of a pleasant dream says: "I have seen a beautiful lady in my dream", that statement has certainly a person as author, even though the person who hears it does not know by any means of valid cognition other than this statement the special cause of the smile of the speaker[173].

The opponent now brings forward a third objection which aims at showing that there is no "speaker" (*vaktā*) at all of the Veda: the "speaker" of the Veda is believed to have direct knowledge of invisible realities such as heaven, Apūrvam etc. But Īśvara cannot have such knowledge; for, when the cause is absent, the effect, too, is necessarily absent. Now, the cause of direct cognition are the senses; but the external senses like eyes, ears etc. of Īśvara, had he possessed them, would not be capable of perceiving these invisible

---

[171] Kir 316, 18—21: *asmaryamāṇakartṛkatvaṃ cānukūlam eva yata eva hi sphuṭataraṃ smaraṇaṃ nāsty ata eva kartā sādhyate, na ca kadācit sphuṭatarāsmaraṇamātreṇākartṛkatvaṃ tathātve tv ityādivākyānām andhakūpānāṃ cākartṛtvaprasaṅgāt.*

[172] Such is the formulation of the full argument as given by the author of the NKusPr (512, 11—12): *vedā na pauruṣeyāḥ, pramāṇāntarāgocarārthatvāt, yan naivaṃ tan naivam, yathā manvādivākyam . . .*

[173] Cf. NKus 512, 4—513, 2.

realities since, like our external senses, they, too, will be incapable of perceiving supra-sensible realities. Nor can the internal sense (Manas) be conceived of as being able to produce the knowledge in question, since this sense can perceive only what is experienced within the body in which it is present, and not what is outside of it.

Such an objection does not take into account the Nyāya-Vaiśeṣika view of Īśvara's knowledge, and Udayana disposes of it briefly pointing out a logical fallacy in the opponent's argument, namely that of unproved substratum (*āśrayāsiddhiḥ*) in that one cannot argue from the senses of Īśvara or knowledge of Īśvara, without having first accepted Īśvara himself who is the substratum or subject of his senses or his knowledge. He observes, moreover, that the objection of the opponent is completely out of place with regard to a knowledge that is eternal, such as is recognized to be Īśvara's; for an eternal knowledge has no senses, external or internal, as cause, nor any cause whatever[174].

The final objection to Udayana's proof is that its logical reason, namely "because (the Vedic sentences have) the nature of sentence" (*vākyatvam*) is, as it is technically termed, ineffective (*aprayojaka-*) to prove that the Vedic sentences are composed by a person. For, argues the opponent, the fact of "being (composed) by a person" (*pauruṣeyatvam*) is effected in the case of the Vedic sentences, not by their "having the nature of sentence" (*vākyatvam*), but rather by "the fact that (their) object belongs to the domain of another means of valid cognition" (*pramāṇāntaragocarārthatvam*). By the expression "another means of valid cognition" (*pramāṇāntaram*) is meant a means of valid cognition other than the verbal testimony[175], which, in the case of the author of the Veda, can only be direct perception (*pratyakṣam*). Thus the objection of the opponent implies that the logical reason of Udayana's proof, "because (the Vedic sentences) have the nature of sentences" (*vākyatvam*) can prove their "being (composed) by a person" (*pauruṣeyatvam*) only when there is a condition (*upādhiḥ*) that the object of these sentences belongs to the domain of direct cognition.

In his answer Udayana at first argues that the logical reason that is alleged to be "effective" to prove that sentences must be composed by a person, is, in fact, not valid, since there is no necessary pervasion of "being (composed) by a person" and "the fact that the object (of the sentences) belongs to the domain of another means of valid cognition"; for the scriptures of the Buddhists, though they possess the character of being composed by a person, do not have their object belonging to the domain of such a means of valid cognition; in fact, according to the Nyāya-Vaiśeṣikas, the scriptures of the Buddhists are not at all valid or authoritative. Moreover, even with regard to scriptures that are accepted as authoritative, the condition set up by the opponent as necessary for being composed by a person is not fulfilled; for, if it were accepted as a necessary condition, then Hindu scriptures ascribed to Manu etc. would have to be considered as not composed by a person (*apauru-*

174 Ibid. 513, 3—6.
175 Ibid. 514, 1.

ṣeya-), since these persons do not have a direct cognition of the objects of their statements[176], but are dependent for their knowledge of the objects of their statements on the Veda. In order to defend the view that the statements of Manu etc. are composed by a person, the opponent now argues that the "fact that (the object of the sentence) belongs to a means of valid cognition other than verbal testimony" (*śabdetarapramāṇagocaratvam*) means only that its object should belong to a domain other than that of the sentence in question. Such a conception of the nature of "being (composed) by a person", answers Udayana, is found also in the case of the Veda, since one and the same object has been spoken of in works of different Vedic branches.

Udayana rejects the conception of "being (composed) by a person" (*pauruṣeyatvam*) as suggested by the opponent and gives his own idea of what it is. "The 'being (composed) by a person' consists, indeed, in being composed by a person who is independent. The independence (of the person consists), indeed, in the desire to say and the effort (to say it), having the cognition of the object for their sole object"[177]. In this definition the author brings out the independence of the person that is said to be the author of a statement from means of cognition such as verbal testimony, where the author himself does not have a cognition of the object, but depends upon the cognition of another. The author of the Veda has such a personal or direct cognition of the objects that are taught that he does not depend upon any other person for his cognition.

We have dwelt at some length on this proof because it is one of the important proofs of the Nyāya-Vaiśeṣikas for establishing Īśvara as the author of the Veda and also, as we remarked earlier, because it was much objected to by opponents from a period much earlier to Udayana. It has been found, though in a slightly modified form, also in the Kiraṇāvalī where, commenting on the Vaiśeṣikasūtra VI, 1, 1 *buddhipūrvā vākyakṛtiḥ* [= "The composition of (Vedic) sentences presupposes an (author endowed with) intelligence"], our author argues:

> "The effecting, (that is to say), the composition of the Vedic sentences presupposes an (author endowed with) intelligence;
> because it has the nature of composition of sentence;
> like the composition of the secular sentences"[178].

If we compare this proof with the one we studied in the Nyāyakusumāñjali we find that the logical reason "the nature of a sentence" (*vākyatvam*) there has been replaced by the "action of the composition of sentence" (*vākyaracanā*). This difference in formulation can be accounted for by the different formulation of the thesis in both the cases; as regards the content of the proof itself there is no difference.

---

[176] Cf. NKus 294, 2—3 where Udayana remarks: *manvādīnām atīndriyārthadarśane pramāṇābhāvāt*. Also 306, 4—5.

[177] Ibid. 513, 12—13: *svatantrapuruṣapraṇītatvaṃ hi pauruṣeyatvam. arthapratityekaviṣayau hi vivakṣāprayatnau svātantryam.*

[178] Kir 316, 16—18: *vedavākyasya kṛtir vākyaracanā buddhipūrvakā, vākyaracanātvāt, laukikavākyaracanāvat.*

Proof 9: (*saṃkhyāviśeṣāt* = from special number).

The existence of Īśvara can be established also from special number[179], says Udayana. Before we proceed to formulate the proof itself, it is necessary to make acquaintance with certain theories of the Vaiśeṣika system on which it is based. The Vaiśeṣikas assume that this material universe having magnitude or greatness (*mahattvam*) has come into being out of the combination of innumerable atoms which are conceived to be devoid of any greatness. As the sufficient reason for the greatness in the effect could not be found in the atoms themselves, these thinkers were obliged to find an answer to the problem as to how greatness is produced in the extended material effects, though their causes, the atoms, are devoid of any greatness. For this purpose they invented an ingenious, though quite arbitrary, theory. As this theory forms the basis of the present proof, it is necessary to mention it here at least in its main outlines.

According to the Vaiśeṣika philosophy size (*parimāṇam*) is that quality on account of which we can speak of a substance as small (*aṇu-*), great (*mahat-*), short (*hrasva-*) or long (*dīrgha-*). Smallness (*aṇutvam*) as well as greatness (*mahattvam*) can be either eternal (*nitya-*) or non-eternal (*anitya-*). Eternal smallness is the size proper to the atoms of the four material elements as well as the Manas, and is technically named spherical or globular (*pārimāṇḍalyam*)[180]. It should well be borne in mind that, in spite of being termed spherical, these atoms and Manas are devoid of parts and are so infinitely small in size that they cannot be perceived by ordinary mortals. When two such atoms combine, they produce a dyad (*dvyaṇukam*) the size of which, too, is smallness (*aṇutvam*), but, unlike that of the atoms, non-eternal (*anitya-*). The dyad, too, is imperceptible to ordinary persons. The size of all other realities is greatness (*mahattvam*). The greatness of a few substances such as Ether (*ākāśaḥ*), Time (*kālaḥ*), Space (*dik*) and Soul (*ātmā*) is said to be supreme greatness (*paramamahattvam*) which is eternal[181]. The greatness of all other substances is produced, and hence non-eternal. The smallest substance that has non-eternal greatness is what is technically known as triad (*tryaṇukam*) which is a compound of three dyads. It is also the smallest compound perceptible to the ordinary beings and is identified with the small dust particles that can be seen in motion when, for example, rays of the rising sun enter a room through a chink on the roof or wall.

The Vaiśeṣikas further maintained that, when compounds are formed, the qualities of the component elements can produce only homogeneous qualities in the compound that originates. Since the triads possess the quality of greatness, however minute it be, the greatness of the compounds that are produced out of them—and thus the greatness of the extended universe, too—could be satisfactorily explained as produced by the same quality in the component

---

179 This special number, as will be clear from the later explanation, is the plural number (*bahutvasaṃkhyā*).

180 Cf. VSu VII, 1, 26: *nityaṃ parimaṇḍalam*.

181 With the term 'supreme greatness' is meant that these substances possessing this quality are all-pervading or omnipresent (*vibhuḥ*). Cf. Kir 35, 7.

triads. But the big problem was to explain the origination of greatness (*mahattvam*) in the triads themselves. The size of the dyads out of which the triads are formed cannot be the cause of the size of the triads; for the dyads are small (*aṇu-*) in size and, since the qualities in the cause can produce only homogeneous quality in the effect, the smallness of the dyads would have produced in the triads only smallness, and not greatness which is of a different kind. Moreover, the smallness of the causes would have produced only still more smallness in the effect[182]. Nor could it be thought that the quality of greatness in the triads arises from the size of the primary atoms (*paramāṇuḥ*) themselves; for, firstly, the size of the atom is infinite smallness (*pārimāṇḍalyam*) and hence it cannot produce greatness which is of a different kind. Secondly, were the smallness of the atoms the cause of the size of the triads, then, it would have produced only still more smallness in the effect, and thus no greatness would have come into being. Hence the Vaiśeṣikas maintained that the triad cannot be formed directly (*āhatya*) from the primary atoms themselves, but only through the intermediary of the dyads[183]. Thus, since neither the size of the primary atoms nor that of the dyads could explain the size of the triads which is the reason for the greatness or extension of all non-eternal things that are said to be great or extended, a cause outside the size of its components had to be sought.

At this juncture another Vaiśeṣika theory found a useful application. According to this theory, non-eternal forms of size *(anityaṃ parimāṇam)* can originate from three causes: number (*saṃkhyā*), size (*parimāṇam*) or accumulation (*pracayaḥ*)[184]. Of these, the size of the component parts cannot explain the size of the dyads or of the triads; for, the size of the primary atoms as well as of the dyads being smallness (*aṇutvam*), it cannot produce the size of greatness (*mahattvam*) in the triads, since, as we remarked earlier, the qualities of the component parts are assumed to be able to produce only qualities of the same kind in the composite product; but smallness and greatness do not belong to the same kind of size[185]. Nor can accumulation be the cause of greatness of the triads; for, although an increase of greatness can be obtained by the accumulation of what is already great (*mahat*), neither the primary atoms nor the dyads can produce any greatness through accumulation, since these are themselves devoid of this quality. Thus by the exclusion of the other possibilities one came to the conclusion that it is the quality called number (*saṃkhyā*) that is the cause of the size of the dyads and triads[186]. When two primary atoms combine to form a dyad, it is the quality of number called

---

[182] Cf. NKusPr 517, 11—12.

[183] Cf. Kir 64, 3ff. E. Frauwallner has pointed out that, in an earlier stage, the Vaiśeṣika philosophers held that triads were formed directly from the atoms without their having to go through the stage of the dyads. Cf. Geschichte II, p. 164.

[184] Cf. VSu VII, 1, 16; PDhS 213, 1—2.

[185] The Vaiśeṣikas classify *parimāṇam* into four kinds or classes: *aṇutvam*, *mahattvam*, *hrasvatvam* and *dīrghatvam*. Cf. PDhS 210, 5—6.

[186] Cf. Kir 65, 3—66, 3 and 214, 12ff.

dual number (*dvitvasaṃkhyā*) that produces the atomic size (*aṇutvam*) of the dyads; for, although the size of the dyad cannot be produced by the size of the primary atoms nor by their accumulation, it has the nature of a size that is produced (*janyaparimāṇatvam*). In the same manner, when three dyads combine together to form a triad, it is the plural number (*bahutvasaṃkhyā*) that produces the quality of greatness in the triad. Udayana formulates this argument in syllogistic form in his Kiraṇāvalī as follows:

> "The size of triads is to be produced by plural number;
> because, though (the other causes of greatness such as) size and accumulation are absent, it is a greatness that is produced.
> That which is not produced by plural (number) is not so;
> like the size of dyads or the size of two cotton threads"[187].

Now, number (*saṃkhyā*) is, according to the Vaiśeṣikas, that quality on account of which we can know and speak of things as one, two, three etc. As unit (i. e. one) number inheres in each individual object, as dual (i. e. two) in two, and as plural in more than two objects. The dual as well as the plural numbers are produced through a process of cognition, technically known as 'relating cognition' (*apekṣābuddhiḥ*) of an observing person[188]. When a person, for instance, observes two pots, there arises in him at first, according to the Vaiśeṣikas, through the contact of his sense of sight with the two pots, the cognition of the generality 'one' inhering in the qualities 'one' inherent in each of the two pots. After that there arises in him the cognition of the quality 'one' which, though itself is a unity, has a plurality for its object of observation. Under the influence of the relating cognition, there arises subsequently duality (*dvitvam*) from the unity existing in the two pots. Afterwards there arises in the observer the cognition of the generality 'two', followed by cognition of the quality 'two', and finally the cognition of both pots as dual. A similar process takes place in the cognition of plural objects[189].

After these preparatory observations on the principles that form the background of our proof, we come now to the proof itself. We must keep in mind that number (*saṃkhyā*) is the sole cause for the origination of the size of the dyads and the triads and that a relating cognition (*apekṣābuddhiḥ*) is indispensable for the origination of the dual and plural numbers. It is this absolute necessity of a relating cognition for the production of plural number (*bahutvasaṃkhyā*) that forms the basis for inferring the existence of Īśvara.

After pointing out that plural number alone can be the cause of greatness (*mahattvam*) in the triads[190], Udayana argues: "This (plural number) has to be produced by a relating cognition, because it has the nature of plural number.

---

[187] Ibid. 214, 14—17: *tryaṇukaparimāṇaṃ bahutvasaṃkhyākāryaṃ, parimāṇapracayāsambhave sati kāryamahattvāt, yat punar na bahutvakāryaṃ na tad evaṃ, yathā dvyaṇukaparimāṇaṃ dvitūlakaparimāṇaṃ veti.*

[188] Ibid. 196, 16—17.

[189] Ibid. 196, 18ff. Also E. Frauwallner: Geschichte II, p. 219f.

[190] NKus 516, 6—517, 1; Kir 213, 13.

But it is impossible that there be relating cognition of people like us with regard to the primary atoms. He who possesses such (a cognition must be) omniscient"[191].

The first part of this proof is clear to us from our preparatory explanation. The reason for postulating the relating cognition of an omniscient person is that no other cognizing being is able to exercise the process of relating cognition on the primary atoms (or subsequently on the dyads) as these are not perceptible to them[192]. Moreover, at the beginning of a new creation, with which this proof is associated, there are no other cognizing agents until the souls are united with a body; but the union with a body presupposes the formation of a body with greatness or extension, and consequently the operation of the relating cognition. It is only a being whose cognition is eternal omniscience that can produce at that time, through his relating cognition, the plural number which, in its turn, produces greatness in the triads, which can account for the existence of objects that have greatness or extension. When such a being exercises his relating cognition on two primary atoms there arises in them the dual number which, in its turn, produces in the dyad, as soon as the two primary atoms combine to form a dyad, the quality of smallness *(aṇutvam)*. When three dyads combine to form the triad there arises in it, by the same process, the quality of greatness (*mahattvam*). When smaller aggregates beginning with triads form still bigger compounds, the greatness of these compounds arises from the greatness of their component parts[193].

Thus, given the existence of great or extended objects, one should necessarily acknowledge the existence of an omniscient being. Without such an omniscient being the universe will not come into existence; for in the absence of such a being, there would not be the relating cognition that produces the quality of number; in the absence of the quality of plural number, there would be no greatness produced in the triads, and consequently no objects having greatness will come into existence[194]. This omniscient being is none other than Īśvara.

The relating cognition (*apekṣābuddhiḥ*) which Udayana assumes as the cause of the number (*saṃkhyā*) that produces the size of the dyads and the triads belongs to the domain of direct perception (*pratyakṣam*), and not to any other means of valid cognition such as inference, comparison or verbal testimony. An opponent argues that, if a relating cognition is deemed to be absolutely necessary, an inferential relating cognition (*ānumānikī apekṣābuddhiḥ*) of people like us should be assumed, without there being any need to assume the existence of an omniscient Īśvara. Udayana points out that such an assumption implies the defect of reciprocal dependence (*itaretarāśrayaḥ*). For, on the one hand, it is only after the extended material object has come into being that one can infer from it that it is composed of primary

---

191 Ibid. 517, 1—518, 1.

192 Kir 213, 14: *dvyaṇukeṣv asmadādīnām apekṣābuddher asambhavāt.*

193 Cf. E. Frauwallner: Geschichte II, p. 222.

194 NKus 518, 1—3; see also Kir 214, 17.

atoms etc., since, anterior to the origination of greatness, the primary atoms or dyads being imperceptible to us, there are no means (*liṅgam*) for inferring them. On the other hand, the very origination of the extended material object from the stage of primary atoms through that of dyads to that of extended material object is possible only if there is a relating cognition[195].

The opponent brings forward a further suggestion that the size of great or extended objects can be explained by the invisible power alone (*adṛṣṭād eva*) without having to postulate any relating cognition. Udayana summarily disposes of this view as unacceptable, since one can call in the agency of this invisible cause for all cases which are difficult to be accounted for, and this would lead to the suppression or denial of all visible causes whatever[196].

With the exposition of the nine proofs we have come to the end of Udayana's first series of proofs for the existence of Īśvara. Before we pass on to the consideration of the second series of proofs a few observations on the first series may not be out of place.

A general glance over these proofs shows that they lead us to the existence of an Īśvara in diverse relationships with the universe, namely as creator, preserver and destroyer of the universe and instructor of the living beings. Thus proofs 1, 2 and 9 based respectively on *kāryam*, *āyojanam* and *saṃkhyāviśeṣaḥ*, lead us to Īśvara as creator of the universe; proofs 3 and 4, based on *dhṛtiḥ* and *saṃharaṇam*, to Īśvara as preserver and destroyer of the universe. The Īśvara that is established by means of the proofs 5, 6, 7 and 8 has the relation of a teacher to the living beings. Of these, the fifth proof (based on *padam*) leads us to the existence of an Īśvara who is the instructor of the living beings in things that are necessary in ordinary daily life, while the remaining three proofs (based on *pratyayaḥ*, *śrutiḥ* and *vākyatvam*), establish the existence of Īśvara as the author of the Śruti or revealed sacred scriptures that teach men their religious duties. Even these last three proofs, though all of them are based on the nature of the Śruti scriptures, differ from each other in as far as the aspect under which these scriptures are considered is different in each of them. Thus the sixth proof bases itself on the Śrutis in as far as they are a source of infallible authoritativeness and absolute credibility. The seventh proof, on the other hand, has its starting point in the Śrutis in as far as they are almost universally accepted as authoritative. The eighth proof makes the fact that the Śrutis contain sentences composed of words as the starting point for establishing Īśvara as their author.

What we said about the proofs 6, 7 and 8 can be applied, *mutatis mutandis*, also to the proofs 1, 2 and 9. For these three proofs, too, lead us to Īśvara as the creator of the universe, but their starting points are different aspects of the created universe. The first proof bases itself on the universe as a finished product. The second and the ninth proofs, on the other hand, have as their

[195] NKus 518, 3—519, 2.

[196] Ibid 519, 2—3. Udayana follows here the principle that when a certain fact can be explained by visible factors, one should not have recourse to the invisible: *dṛṣṭadvāreṇaivopapattāv adṛṣṭakalpanānavakāśāt, anyathā bheṣajādiṣv api tathā kalpyeta* (Kir 12, 8—10).

point of departure the universe in its process of formation. While the second proof takes the process of combination of atoms etc. as its basis, the ninth proof bases itself on a particular aspect of the combination of the atoms.

Of all the proofs we have considered so far, that which appears to us to be the least convincing is the last one based on the quality of number. The whole theory of number as one of the causes producing greatness is very arbitrary[197] and the proof based on it will not have any validity for those who do not accept its premisses. But the only school of thought, even in Indian philosophy, that accepts this theory is the Nyāya-Vaiśeṣika system. Rightly did H. JACOBI observe concerning this proof: „Wenn man Udayana durch diese Vorgänge der Vaiśeṣika Metaphysik gefolgt ist, wird man vielleicht seinen Scharfsinn bewundern, aber über den Beweis selbst den Kopf schütteln"[198].

Interesting to notice is the attempt of Udayana to accomodate and harmonize his Īśvara doctrine with the accounts found in the Hindu scriptures, Śruti as well as Smṛti, where various deities are mentioned with functions or characteristics ascribed by him to Īśvara. For this purpose he quotes, at the close of most of the proofs we have seen, scriptural passages in which the functions of the Īśvara he has been speaking about are ascribed to other deities. He tells us that such passages should be interpreted as referring to Īśvara himself[199]. In some cases, where it is possible, he identifies with Īśvara the Supreme Being, Brahman, spoken of in the scriptures[200]. But in all his proofs it is the rational argument that has priority, and confirmations through scriptural passages are very brief and reduced to a minimum.

2. The Second Series of Proofs

After exposing the above proofs for the existence of Īśvara, the author of the Nyāyakusumāñjali brings forward a second series of proofs with the same logical reasons (*hetuḥ*) as in the preceding series of proofs. This identity of logical reasons in both the series is merely formal in as far as the same Sanskrit expression is used in both the cases. In reality, however, these terms representing the logical reasons have been given a new content through a new interpretation[201] by applying the rhetorical ornament called *śleṣaḥ* or *double entendre*. Perhaps Udayana has gone a little too far, at least from the point of view of philology, in giving new interpretations to some terms[202].

---

[197] Cf. E. FRAUWALLNER: Geschichte II, p. 164. B. FADDEGON characterises the *apekṣābuddhiḥ* of Īśvara as "an artifice to get rid of the self-contradiction in the idea that corporeal bodies with extension are formed out of *paramāṇus* without extension" (The Vaiçeṣika-System, p. 148).

[198] H. JACOBI: Gottesidee p. 62.

[199] Cf. NKus 503, 11; 506, 3—4; 506, 16—17; 507, 7; 508, 20.

[200] Ibid. 569, 1—4. See also Kir 151, 6—7 where, referring to the Parabrahman of the Vedāntins, Udayana remarks: *parabrahmaṇi ceśvarād anyasmin pramāṇābhāvāt.*

[201] Cf. NKus 519, 4: *athavā kāryetyādikam anyathā vyākhyāyate.*

[202] For example, in interpreting *āyojanam* as *vyākhyānam* or *saṃkhyā* as *samākhyā.*

The first verse of the fifth Stabaka containing the logical reasons of the proofs may be thus translated according to the interpretation given in the second series of proofs:

"An omniscient (and) immutable (Īśvara) can be established from intention, from explanation, from accurate determination (?) etc., from word, from verbal suffix, from (praises found in) the Śruti texts, from association of word-meanings and from number (and name)".

The exact significance of the translation of the logical reasons in this passage will be explained in the exposition of the proofs themselves. Only one remark may be made at this stage, namely, that in the second series of proofs these reasons are all applied to the Veda which is made the basis and the *point de départ* of the arguments.

With these preliminary observations we shall now pass on to the exposition of the proofs themselves.

Proof 1: (*kāryāt* = from intention)

While in the first series of proofs the reason *kāryāt* was applied to the nature of earth etc. as 'produced', it is used here in the sense of "intention" (*tātparyam*)[203] that underlies some Vedic statements.

The Vedic texts contain statements some of which refer to things that are to be accomplished (*bhāvyārthaḥ*) and others to facts that are already accomplished (*bhūtārthaḥ*). To the first class belong statements such as "He who desires heaven should offer the Agnihotra sacrifice" (*svargakāmo agnihotreṇa yajeta*). They enjoin the performance (*pravṛttiḥ*) of an action for a desired end. To this class belong also the statements that enjoin a person to abstain from an action (*nivṛttiḥ*), such as, for example, "One should not eat Kalañja[204a]" (*kalañjaṃ na bhakṣayet*) (Taitt. Saṃ. 2, 5, 5, 6). These kinds of statements known respectively as injunctions (*vidhiḥ*) and prohibitions (*pratiṣedhaḥ* or *niṣedhaḥ*) are directly (*āhatya*) related to an action either to be performed or to be abstained from. The second class consists of Vedic statements that enunciate what is already accomplished (*bhūtārthaḥ*) and are not directly related to an action to be performed or to be avoided; nevertheless they, too, are indirectly and ultimately directed towards the same end on account of the intention (*tātparyam*) that is implied in them[204]. For the power of an injunction, positive (*vidhiḥ*) as well as negative (*pratiṣedhaḥ*), may, under certain circumstances, become so weakened in men that they stand in need of some additional incentive for performing or abstaining from an action that has been enjoined or forbidden. This incentive is offered by this second class of Vedic statements which either praise (*stutiḥ*) the action enjoined to be performed or condemn (*nindā*) that which is forbidden. It is, indeed, known from experience that praise of an action or what is related to it encourages a person to perform it, and condemnation of it dissuades him from it. Applying this principle to the Veda, we can conclude that the statement of praise found in

[203] Cf. NKus 522, 9.
[204] Cf. MSu I, 2, 7 and ŚBh on it; NKus 520, 2—3.
[204a] Cf. Note 249 on p. 124.

the Veda "Vāyu is indeed the swiftest deity" (*vāyur vai kṣepiṣṭhā devatā*: Taitt. Saṃ. 2, 1, 1, 1) serves to encourage a person to the performance of a sacrifice to the god Vāyu enjoined by the Vedic injunction that immediately precedes it: "One desirous of prosperity should sacrifice a white (animal) to Vāyu" (*vāyavyaṃ śvetam ālabheta bhūtikāmaḥ*). In the same manner, all the Vedic passages that praise or condemn an action—such passages are technically known as Arthavādas or explanatory passages[205]—are ultimately directed towards the injunctive passages of the Veda.

In a subsequent proof[206] Udayana will show that the injunctive passages of the Veda necessarily imply the existence of an author. In the present proof he considers only the Arthavāda passages of the Veda and shows that these, too, argue for the existence of an author.

We have already remarked that the injunctive passages of the Veda are immediately directed towards action (*kāryam*), either in the form of positive performance (*pravṛttiḥ*) or in that of negative avoidance (*nivṛttiḥ*), and that Arthavāda passages, on the other hand, are directed towards action only mediately through their purport (*tātparyataḥ*). Udayana now enters into an excursus to determine the exact meaning of the word *tātparyam*. After excluding the other possible significations he establishes that the term *tātparyam* can mean here only "intention" (*uddeśaḥ*) which is defined as that in view of which a word is employed[207]. Such, indeed, is the meaning of the word *tātparyam* in ordinary usage, too. For in ordinary life a statement in praise of a certain object is made in order to encourage a person to acquire it; in other words, it has acquisition (*upādānam*) as its intention. In the same way a statement of censure or condemnation of a thing is intended to dissuade a person from acquiring it; it has avoidance (*hānam*) as its intention. Since in the ordinary usage statements of praise are intended to encourage a person to acquire an object or to perform an action, and the statements of censure are intended to deter a person from acquiring an object or from performing an action, the Vedic sentences of praise or of censure must also have the same intention[208]. But intention of a statement presupposes a person who is its author. As these Vedic statements thus express the intention of a person it follows that the Arthavāda passages in the Veda presuppose a person whose intention is expressed in them.

Udayana formulates the proof in syllogistic form as follows:

> "The statements of praise that are (found) in the Veda presuppose the intention (of a person that the thing praised is) to be acquired;

---

[205] Note, however, that Arthavāda includes, besides *stutiḥ* and *nindā*, also *parākṛtiḥ* and *purākalpaḥ*. Cf. P. V. Kane: History of Dharmaśāstra, Vol. V, Part II, p. 1241—1242.

[206] Cf. the proof based on *pratyayaḥ*, pp. 122ff.

[207] Cf. NKus 521, 13.

[208] It is generally accepted that words have the same signification in both the ordinary usage (*loke*) and in the Vedic usage (*vede*). Cf. NKus 521, 16; 524, 23—24; 568, 4—5; 571, 2—3.

because they have the nature of statement of praise,
like the statement (of praise) in ordinary usage: 'The mango fruit is savoury through ripening', etc.
In the same manner, the statements of censure (that are found in the Veda) presuppose the intention (of a person that the thing censured is) to be avoided;
because they have the nature of statement of censure,
like the statement (of censure in ordinary usage:) 'The fruit of the bread-fruit tree is tasteless through ripening' etc."[209].

In order to confirm the validity of his reasoning Udayana observes that, if the Arthavāda passages in the Veda did not express the intention of an author, they would be devoid of any purpose, a consequence which the Mīmāṃsaka opponents are unwilling to accept[210]. Moreover, if the Arthavāda passages of the Veda did not serve to express the intention of an author, he remarks, the Mīmāṃsakas would have to give up their theory of Śrutārthāpatti or implication based on verbal testimony (lit. 'on what is heard'). To understand this argument it should be remembered that the Mīmāṃsakas admit implication (*arthāpattiḥ*) as a distinct means of valid cognition which they divide into two main classes: implication based on what has been seen (*dṛṣṭārthāpattiḥ*) and that based on what has been heard, namely on verbal testimony (*śrutārthāpattiḥ*). It is only the second kind of implication that interests us here. In ordinary life when someone says "Devadatta who is fat does not eat during the day" (*pīno devadatto divā na bhuṅkte*), the listener concludes, on the basis of the implied intention of the speaker, that, as fatness is incompatible with fasting and since Devadatta fasts during the day, he "eats at night" (*rātrau bhuṅkte*). In the same manner, when a person says "water", the person who hears this word understands what is implied in it; he mentally completes the unuttered words 'Bring me' by surmising the intention of the speaker, and brings him water. In the Vedas also there are passages in which the statements are incomplete. The Mīmāṃsakas apply the above principle of completing these statements on the basis of Śrutārthāpatti. Thus, for example, in the Vedic statement "One should offer the (sacrifice called) Viśvajit" (*viśvajitā yajeta*), the injunction is incomplete, and so one adds, on the basis of implication of what has been heard or read in the Veda, the rest of the passage in the context (*vākyaśeṣaḥ*), "he who desires heaven" (*svargakāmaḥ*), or "for the purpose of (obtaining) heaven" (*svargārtham*) in order to get the complete injunction "He who desires heaven should offer the (sacrifice called) Viśvajit"[211]. Just as in ordinary usage the listener completes a statement that is

---

[209] NKus 521, 19—522, 3: *vaidikāni praśaṃsāvākyāni upādānābhiprāyapūrvakāṇi praśaṃsāvākyatvāt, pariṇatisurasam āmraphalam ityādi lokavākyavad iti. evaṃ nindāvākyāni hānābhiprāyapūrvakāṇi nindāvākyatvāt, pariṇativirasaṃ panasaphalam ityādi vākyavat.*

[210] Cf. NKus 522, 3: *anyathā nirarthakatvaprasaṅgaś ca vipakṣe bādhakam uktam.* According to the Mīmāṃsakas every part in the Veda has a purpose. Cf. P. V. KANE: History of Dharmaśāstra, Vol. V, Part II, p. 1223.

[211] Cf. ŚD 228, 5ff.; NKus 522, 4ff.

heard only because he recognizes the implicit intention of the speaker, so also the completion of the Vedic injunctions that are incompletely stated is possible only on the supposition that the statement implies the intention of a speaker or author of the Veda. Were there no author of the Veda, there would be no intention of the speaker, and consequently the implication based on scriptural testimony which the Mīmāmsakas defend, would be done away with. "Hence either one should accept that the Vedas are (composed) by a person or one should reject implication based on testimony"[212].

Thus the existence of a person whose intention is expressed in the statements of praise or of censure found in the Veda is necessarily to be admitted. And this person is no other than Īśvara.

The Mīmāṃsakas, no doubt, admit that the Vedic sentences have an intention (*tātparyam*); but, while the Nyāya-Vaiśeṣikas consider this intention to be that of Īśvara, the author of the Veda, the Mīmāmsakas understand by it not the intention of a person who is their author, but an intention innate in them through the natural capacity of the words themselves to express a meaning, independent of the intention of any author. For the Nyāya-Vaiśeṣikas the intention expressed in a statement always presupposes a person since, in their view, the signification of words is not co-natural, but depending on convention (*samayaḥ*) made by a person.

Proofs 2, 3 and 4.

Before entering into these proofs themselves, a few observations on their structure seem necessary. We have seen that in the first series of proofs Udayana brought forward no less than nine proofs following the order given in the introductory verse of the fifth Stabaka. Each proof was formally introduced there by an explicit mention of its logical reason (*hetuḥ*) such as *āyojanāt khalv api, dhṛteḥ khalv api, saṃharaṇāt khalv api* etc. In the second series, too, he introduces each proof by mentioning its logical reason, except in the case of the logical reasons *dhṛtyādeḥ* of proofs 3 and 4, explained in the first series as *dhṛteḥ* and *saṃharaṇāt*. The second proof is formally introduced by *āyojanāt khalv api*. But the next proof that is formally introduced in the usual manner is that based on *padam*: *padāt khalv api*, so that there is no introduction of the proofs based on *dhṛtyādiḥ*.

Although there is no formal or explicit introduction of the proofs based on *dhṛtyādiḥ* (i. e. based on *dhṛtiḥ* and *ādi*), nevertheless there is every reason to believe that Udayana did not leave these proofs out of consideration. In fact the present author could not find a good reason why the author of the Nyāyakusumāñjali should exclude them from his orderly series. Moreover, the explicit statement of Udayana at the beginning of his exposition of the second series of proofs that he is going to interpret the logical reasons, already explained in the first series, in a different way: "Or, 'effect' etc. is (going to be) explained in another manner"[213] allows one to conclude that he

---

[212] Kir 326, 9—11: *tasmāt svīkaraṇīyaṃ vedasya pauruṣeyatvaṃ pratihartavyā vā śrutārthāpattiḥ* . . .

[213] NKus 519, 4.

is going to explain all the logical reasons in the second series also. Hence we assume that, despite the absence of an explicit introduction of the proofs, our author deals also with the logical reasons *dhṛtyādeḥ* together with the second proof based on *āyojanam*. Our surmise is further strengthened by the testimony of the commentators of the Nyāyakusumāñjali who, though not quite in agreement in their interpretation of *dhṛtiḥ* and *ādi*, agree therein that Udayana includes also these two proofs in his exposition of the second proof[214].

With these preliminary remarks we shall now pass on to the proofs themselves. Of the three proofs in question, the first one based on *āyojanam* is at first distinctly dealt with in the usual manner. The term *āyojanam* is interpreted here to mean "explanation" (*vyākhyānam*)[215]. Udayana formulates this proof as follows:

"Indeed, also from the explanation (of the Veda can the existence of Īśvara be inferred). For no one understands from an unexplained Veda (its) meaning. And the explanation of (a person) who perceives only a part (of the Vedas and their meaning) cannot be looked upon with respect (i. e. as authoritative). For in accordance with the maxim: 'A word that is untouched by the relation of priority and posteriority produces a cognition other (than what was meant by the speaker, namely an erroneous cognition)'[216], there would be no confidence (in the explanation of a person who perceives only part of the Vedas and their meaning). He who hears (only) a part (of what is uttered) would have the cognition of a meaning other (than what was intended by the speaker) even from a sentence having (only) three or four words[217]. How much more (will it be so in the case of the Vedic sentences the object of which is) beyond the range of the senses and can hardly be grasped (even) through association with other sentences? Consequently one single person who perceives all the Vedas and their meaning has to be admitted. Otherwise there would be the series of blind men"[218].

---

[214] It is the statement of Udayana *sa ca śrutādhītāvadhṛtasmṛtasāṅgopāṅgavedavedārthaḥ* ... that introduces, in the view of the commentators, the proof based on *dhṛtyādeḥ*. Commenting upon this passage Vardhamāna says: "[With the words] *sa ca* he explains also [the term] *dhṛtyādeḥ* [found] in the Kārikā that begins with [the word] *kārya*". (Reference is to the first Kārikā of the fifth Stabaka, NKus 479, 7): *kāryetyādikārikāyāṃ dhṛtyāder ity api vyācaṣṭe sa ceti.*)

[215] Cf. NKus 519, 5; 522, 10. Śaṅkaramiśra explains: *āyojanaṃ samastavedavyākhyānam* (NKusAm 363, 17).

[216] ŚV 655, 6 (= Sambandhākṣepaparihāraḥ, verse 63b).

[217] Śaṅkaramiśra gives the example of a person who, without hearing the first words *vimalaṃ jalam* of the sentence uttered by a person, hears only the rest of the sentence: *nadyāḥ kacche mahiṣaś carati*, and thereby understands the statement of the speaker in a manner very different from the intended significance. Cf. NKusAm 363, 19—20.

[218] NKus 522, 10—15: *āyojanāt khalv api. na hi vedād avyākhyātāt kaścid artham adhigacchati. na caikadeśadarśino vyākhyānam ādaraṇīyam, paurvāparyāparāmṛṣṭaḥ śabdo 'nyāṃ kurute matim iti nyāyenānāśvāsāt. tricaturapadakād api vākyād ekadeśaśrāviṇo 'nyathārthapratyayaḥ syāt, kim utātīndriyād antaravākyasambhedaduradhigamāt. tataḥ sakalavedavedārthadarśī kaścid evābhyupeyo 'nyathā-'ndhaparamparāprasaṅgāt.*

The idea behind this argument is that the Vedic statements which are accepted even by the opponents as infallibly authoritative need to be explained by a person who knows all the Vedas and perceives directly all that is taught in them. An ordinary person will not be able to give such an explanation, since the Vedas treat of objects inaccessible to his senses. Above all, a correct explanation of even a part of the Veda can be given only by a person who has grasped correctly all that has been taught in all the Vedas. The topics or objects spoken of in one Veda often recur in other Vedic texts, and hence a person who gives an authoritative explanation of the Veda must possess a correct knowledge of all that is taught in all the Vedas. Such a correct knowledge can be had only by a person who directly perceives all the contents of all the Vedas. He who possesses direct perception of all the Vedas and who first explains them correctly is none other than Īśvara.

If one does not admit such an explainer of the Vedas, remarks Udayana in confirmation of his argument, there would follow the defect of a continuous series of blind men leading each other (*andhaparamparāprasaṅgaḥ*)[219]. Hence no person like us can be considered to be the first explainer of the Vedas. If the first explainer of the Vedas were not one who has perception of all that is taught in all the Vedas, the present explanation of the Vedas that depends upon it would be without an authoritative basis for its validity.

Immediately after the passage which we translated above Udayana continues:

"And this person (who sees all the Vedas and their objects), whether he possesses (the knowledge of) the Vedas together with all their branches and sub-branches (as well as) of the objects (treated therein) through hearing, study, accurate determination (and) remembrance, or in (a manner) contrary to this[220], cannot but be an omniscient person. For which person who has not directly perceived the whole (Veda) and the religious practices pertaining to it (is able to) ascertain the exact extent of these sacred scriptures (lit. 'that this sacred text is only so much')? And which person of inferior vision (*arvāgdṛk*) will (be able to) study or to teach all the sacred texts either according to their text or according to their meaning?"[221]

---

[219] In the view of the Mīmāṃsakas the eternal Veda is transmitted from teachers to their students in an uninterrupted series. Cf. ŚV 949, 1—2:

vedasyādhyayanaṃ sarvaṃ gurvadhyayanapūrvakam /
vedādhyayanavācyatvād adhunādhyayanaṃ yathā //

[220] Meant is: "whether he possesses (the knowledge of) the Vedas together with all their branches and sub-branches (as well as) of the objects (treated therein) without hearing, study, accurate determination (and) remembrance, through innate or natural knowledge of them".

[221] NKus 522, 16—18: *sa ca śrutā'dhītāvadhṛtasmṛtasāṅgopāṅgavedavedārthas tadviparīto vā na sarvajñād anyaḥ saṃbhavati. ko hy apratyakṣīkṛtaviśvatadanuṣṭhāna etāvān evāyam āmnāya iti niścinuyāt. kaś cā'rvāgdṛg niḥśeṣāḥ śrutīr granthato 'rthato vā'dhīyīta adhyāpayed vā.*

The words "either according to the text or according to their meaning" may require an explanation. "According to the text" means here "according to the correct reading of the text"; "according to the meaning" means "according to the exact meaning of the text".

It is in this passage that the commentators trace the exposition of the third and fourth proofs indicated by the expression *dhṛtyādeḥ* in the introductory verse of the fifth Stabaka. That these proofs are not so clearly indicated in this passage seems to be borne out by the fact that the commentators are not agreed as to how the two proofs are to be explained. Although all of them are agreed in explaining the logical reason *dhṛtyādeḥ* of the first verse as *dhṛtiḥ* and *ādi*, and not as *dhṛtiḥ* and *saṃharaṇam* as was done by Udayana himself in the first series of proofs, they differ in their explanation as to what is meant here by *dhṛtiḥ* and *ādi*. As far as I can make out, the author of the Prakāśa does not tell us in his commentary in what way he understands this passage to be an explanation of the proofs based on *dhṛtiḥ* and *ādi*. The later commentators seem to have felt a certain lack of clarity in explaining these two proofs as contained in this passage. In any case they have tried to indicate which words in Udayana's passage stand for and explain *dhṛtiḥ* and *ādi*. Guṇānanda, who wrote a commentary on the whole of the Nyāyakusumāñjali, finds in the Vedas, which are objects that are fixed or retained in mind, an indication of *dhṛtiḥ*, and in study (*adhyayanam*) an indication of the word *ādi*[222]. Haridāsa Bhaṭṭācārya who comments only on the Kārikās of the Nyāyakusumāñjali speaks of *dhṛtiḥ* and *ādi* as referring respectively to the preservation (retaining in memory) (*dhāraṇam*) and performance (*anuṣṭhānam*) without further explanation[223]. Rāmabhadra Sārvabhauma who, too, comments only on the Kārikās, remarks that *dhṛtiḥ* means here "retaining (in memory) all the Vedas" (*samastavedadhāraṇam*) which is not dependent upon us, while the interpretation of *ādi* is to be sought in "the instruction in the Veda with its thousand branches"[224].

The diverse interpretations of these commentators reveal that Udayana did not clearly indicate here how we are to understand the proofs based on *dhṛtyādiḥ*. One wonders whether Udayana's own passage does not admit of other interpretations than the ones given by the above commentators, especially since a certain arbitrariness is found in all these explanations. For example, would it not be possible to interpret the compound "whether he possesses (the knowledge of) the Vedas together with all their branches and sub-branches (as well as) of the objects (treated of therein) through hearing, study, reflection (and) remembrance" (*śrutādhītāvadhṛtasāṅgopāṅgavedavedārtha-*) as standing for the argument based on *dhṛtiḥ* and "whether in a manner contrary to this" (*tadviparīta-*) for that based on *ādi*? Similarly one can ask oneself whether the words "who ... will (be able to) study all the sacred texts ..." (*kaḥ ... adhīyīta*) indicate the proof based on *dhṛtiḥ*, while "who ... will (be able to) teach all the sacred texts ..." (*kaḥ ... adhyāpayet*) refer to that based on *ādi*.

---

[222] NKusVi 366, 32—34: *tathā ca vedā vaktraprayuktā dhṛtiviṣayās tatprayuktādhyayanaviṣayā iti ... dhṛtyādir ity ādigrahaṇād adhyayanaparigrahaḥ.*

[223] Cf. the edition of COWELL: The Kusumánjali 53, 3—4: *evaṃ dhṛtir dhāraṇam, dhṛtyāder ity ādigrahaṇāt anuṣṭhānasaṅgrahaḥ.*

[224] NKusKaVy 86, 19—20: *dhṛtiḥ samastavedadhāraṇam tad api nāsmadādyadhīnam. ādipadāt sahasraśākhavedādhyāpanaṃ saṃgṛhītam.*

Even though the exact structure of the two proofs based on *dhṛtiḥ* and *ādi* is not easy to be traced in this passage, the idea behind it seems to be clear. The words introducing this passage: "And this person ..." (*sa ca*) show us its connection with the previous passage in which we were told that the first explainer or interpreter of the Veda must be a person who has directly perceived all that is treated of in all the Vedas. Such an explanation or interpretation presupposes a kind of cognition which, be it obtained by the methods of hearing, study, reflection and remembrance as in the case of ordinary persons or be it otherwise, cannot be possessed by anyone other than an omniscient person. For he alone is able to know fully all the Vedas, both according to their texts and according to their meaning, and explain it to others. By excluding such a cognition from persons of inferior vision such as we are, Udayana establishes that the omniscient in question could be none other than Īśvara.

Udayana now enunciates his argument in syllogistic form:

"Here, too, the application (is as follows):

The Vedas have been once explained by one who has knowledge of the meaning (or object) of all the Vedas;

because, even when there is uncertainty (lit. 'wavering') in the minds of the performers, there is performance of a stable object (or rite).

Whatever is such, has been explained by one who knows its meaning (or object),

like the Saṃhitās of Manu etc."[225].

One who is acquainted with the works of Udayana knows that the author usually enunciates a formal proof with the introductory words *atrāpi prayogaḥ* as the conclusion in syllogistic form of an argument he has been explaining. We have pointed out that, in the view of the commentators, the short passage preceding this syllogistic formulation contains 'in disguise' (*chalataḥ*, as Guṇānanda remarks)[226] the proofs based on *dhṛtyādiḥ*. Although the thesis (*pratijñā*) of this syllogistic argument resembles very closely that of the previous proof, the logical reason (*hetuḥ*) here is different, and hence we can say that, despite the fact that the passage in question reads as a continuous whole[227] without the usual way of introducing a new proof, we are justified in finding in the latter syllogistic formulation a proof based on *dhṛtyādiḥ*.

The argument of Udayana is based on the fact that, even though there might be divergence of views among the exponents of the Vedic texts, such as, for example, regarding the details of performing certain sacrifices, still there is unanimity regarding the performance of the different kinds of sacrifices, sacred ceremonies (*saṃskārāḥ*), acts of worship etc. Such a certainty can be

---

[225] NKus 522, 19—523, 2: *atrāpi prayogaḥ — vedāḥ kadācit sarvavedārthavidvyākhyātāḥ, anuṣṭhātṛmaticalane 'pi niścalārthānuṣṭhānatvāt, yad evaṃ tat sarvaṃ tadarthavidvyākhyātaṃ, yathā manvādisaṃhiteti.*

[226] NKusVi 366, 31—32.

[227] The words *sa ca* (NKus 522, 16) shows that the passage that follows is connected with the preceding.

explained, believes Udayana, only on the supposition that the Vedas have been once (*kadācit*), that is to say, at the beginning of creation, explained by one who has complete and perfect knowledge of all that is contained in all the Vedas. Such a first explainer (*vyākhyātā*) can only be Īśvara.

In confirmation of his argument Udayana adds that, if the Vedas were not once (i. e. at the time of creation) explained by a person who knows all that is contained in all the Vedas, there would be no proper instruction, and consequently, in the absence of certainty as to what exactly is to be performed, there would follow either non-performance (*ananuṣṭhānam*) or irregular or unsteady performance (*avyavasthā*) of the rites prescribed in the Vedas. It cannot be assumed that the performers (*anuṣṭhātā*) themselves would also be the instructors (*ādeṣṭā*) of the religious prescriptions even from the very beginning of creation; for these performers being non-omniscient, their knowledge of the Vedic teachings would be uncertain and their instruction would not convey certainty. Nor can it be thought, as the Mīmāṃsakas do, that the Vedic practices are eternal like the Vedas themselves; for, even disregarding the fact that the Vedic practices cannot be eternal since they would be interrupted during the period of dissolution, they would have to be considered either as independent (*svatantra-*) or as dependent upon the knowledge of Vedic meanings (*vedārthabodhatantra-*). In the first case, the Vedic practices would not have a sufficient foundation; in the second case, there would be uncertainty, if the knowledge of the Vedic meanings is derived from a non-omniscient instructor. Hence the steady performance of Vedic rites with certainty of their validity can be adequately accounted for only if one admits an omniscient person who knows all the Vedas and explains them at the beginning of creation to the human beings. Such a person is Īśvara.

Proof 5: (*padāt* = from word)

While the term *padam* was interpreted in the first series of proofs to mean human usages, here it is explained in its ordinary sense of 'word'. As will be seen from the exposition of this proof, Udayana considers certain groups of words in the Veda that refer to Īśvara and makes them the basis for establishing his existence.

a) *Words like "Praṇava", "Īśvara" or "Īśāna":* In the Vedic texts one comes across words like *praṇavaḥ* (i. e. the sacred syllable *Oṃ*), *īśvaraḥ* or *īśānaḥ*[228]. That these words have a meaning (*arthavat*) is clear from the fact that they are employed without contradiction (*avigānena*) in Śruti-, Smṛti-

[228] For the term *īśvaraḥ*, cf. Taitt. Br. I, 3, 10; BĀUp. I, 4, 8; Śvet Up. VI, 7. On the notion of Īśvara as found in Vedic texts cf. J. GONDA: Change and Continuity in Indian Religion, pp. 137—140. Cf. also his article: The concept of a personal God in ancient Indian religious thought, in: La Réalité Suprême dans les religions non-chrétiennes. (Studia Missionalia, Vol. XVII, Rome 1968) pp. 111—136. For the term *īśānaḥ*, cf. BĀUp. I, 4, 11; IV, 4, 15; Śvet Up. III, 12; III, 17; IV, 11. See also J. GONDA: Change and Continuity in Indian Religion, pp. 140ff. For the term *praṇavaḥ* (= *oṃ*) see Praśna Up. V, 2; V, 5; Taitt. Up. I, 8, 1.

and Itihāsa texts, just as one uses meaningful words like 'pot' or 'cloth' in ordinary life. The question as to what the precise meaning or object (*arthaḥ*) of these words is can be answered in two ways. The first way of determining the meaning is by means of the explanatory passages (*arthavādaḥ*). The meaning of the word *svargaḥ* (heaven), for example, can be determined from the explanatory passage: "That happiness which is not mingled with pain and which will not be lost immediately afterwards and which is present according to desire is the place (indicated) by the word 'heaven'"[229]. In the same manner the meaning of the words Īśvara etc. can be determined from explanatory passages such as "But the other is the foremost Person called Paramātmā (Supreme Soul), the immutable Īśvara, who, having entered the three worlds, maintains (them)"[230]. The second way of determining the meaning of the words Īśvara etc. is by taking into account the remaining part of the passage (*vākyaśeṣaḥ*). For example, although the word *yavaḥ* is generally used by the Āryas to mean 'barley' and by the Mlecchas to mean 'panic seed', yet its meaning in the statement *yavamayaś carur bhavati* (= The [oblation called] Caru consists of *yavaḥ*) is known to be 'barley' from the passage that follows: *yatrānyā oṣadheyā mlāyante athaite modamānā ivottiṣṭhanti* ('whereas the other plants fade, these stand upright as though rejoicing')[231]. In the same manner, after prescribing the practice of meditation on Īśvara (*īśvarapranidhānam*) the passage that follows says: "Those who are well versed in rituals (lit.: 'those that know the injunctions') say that omniscience, contentment, eternal knowledge, independence, a power that remains undiminished at all times, a power that is endless, are the six limbs[232] of the omnipresent Maheśvara"[233]. From this passage which follows the injunction of meditating upon Īśvara we know that it is such a person endowed with the above-mentioned six qualities that is the object to be meditated upon.

Thus from explanatory passages (*arthavādaḥ*) and from the passage that follows (*vākyaśeṣaḥ*: lit. 'remaining part of the statement') we can determine the meaning (*arthaḥ*) of the words like *praṇavaḥ*, *īśvaraḥ* or *īśānaḥ*. As these words are used unanimously (*avigānena*) in the different holy scriptures as having an object (*arthavat*), that is to say, designating a person endowed with certain specific attributes, that person necessarily exists. In answer to an objection of the Mīmāṃsakas that such an object (*arthaḥ*) called Īśvara is contradicted by the means of valid cognition, Udayana answers that he has

---

229 The oft-quoted definition of *svargaḥ* runs:
yan na duḥkhena saṃbhinnaṃ na ca grastam anantaram /
abhilāṣopanītaṃ ca tat sukhaṃ svaḥpadāspadam //

230 Bh. Gītā XV, 17.

231 Cf. NKusAm 367, 29—33; K. KUNJUNNI RAJA: Indian Theories of Meaning, pp. 30—31; P. V. KANE: History of Dharmaśāstra, Vol. V, Part II, p. 1285.

232 NKusPr and NKusAm explain the term *aṅgāni* (which I translated literally by 'limbs') to mean *dharmāḥ*. Cf. NKusPr 524, 29—30; NKusAm 368, 4.

233 Quoted in NKus 524, 1—2:
sarvajñatā tṛptir anādibodhaḥ svatantratā nityam aluptaśaktiḥ /
anantaśaktiś ca vibhor vidhijñāḥ ṣaḍ āhur aṅgāni maheśvarasya //

shown earlier (in the third Stabaka of his Nyāyakusumāñjali) that none of the means of valid cognition can invalidate or disprove the existence of Īśvara. If the Mīmāṃsakas insist that there is no means of valid cognition for establishing the existence of an object called Īśvara, our author retorts that ordinary people have no means of cognizing the existence of heaven, and yet the Mīmāṃsakas advocate its existence.

At the conclusion of his exposition, Udayana formulates the proof as follows:

> "That word which is applied by the wise (or the elders) to a certain (object), without (its having) another (significative) function[234], is expressive of that (particular object);
>
> like the word 'heaven' applied to a particular (kind of) happiness is expressive of that (object called 'heaven');
>
> And this (namely, words like *praṇavaḥ*, *īśvaraḥ* and *īśānaḥ*) is applied (by the wise or elders) to the maker of the universe, (without its having a function to signify any object other than the maker of the universe.
>
> Therefore the words like *praṇavaḥ*, *īśvaraḥ* and *īśānaḥ* are expressive of the maker of the universe)"[235].

In confirmation of his argument Udayana adds: "Otherwise, as (these words, *praṇavaḥ*, *īśvaraḥ* and *īśānaḥ*) would turn out to be without a meaning, it would be impossible to utter (them) together with groups of words that have a meaning"[236].

Since the wise or the elders (*vṛddhaḥ*) apply words such as *pranavaḥ*, *īśvaraḥ* and *īśānaḥ* to denote only the creator of the universe, and no object other than him, these words express the creator of the universe. As these words are meaningful, there must exist a creator of the universe, namely Īśvara, who is expressed by them.

What has been said of the words *praṇavaḥ*, *īśvaraḥ* and *īśānaḥ*, observes Udayana, is to be applied also to other words such as Rudra, Upendra, Mahendra etc. that express special deities[237]. By applying the explanatory passages (*arthavādaḥ*) or the remainder of the passage (*vākyaśeṣaḥ*) we can know that the object or person to which these words are applied is none other than Īśvara, the creator of the universe.

b) *The word 'I' found in the Vedas:* Udayana now chooses the pronominal word 'I' with its derivatives found in Vedic texts and deduces from them an author of the Veda. Just as in ordinary speech, he says, there is also in Vedic texts the usage of the word 'I' (*asmatpadam*). In ordinary speech, the word

---

[234] i. e. without that word being applied to signify any other object.

[235] NKus 524, 11—13: *yaḥ śabdo yatra vṛddhair asati vṛttyantare prayujyate sa tasya vācakaḥ, yathā svargaśabdaḥ sukhaviśeṣe prayujyamānas tasya vācakaḥ, prayujyate cāyaṃ jagatkartarīti.*

[236] Ibid. 524, 13—14: *anyathā nirarthakatvaprasaṅge sārthakapadakadambasamabhivyāhārānupapattir iti.*

[237] Ibid. 524, 14.

'I' is never applied to unconscious (*acetana-*) beings, since it is absolutely inapplicable to them. Nor does it signify self in general (*ātmamātram*), that is to say, any person in general, since it would then be applicable also to other selves or other persons. On the contrary, it has been established by the methods of concomitance and non-concomitance, that the word 'I' refers solely to that person who utters the statement in question independently (*svātantryeṇa*) or as his own, and not as repeating the words of another speaker. For example, when in the Raghuvaṃśa the poet Kālidāsa says: "You must tell that king (i. e. Rāma) in my name" (*vācyas tvayā madvacanāt sa rājā*), the pronoun 'my' (in *madvacanāt*) refers not to the poet Kālidāsa himself who formulates it in the epic, but to Sītā who first uttered it as the independent speaker of that statement.

Just as in ordinary usage the word 'I' refers only to the first independent speaker who expresses his own idea, the word 'I' found in the Vedic texts, too, refers solely to the first independent speaker of the Veda. It cannot be thought that the word 'I' in Vedic texts refers to any person who utters it, for example, the person reciting those passages. Otherwise, when one recites the scriptural passage "He should worship me" (*mām upāsīta*), the person who merely recites it would have to be worshipped. Or, when teachers and disciples repeat the passage "I am the source of all things; all things come forth from me", they will be ascribing to themselves the nature of Īśvara. If the reciters themselves of these passages were referred to by the pronoun 'I', there would be, as Udayana says, with regard to the meditation of Īśvara prescribed by the Vedic texts, "a sport of mad persons" (*unmattakeliḥ*), and verbal communication in ordinary life would be impossible. Hence, it is not the reciter who merely repeats (*anuvaktā*) the words said by another that is referred to by the pronoun 'I' (and its derivative cases, like 'me', 'from me' etc.) in the Vedic passages, but their original speaker (*vaktā*) who first uttered them, referring them to himself[238]. In the case of the Vedic word 'I' and its derivative cases, such a speaker can only be Īśvara, the author of the Vedas.

Udayana formulates this argument in syllogistic form as follows:

> "The word 'I' (found) in the Veda expresses its own speaker;
> because it has the nature of the word 'I';
> like (the word 'I' used) in ordinary speech"[239].

c) *Some other words, pronouns and interjections found in Vedic texts:* Udayana now applies the same argument to the pronouns such as "he who" (*yaḥ*), "who" (*kaḥ*: interrogative)[240], "he" (*saḥ*) etc. found in the Veda and

[238] To put it in terms used by Donald D. Evans in his book: The Logic of Self-involvement (see pp. 11—15 and 92—93), the word 'I' found in the Veda is "self-involving" or "self-referring".

[239] NKus 524, 23—24: *vede asmacchabdaḥ svaprayoktṛvacanaḥ, asmacchabdatvāl lokavad iti.*

[240] The Ṛgvedic hymn X, 121 inquiring after the creator of the universe is an instance where *kaḥ* is found in a Vedic passage. O. Strauss (Indische Philosophie, pp. 26—27) points out that the pedantry of later Hindu theologians made of this *kaḥ* a name of God.

argues that, as these pronouns also refer to an author of the Veda, they imply his existence. For these words imply the introduction of cognition, interrogation due to desire to know, remembrance etc. which are subjective aspects or attributes of a speaker, and therefore imply his existence. Words expressing doubt (*saṃśayaḥ*), too, are to be explained in the same way. It cannot be argued that the ascription of desire to know, doubt etc. are unbecoming in a being such as the author of the Veda who is said to be omniscient; for though he is omniscient, he makes use of expressions implying non-omniscience for the sake of instructing the living beings that are ignorant. It is only because they are indispensable as pedagogical means that these cognitional states of desire for cognition, doubt etc. can be applied to the author of the Veda, and not because he is non-omniscient[241].

The interjections found in the Veda such as *dhik*, *aho*, *bata* and *hanta*, expressing respectively reproach, surprise, pain and regret, are also to be applied to the author of the Veda in a similar way. They, too, therefore imply the existence of Īśvara[242].

Proof 6: (*pratyayāt* = from verbal suffix.)

In the first proof of the second series Udayana established the existence of Īśvara from the Arthavāda or explanatory passages of the Veda. But the core of the Vedic texts is said to be the injunctions, the most fundamental element of which is the verbal form, mostly expressed in the optative mood or *liṅ*. In the proof to be considered now Udayana interprets the term *pratyayaḥ*—which expresses the logical reason—in its grammatical meaning of 'verbal suffix'. Meant here is primarily and principally the verbal suffix of the optative mood or *liṅ*. No doubt, Udayana includes here also the other verbal suffixes expressing injunction, such as the verbal suffixes of *liḍ*, *-tavya*, *-anīya*, *yab* etc.[243]; for these, too, may be used to convey an injunction and are reducible to the optative. Moreover, it should be remembered that, as these verbal suffixes express not only positive commands to perform some action, but also negative commands to avoid some action, Udayana here makes both the positive injunctions (*vidhiḥ*) and the negative injunctions (*niṣedhaḥ*) the basis for proving the existence of Īśvara.

The major part of the exposition of this proof, which in length surpasses all the others, is devoted to an analysis of the nature of injunction or *vidhiḥ*. The activity (*pravṛttiḥ*) that results from a positive injunction, observes Udayana, is not mere motion (*spandamātram*), since in injunctions such as "The Self must be cognized" (*ātmā jñātavyaḥ*) such motion is absent. Nor does it consist in mere desire (*icchāmātram*); for, were the desired fruit (such as heaven) obtainable by mere wish, no one would engage himself in the very complicated and often expensive rites that are said to be the means of obtaining them. Hence what constitutes the activity that results from an injunc-

[241] Cf. NKus 525, 1—6.
[242] Ibid. 525, 6—7.
[243] Ibid. 525, 8: *liṅgādipratyayāḥ* . . . See also NKusAm 370, 2.

tion is the effort (*prayatnaḥ*) which is found even in injunctions such as "The Self must be cognized", "Be compassionate towards the beings" (*bhūtebhyo dayāṃ kuru*) etc., where no motion or external activity is found[244]. In other words, activity (*pravṛttiḥ*) demanded by the injunction is effort (*prayatnaḥ*).

Now the activity with regard to something enjoined does not proceed from the mere fact that there are injunctions, but only in as far as they are cognized. If we analyse the psychological process that leads to the activity enjoined by an injunction, we observe that it takes its origin from desire (*icchā*). On the other hand this desire itself arises from the cognition (*jñānam*) that the action has been enjoined, and that it is the means for attaining the desired end. Thus injunction or *vidhiḥ* is the object, the knowledge of which produces the desire which, in its turn, gives rise to effort (*prayatnaḥ*) or activity (*pravṛttiḥ*). Such was the traditional teaching of the school. Udayana diverges from this view and maintains that the injunction which, though variously termed as *vidhiḥ*, *preraṇā*, *pravartanā*, *niyuktiḥ*, *niyogaḥ* or *upadeśaḥ*, denotes one and the same thing, is that which makes known (*jñāpaka-*) to the hearer, or makes him infer, that the prescribed action is the means to attain the desired end[245].

In order to justify and defend his view of *vidhiḥ* against that of the others, Udayana enters into a long discussion on its nature. Following his usual method he proposes different possible answers to the question of the nature of *vidhiḥ* and rejects them one by one, leaving his own view as the only right one. He says that *vidhiḥ* could be (1) either the attribute of the agent (*kartṛdharmaḥ*); (2) or the attribute of the action (*karmadharmaḥ*); (3) or the attribute of the instrument (*karaṇadharmaḥ*); (4) or finally the attribute of the person that enjoins (*niyoktṛdharmaḥ*). He then considers in great detail the first three alternatives, one by one, analysing them by proposing various alternative answers, and shows that none of them can be said to constitute *vidhiḥ*[246]. We shall not enter into this discussion as it would take us far away from our present purpose and also because it is not necessary for the understanding of the proof we are studying. Having rejected the first three possible explanations of *vidhiḥ*, Udayana exposes his own view, namely that *vidhiḥ* is the wish or intention of the speaker (*vaktur abhiprāyaḥ*) with regard to the performance of, or the abstaining from, certain actions (*pravṛttinivṛtti*) expressed by means of the optative mood or other verbal suffixes such as *-tavya*, *-anīya* etc. which express the same meaning. The agent acts according to the commands expressed by optative mood and other suffixes that express command because he infers that performance of or abstaining from the action mentioned in the command is the means to obtain the desired end[247].

The wish or intention of the speaker is expressed in different ways. The expression of the wish that the action in question should be performed (or avoided) by the speaker himself is expressed in the optative first person of the

---

244 NKus 525, 12—15; NKusPr 525, 26ff.
245 NKus 525, 16—526, 3; NKusVi 371, 1.
246 NKus 526, 3—567, 2.
247 Ibid. 567, 4—5.

verb. The wish that a certain action be performed (or avoided) by the person who is addressed is expressed in the optative second person of the verb, while the wish with regard to the other persons is expressed in the optative third person.

In ordinary life (*loke*) the injunction "He who desires fire should rub two pieces of wood" (*agnikāmo dāruṇī mathniyāt*) expresses the wish or the intention of the speaker: "The activity of rubbing two pieces of wood by a person who wants fire is desired by me" (*agnikāmasya dārumathane pravṛttir mameṣṭā*). The person who hears this injunction then infers: "Indeed, the activity of rubbing two pieces of wood is the means for obtaining fire". Thus the person who hears an injunction understands that, when a trustworthy teacher enjoins a person the performance of some action, that performance is for him the cause or means that is desired by the teacher in order that he may obtain what he desires. For example, when my father wishes that certain things should be eaten by me, the eating of those things is conducive to my good. In the same manner, negative injunctions or prohibitions (*niṣedhaḥ*) in ordinary life, such as "One should not eat poison" (*viṣam na bhakṣayet*) express the wish or intention of the speaker: "The activity of eating poison is not desired by me" (*viṣabhakṣaṇagocarā pravṛttir mama neṣṭā*). The person who listens to this prohibition infers that the action of eating poison is certainly undesirable, and that, even if he likes the food containing poison, eating it will be for him the cause of great misfortune, since it has not been wished by the trustworthy author of that prohibition. For example, however much his own children might desire to eat mud or poison, he himself does not desire them to do so, as it would cause serious consequences to their health[248].

Udayana does not, as one would have expected, explicitly formulate the application of the above examples of positive and negative injunctions taken from ordinary life to those found in the Vedic texts, probably because the application is quite evident and easy. He says that the Vedic injunctions such as "He who desires heaven should sacrifice" (*svargakāmo yajeta*) express the desire or intention of their author that the activity of sacrifice by a person who desires heaven is desired by him as the means for obtaining heaven. Similarly, the Vedic prohibitions such as "One should not eat Kalañja"[249] (*kalañjaṃ na bhakṣayet*) express the wish or intention of their author that the action of eating Kalañja is not desired by him, as it would lead to evil consequences.

Since both the positive and the negative injunctions in the Veda thus imply the wish of a person who is their author, it necessarily follows that the Vedas should have an author. This author is Īśvara.

Such a conclusion is not acceptable to the Mīmāṃsakas. Although they are willing to concede that injunctions and prohibitions in ordinary life express the wish or intention of a speaker who is their author, they deny the application of this principle to the Vedic injunctions and prohibitions on the ground that there is no author of the Veda. In answer to the observation of Udayana

[248] Ibid. 567, 6—15.

[249] *kalañjam* is the flesh of an animal struck with a poisonous weapon.

that there is no reason for denying an author of the Veda, they state that there is also no positive argument for proving the existence of such an author. At this point the author of the Nyāyakusumāñjali rejoins: "Let there be no other (proof for the existence of an author of the Veda; but) the very injunction (in the Veda), indeed, is a proof for the Virgin (called) Śruti having a union with a person, just as the embryo (is the proof that an unmarried girl has had a union with a man)"[250]. Udayana means that since the Mīmāṃsakas admit positive and negative injunctions in the Veda and devote themselves to a minute study of them, they must also admit that these injunctions have a necessary relation to a person who is their author, in as far as they express his wish. He points out, moreover, that, in case the opponents are not willing to accept this conclusion, they will also have to give up the view that the words in the Veda have the same meaning as in the ordinary usage[251].

Unwilling to accept an author of the Veda and yet unable to deny the fact that injunctions in ordinary usage express the wish of their author, the Mīmāṃsaka now tries to argue that the injunctions in the Veda represent the wish (*abhiprāyaḥ*) of the teachers (*upādhyāyaḥ*) of the Veda who repeat them, and that there is no need of admitting an independent (*svatantra-*) author called Parameśvara. Udayana rejects this argument on the ground that the Vedic injunctions cannot be said to express the wish of the teachers of Veda, since these merely repeat or recite (*anuvaktṛtā*) the wish of another person who is the real author of the Veda, just as parrots repeat the words they have heard from another person. In other words, these Vedic teachers are not independent authors of the Veda; they are dependent in their recitation or repetition of the Veda upon another who, in his turn, is not dependent upon any other author. If the person who merely repeats or reads out the wish of another were himself the independent author of the statement he repeats or reads out, one would have to admit that, when a courtier merely repeats the words of the king to another person, the order thus conveyed is not that of the king, but of the courtier himself who, in fact, merely repeats the wish or will of the king. Hence the injunctions in the Veda necessarily presuppose an author who is none other than Īśvara.

Proof 7: (*śruteḥ* = from [praises found in] the Śruti-texts)

In the first series of proofs Udayana had proved the existence of Īśvara from the fact that the sacred texts called Śruti or "revealed" texts were composed by an omniscient person on the ground that they possess 'the nature of the Veda' (*vedatvam*) which consists in the fact that the Vedic statements are accepted by the large mass of people (*mahājanaparigṛhīta-*), while no

---

[250] NKus 568, 3—4: *mā bhūd anyat, vidhir eva tāvad garbha iva puṃyoge pramāṇaṃ śrutikumāryāyāḥ*. To understand this simile properly, it should be remembered that the Sanskrit word *puṃs* which is used here means a man as well as a person in general.

[251] The Mīmāṃsakas maintain the view: *ya eva laukikā śabdāḥ, ta eva vaidikās ta evaiṣām arthāḥ*. This view quoted by Udayana in NKus 568, 4—5 is found in ŚBh to MSu I, 3, 30 (ŚBh 79, 5).

other basis for their acceptance can be perceived. Here he considers the Śrutis or revealed texts in as far as they are related to Īśvara (*parameśvaragocara-*) and argues from this aspect of theirs for the existence of Īśvara.

"There are, indeed, no parts of the Veda at all", observes he, "where the Supreme Lord is not praised. Thus (he is praised) in the Hymns to the Puruṣa as being the Creator, in the Rudra-(Mantras) as being the universal display of majesty[252], in the Maṇḍala-Brāhmaṇas as Śabdabrahman (i. e. the Brahman or the Absolute in the form of Śabda or Sound), in the Upaniṣads, on account of the existence of the world of manifoldness (*prapañcaṃ puraskṛtya*), as being devoid of manifoldness, in the Injunctive Mantras as being the Sacrificial Person, in the Upākhyānas as being (different) bodily manifestations, and in all (these texts he has been praised) as one to be worshipped"[253].

Important to note in this passage is that Udayana mentions in it the different types or groups of sacred scriptures that have unquestioned authoritativeness even for his opponents, namely the Saṃhitās, the Brāhmaṇas, the Upaniṣads and the Upākhyānas[254]. In order to show that all these texts have Īśvara for their object, he makes mention of those passages in the scriptures which deal directly with Īśvara under his different aspects as Puruṣa, Rudra, Śabdabrahman, transcendent quality-less Brahman etc. Important to note is that Īśvara not only is mentioned in them, but is also mentioned in all these texts as one worthy of being worshipped (*upāsyatvena*). The fact that Īśvara is praised as one deserving worship in all these texts that are accepted as authoritative shows, in the view of Udayana, that he must be existent.

Though the Mīmāṃsakas accept the authoritativeness (*prāmāṇyam*) of these texts, nevertheless, as deniers of Īśvara, they interpret them differently. They argue that the passages such as the Hymn to the Puruṣa (*puruṣasūktiḥ*), brought forward by the Nyāya-Vaiśeṣikas as referring to Īśvara, being mere statements of facts, have a purport other than is meant in their primary meaning. It is only the *vidhi*-s that have a primary purport for themselves. Such a view is not acceptable to Udayana; for even if a statement may have a secondary meaning or purport, the primary meaning has precedence over the secondary. Were it not so, even statements that explain or describe the nature of heaven, hell, Vrātya or Brāhmaṇa would have to be considered as invalid.

---

[252] *vibhūtiḥ* is the term applied to Viṣṇu's "divine and universal power and dignity". Cf. J. Gonda: Viṣṇuism and Śivaism, p. 15; and: Aspects of Early Viṣṇuism, p. 121. The term is used also for the bodily manifestations or incarnations of God. Śaṅkaramiśra in his NKusAm 350, 20—21 says: *vibhūtir iti brahmādy avatārādīty arthaḥ.*

[253] NKus 569, 1—4: *na santy eva hi vedabhāgā yatra parameśvaro na gīyate. tathā hi sraṣṭṛtvena puruṣasūkteṣu, vibhūtyā rudreṣu, śabdabrahmatvena maṇḍalabrāhmaṇeṣu, prapañcaṃ puraskṛtya niṣprapañcatayopaniṣatsu, yajñapuruṣatvena mantravidhiṣu, dehāvirbhāvair upākhyāneṣu, upāsyatvena ca sarvatreti.*

[254] With *upākhyānam* is meant the 'narrative' literature (Epics and Purāṇas) which is considered to be of divine origin and is for Hinduism almost as sacred as the Veda was for Brāhmaṇism. On the important position of Purāṇas in the Indian sacred literature cf. M. Winternitz: Geschichte der indischen Literatur, Vol. I, pp. 440—449.

If the Mīmāṃsakas believe that these statements are valid, since there is nothing to contradict them, the same can be said also of the passages referring to Īśvara. Nor can the Mīmāṃsakas deny Īśvara on the ground that he is not seen[255]; for, on the same principle they would equally have to deny heaven, since that, too, is not seen by us. If they would justify the validity of the statements on heaven on the ground that, were it non-existent, the injunctions relating to heaven such as "He who desires heaven should offer sacrifice" would be useless (*anarthaka-*), the same can be said also of Īśvara; for, if Īśvara were non-existent, then the Vedic statements wherein Īśvara is enjoined to be worshipped would be untrue, and consequently no reasonable person would worship him.

What Udayana wants to show in this discussion with the Mīmāṃsakas is that, if the opponents want to explain away the passages of the sacred scriptures wherein Īśvara is asked to be worshipped as invalid or having another sense than is primarily signified by them, they will have to admit that, for the same reasons, the passages relating to heaven, hell etc., too, are not valid and have a meaning other than what is assumed by them. Since the opponents accept the passages relating to heaven, hell etc. as infallibly true and believe in the existence of these invisible realities, they should also accept the passages relating to the worship of Īśvara as infallibly true and admit that Īśvara exists.

If we compare this proof with the fourth proof in the second series (based on *padam*) we find some common points. Nevertheless this proof differs from the other because while in the earlier proof the existence of Īśvara was established from the fact that words such as Praṇava, Īśvara, Īśana etc. are meaningful and hence designate a reality, here the argument is based, not on the words expressing Īśvara as such, but on the fact that Īśvara is mentioned in the different sacred scriptures as one who is to be worshipped (*upāsyatvena*).

Proof 8: (*vākyāt* = from association of word-meanings.)

Udayana had argued in the first series of proofs that, since the Vedic sentences have the same nature as the ordinary sentences, they should have, like the latter, a composer or author. In the present proof he goes a little deeper into the nature of the Vedic sentences. He interprets here the term *vākyatvam* ("the nature of sentence") in the sense of "the expression (or enunciation) of association or dissociation" (*saṃsargabhedapratipādakatvam*). That a sentence, though constituted of different word-meanings (*padārthaḥ*) produces a unified meaning was accepted by all. There was, however, difference of opinion as to what this meaning was. There were some—to this group belonged the Mīmāṃsakas—who believed that the sentence expressed association (*saṃsargaḥ*) of word-meanings. Udayana himself seems to have followed this view[256].

---

[255] Cf. ŚV 651, 2 (= Sambandhākṣepaparihāra, verse 46b).

[256] In NKus 520, 6—7 Udayana defines *vākyam* as . . . *ākāṅkṣādimattve sati anvayaśaktiḥ padānāṃ padārthānāṃ vā vākyam.*

Others, on the contrary, were of the view that a sentence expresses dissociation or exclusion of the word-meanings from other word-meanings[257].

Udayana bases his argument for the existence of Īśvara on the fact that the association of word-meanings in the Vedic sentences presupposes, as in the case of secular or ordinary sentences, a cognizer of that association:

"That group of words which expresses the association or dissociation of certain (word-meanings) presupposes the cognition of the association independent of that (group of words). As in the case of the ordinary (group of words), so, too, (is) the case with Vedic (groups of words)"[258].

Udayana disposes of this proof in three lines. The commentators, too, are very modest in their explanation of this passage. The underlying idea in this argument is that the association of words in a sentence in such a way as to give one unified meaning presupposes in its composer a cognition of the associability of those words independent of and prior to the association of the same words in the sentence in question. In the case of the Vedic sentences, the cognition of the words used in them can be known only by a being whose knowledge is independent of any other source, in other words, a being endowed with eternal omniscience[259].

Proof 9: (*saṃkhyāviśeṣāt.*)

In the first series of proofs the term *saṃkhyā* was interpreted as 'number' produced by the relating cognition (*apekṣābuddhiḥ*) and thus under the aspect of a product (*kāryatayā*). Here, on the other hand, Udayana considers *saṃkhyā* in as far as it is to be expressed or to be communicated (*pratipādyatayā*)[260]. He gives a double interpretation of the word *saṃkhyā* even under this aspect: *saṃkhyā* in as far as it is expressed in the verbal forms of the first person and *saṃkhyā* interpreted as *samākhyā* or name. Thus, properly speaking, there are two distinct proofs here, although he groups them together under the common logical reason *saṃkhyā*.

a) *saṃkhyāviśeṣaḥ* in as far as it expresses the number in the verbal form of the first person: "It is very well known that the number expressed by the (verbal form of the) first person goes together with the speaker. And there is abundant use of it in the Veda. Hence also that (number) expressed

---

[257] Cf. K. Kunjunni Raja: Indian Theories of Meaning, pp. 191—193; P. Hacker: Untersuchungen über Texte des frühen Advaitavāda, I. Die Schüler Śaṅkaras, p. 75.

[258] NKus 571, 1—3: *yat padakadambakaṃ yat saṃsargabhedapratipādakaṃ tat tadanapekṣasaṃsargajñānapūrvakaṃ, yathā laukikaṃ, tathā ca vaidikam iti prayogaḥ.*

[259] The explanation of this proof given by Haridāsa Bhaṭṭācārya (see Cowell's edition of his commentary on the Kārikās of the NKus 63, 11—64, 2) is completely different from that given by Udayana. In fact, although he introduces the proof with the *hetuḥ* "from sentence" (*vākyāt*), the explanation he gives and the example he uses correspond to Udayana's explanation of the proof based on *kāryatvam* in the second series of proofs.

[260] Cf. NKus 572, 4.

by it (= the verbal form of the first person found in the Veda) must go together with that same (speaker or author of the Veda).

Otherwise there would be absence of connection (between them)"[261].

As he has done earlier, Udayana makes here also the language of ordinary life the basis for his argument. In ordinary language it is known to everyone that the number expressed by the first person refers to the speaker of that statement, and not to any other. In the Vedic texts there are verbal forms in the first person such as *syām* "may I be", *abhūvam* "I was", *bhaviṣyāmi* "I shall be" etc.[262]. Since the Vedic words are to be explained, as far as possible, in the same sense as the words in ordinary speech, it is to be concluded that the number expressed by the verbal forms in first person found in the Vedic texts refers to the speaker or author of the Veda. Consequently the verbal forms of the first person found in the Vedic texts necessarily imply the existence of the author of those texts.

In the Kārikā summarizing this argument Udayana mentions only three verbal forms, *syām, abhūvam* and *bhaviṣyāmi*, indicative of three tenses, but, as is indicated by the word *ādi* that follows these three words, he includes also other tenses in the first person found in the Vedic texts. He speaks only of the singular forms, probably because Īśvara, the author of the Veda to whom these forms refer, is one. Or, in case plural forms are also to be applied, they will have to be interpreted in the singular as referring to one single author of the Veda.

b) *saṃkhyāviśeṣaḥ* in the sense of particular names (*saṃjñāviśeṣaḥ*). "Or, it is the particular name that is meant by (the term) *saṃkhyāviśeṣaḥ*", continues Udayana. "For particular names of particular (Vedic) branches such as Kāṭhaka, Kālāpaka etc. have been handed down by tradition. But (*ca*) these (names) are not based on the mere (fact of) oral teaching[263]; for there are innumerable oral teachers. Nor (are these names) based (on the fact that certain teachers) have taught in a manner superior (to that of the others); for, if (these teachers, Kaṭha, Kalāpa etc. were) superior even to (their) preceptors, (and that would, then, be the reason for the Vedic branches being named after them), there would rather be the fault that they might have changed (something in the Vedic text that has been taught to them by their teachers[264]); if, however (*ca*), they followed their (= of their teachers) text (exactly), they would not be superior to them. And what factor is there to

---

[261] Ibid. 572, 4—6: . . . *uttamapuruṣābhihitā saṃkhyā vaktāram anvetīti suprasiddham. asti ca tatprayogaḥ prāyaśo vede. tatas tadabhihitayā tayā 'pi sa evānugantavyaḥ, anyathā 'nanvayaprasaṅgāt.*

[262] For example, ChUp. VI, 2, 3: *tad aikṣata bahu syāṃ prajāyeyeti.* See also Taitt. Up. II, 6, 1.

[263] That is, on the mere fact that the Vedas have been orally transmitted by teachers.

[264] Śaṅkaramiśra interprets it differently in his NKusAm 422, 5—6: *adhyāpakāpekṣayā prakarṣaś ced vivakṣitas tadā pūrvapūrvādhyāpakāpekṣayā yaḥ kaścit pūrvotkṛṣṭas tasyaiva nāmnā samākhyā syād ity arthaḥ.*

determine how many eminent teachers there are in this worldly existence which is beginningless? Nor is it correct (to assume) that the name (Kāṭhaka, Kālāpaka etc.) is of the first proclaimer (of the Vedic branch in question), since you (Mīmāṃsakas) do not admit that (there is a first proclaimer of the Veda). Or, if you do admit (a first proclaimer of the Veda, then) he is none else than our (Īśvara, whom we regard as the) author of the Veda. Hence dissension (on this point) is useless"[265].

In this passage Udayana works out into a proof an idea that had been brought forward by earlier thinkers to argue that the Veda has a person as author (*pauruṣeya-*). We come across this idea at least as early as Śabara's commentary on the Mīmāṃsāsūtra I, 1, 27 as the view of 'some' (*kecit*) who consider the Vedas as produced (*kṛtaka-*), and not eternal (*nitya-*), as the Mīmāṃsakas had held. These thinkers had maintained that the names of the Vedic branches (*vedaśākhā*) such as Kāṭhaka, Kālāpaka, Paippalādaka, Maudgala etc. could not be derived except from their relation to persons such as Kaṭha, Kalāpa, Pippalāda, Mudgala etc. indicated by those names. Probably these thinkers wanted only to argue that the Vedas were not eternal, but composed by persons such as Kaṭha etc. An identification of these persons with Īśvara. as the later Nyāya-Vaiśeṣikas did, was probably not made at that time. The advocates of the eternity of the Vedas had argued that the assumption of persons such as Kaṭha, Kalāpa etc. as authors of the Veda was unacceptable to them. For name (*samākhyā*) is used in order to determine the particularity, after the generality has been established. Since the generality —in our present context it means an author in general (*kartṛsāmānyam*)— is here not established, a particularity of it, namely a particular author like Kaṭha, Kalāpa etc., cannot be determined[266]. The Mīmāṃsakas would admit no person, human or divine, as the author of the Veda. In their view the study of the Vedic texts was at all times dependent upon a teacher who, in his turn, had studied from another teacher[267], this uninterrupted succession of teachers and disciples going on without a beginning. Every teacher taught the texts to his students in exactly the same way as he had been taught by his own teacher, and there was no question of a first teacher who, independent of another teacher, himself composed the Veda. Consequently, they concluded, the names of the Vedic branches Kāṭhaka, Kālāpaka etc. are derived from the names of the teachers of these branches[268]. It is this view that is rejected by Udayana in that part of the passage quoted above, where he states the opinion of the Mīmāṃsakas that the names of the particular Vedic branches are derived

---

[265] Cf. NKus 572, 7—13.

[266] Cf. ŚV 950, 6—951, 4. (= Vedanityatādhikaraṇam, verses 1—3) See also Pārthasārathimiśra's commentary on it.

[267] See note 219; see also ŚD 469, 18—470, 3: *sarvapuṃsānām adhyayanam adhyayanāntarapūrvakam, sarve hi yathaiva guruṇā'dhītaṃ tathaivā'dhijigāṃsante, na punaḥ svātantryeṇa kaścid api prathamo'dhyetā vedānām asti yaḥ kartā syāt*, ...

[268] Cf. MSu I, 1, 30: *ākhyā pravacanāt* and Śabara's commentary on it; further ŚV 951, 5f. (= Vedanityatā'dhikaraṇam, verse 4ff.); ŚD 470, 3—7 and 50, 18—22; PrP 247, 2—3.

from the mere fact of teaching (*pravacanamātranibandhana-*). He rejects their explanation as unacceptable because, as there is an endless (*ananta-*) number of teachers of each of these Vedic branches, they cannot be named each after one person[269].

In order to get over this difficulty, which was put to them by authors even earlier than Udayana, the Mīmāṃsakas had answered that, although the Vedic branches had an innumerable number of teachers, each of these branches acquired its name from that teacher who, among its numberless teachers, taught it in the most eminent manner (*prakṛṣṭavacananimitta-*). In order to show that there were such teachers Śabara quotes a passage wherein it is said that Vaiśampāyana studied all the Vedas, while Kaṭha taught only the one Vedic branch now called Kāṭhaka. It is quite natural that a person who studies only one branch of the Veda, neglecting the others, would acquire a superior knowledge of it and be a better teacher than others who study the entire Veda[270]. Udayana raises objections even against such an explanation. For, to say that Kaṭha, Kalāpa etc. excelled all other teachers, he argues, would imply that they have made some changes in the text of the Veda on account of which they would be held superior to the others. Had they merely followed the text of the Veda exactly as they had learned it from their teachers, they would not be considered superior to them. But any change, however minute it be, in the text of the Veda would affect its authoritativeness[271]. Hence, Udayana continues, it is not right to explain the names of the particular Vedic branches as derived from the name of the most eminent teachers of each of those branches. Moreover, he asks, what criterion is there to determine how many such superior teachers (*prakṛṣṭāḥ pravaktāraḥ*) there are, since the Saṃsāra is beginningless? The adversaries are not willing to accept that, though there are numberless proclaimers of the Veda, the names of the Vedic branches are derived from a first proclaimer. Were they to admit it, then, that first proclaimer would be none other than the author of the Veda (*vedakāraḥ*) postulated by the Nyāya-Vaiśeṣikas[272].

The Mīmāṃsakas had tried to explain the names of the Vedic branches in other ways also[273]. One of these explanations was that the name Kāṭhaka, for instance, was derived from an intermediary caste (or sub-caste) among the Brāhmins (*brāhmaṇāvāntarajātiḥ*) called Kaṭha the members of which studied and practised only what is contained in that particular Vedic text. Udayana rejects this theory as unacceptable, since the Kāṭhaka Vedic text

---

269 Cf. NKus 572, 8—9. See also ŚD 467, 5—7. Note that here the view of a Pūrvapakṣin, most probably of a Nyāya-Vaiśeṣika, is spoken of.

270 Cf. ŚBh to MSu I, 1, 30: *smaryate ca vaiśampāyanaḥ sarvaśākhādhyāyī, kaṭhaḥ punar imāṃ kevalāṃ śākhām adhyāpayāṃbabhūveti*. See also ŚD 470, 5—7; NR 952, 14—16; PrP 247, 3—5.

271 We know that various means such as the *padapāṭhaḥ* were used by the Vedic teachers in order to preserve the original text of the Veda without any modification.

272 Cf. NKus 572, 9—13.

273 Cf. NR 952, 17ff.

is studied and practised not only by the Brāhmins, but also by the Kṣatriyas and the Vaiśyas. If the Kāṭhaka texts were studied and practised exclusively by the particular Brāhmin sub-caste called Kaṭha, as the Mīmāṃsakas maintain, then the Kṣatriyas and the Vaiśyas would not have done so. Moreover, no Vedic text can be said to be only for the Brāhmins, since the Kṣatriyas and the Vaiśyas, too, have the same Veda as the Brāhmins. Besides, it cannot be maintained that the Kaṭha Brāhmins study only the Kāṭhaka Vedic texts and perform solely what is prescribed in them; for it is often observed that a person changes at discretion the Vedic branch and passes over from the study and practice of one branch of the Veda to another[274]. It cannot be argued that, although at present we observe transition from one Vedic branch to another, in very ancient times the Kaṭha Brāhmins studied only the Kāṭhaka texts; for if there is no such rule at present, we cannot legitimately assume that it existed at an earlier period. Nor is there any evidence that there was an intermediary Brāhmin caste called Kaṭha[275].

Having thus rejected the explanations of his opponents as inadmissible Udayana concludes: "Therefore the only right (explanation is) that this connection of a particular name (such as Kāṭhaka with a particular Vedic branch) is solely (*eva*) based on the utterance (*vacanam*) of the first teacher"[276]. By this statement Udayana affirms that the names of the Vedic branches such as Kāṭhaka can be derived neither from the name of any teacher in general of that Vedic branch nor even from the name of the foremost among them, as the Mīmāṃsakas tried to explain, but only from the first teacher (*ādyapravaktā*) who is not dependent upon any other previous teacher.

It may be of interest to point out here that the conclusion of Udayana has been differently explained by his commentators. Thus the author of the Prakāśa explains it to mean that the Vedic branches Kāṭhaka etc. are called so because they were composed at the beginning of the creation by Īśvara himself assuming the bodies of persons such as Kaṭha[277]. Such is also the interpretation given by Haridāsa Bhaṭṭācārya and Rāmabhadra Sārvabhauma[278]. Śaṅkaramiśra, however, gives a different interpretation: the Vedic branches in question have their names from the names of the persons

---

[274] A person belongs to that Vedic branch according to which sanctifying ceremonies (*saṃskārāḥ*) have been performed on him. Hence even a person not belonging to the Kāṭhaka Vedic branch becomes a follower of that branch, if the sanctifying ceremonies are performed on him according to it.

[275] Cf. NKus 572, 14—573, 5.

[276] Ibid. 573, 5—6: *tasmād ādyapravaktṛvacananimitta evāyaṃ samākhyāviśeṣasambandha ity eva sādhv iti.*

[277] NKusPr 573, 14—15: *kaṭhādiśarīram adhiṣṭhāya sargādāv īśvareṇa yā śākhā kṛtā sā tatsamākhyeti pariśeṣa ity arthaḥ.*

[278] Cf. E. Cowell's edition of Haridāsa Bhaṭṭācārya's commentary 64, 11—14: *tasmād atīndriyārthadarśī bhagavān eva kāruṇikaḥ sargādāv asmadādyadṛṣṭākṛṣṭakāṭhakādiśarīraviśeṣam adhiṣṭhāya yaṃ śākhām uktavān tasyāḥ śākhāyās tannāmnā vyapadeśa* (wrongly printed *vyavadeśa*) *iti* . . .; NKusKaVy 108, 7—10 reproduces the words of Haridāsa Bhaṭṭācārya without any modification.

to whom Īśvara taught them first[279]. Guṇānanda, the author of the Vivekaṭīkā, seems to follow the view of Śaṅkaramiśra[280].

A review of the second series of proofs brings out one feature in full relief: while the first series of proofs establishes the existence of Īśvara under different aspects of his relation to the universe, namely as creator, preserver and destroyer of the universe, as the teacher of the living beings, and as the author of the Veda, the second series of proofs aims, without exception, to establish the existence of Īśvara as the author of the Veda. This is not without a ground. The first series of proofs were addressed to the opponents of Īśvara doctrine in general, regardless of the question whether or not they believed in the validity or authoritativeness (*prāmāṇyam*) of the Veda. But the latter series of proofs take for granted that the opponents to whom they are addressed accept the authoritativeness of the Vedic scriptures and hence they are intended for those adversaries who believed in the Veda. Though there were Brāhmaṇic schools like Sāṃkhya which, while accepting the authoritativeness of the Veda, denied the existence of Īśvara, Udayana does not seem to have intended the latter series of proofs for them; for neither in the exposition of the proofs nor in the discussions after their formulation are the Sāṃkhyins or their doctrines spoken of. On the other hand, we see that the Mīmāṃsaka doctrines, especially those concerning the authoritativeness of the Veda, are constantly referred to, implicitly or explicitly, in the formulation of these proofs as well as in their further elaboration and discussion. Hence we can conclude that the second series is meant for the Mīmāṃsakas in particular. We have already referred to the fact that our author considered the Mīmāṃsakas as the foremost opponents of the Īśvara doctrine within the fold of Hinduism, and hence it is easy to understand why he brings forward a series of proofs for them, arguing that, since they admit the Vedic scriptures as infallibly valid, they should also recognize an author for them.

It is striking that, although Udayana shows in these arguments the necessity of accepting a person as the author of the Vedas, he does not proceed further to argue that this person is Īśvara himself. As a matter of fact, there is no need of such an explicit formulation; for he has made clear that the person who is said to be the author of the Veda cannot but be omniscient, since he perceives all that is taught in the Veda, including those realities that are invisible to ordinary persons. But such an omniscient being, at the beginning of creation, cannot but be Īśvara. The fact that he does not, in the second series of proofs, argue that the author of the Veda is identical with the creator of

---

[279] NKusAm 422, 12—13: *ādyeti. ādau yaḥ pravaktā īśvaras tena yā śākhā prathamaṃ yasmai proktā sā tannāmnā prasiddhety arthaḥ.*

[280] NKusVi 424, 3—5: *ādyena itarajñānānadhīnatajjñānavatā pravaktādhyāpakena yannāmno yā śākhā'dhyāpitā sā tena vyapadiśyata iti niyama ity arthaḥ.* The word *yannāmno* in this passage seems to me incorrect. Probably it is a misprint for *yannāmne*, and in that case Guṇānanda's view will correspond to that of Śaṅkaramiśra. Another possible interpretation is to take it as a misprint for *yannāmnā*. If it is so, then, his view will correspond to that of Vardhamāna and Haridāsa Bhaṭṭācārya.

the universe can also be explained in the same way. The author of the Veda should be eternal and omniscient; so should be the creator of the universe. But there is no need of admitting more than one eternal and omniscient being to explain the created universe as well as authoritativeness of the Vedas. Hence, even though Udayana does not explicitly identify the author of the Vedas with the creator of the universe, as Jayanta did[281], the whole tenor of his proofs in general bears out this fact.

Another point to be observed is that, as in the first series of proofs, here, too, not all the proofs have been dealt with equal elaboration. As is clear, not all the proofs are of equal importance; some of them are more important than the others because they are more fundamental or more often used by the Nyāya-Vaiśeṣika authors. Such is, for example, the case of the first proof of the first series based on *kāryatvam* which has received the longest and the most thorough explanation at the hands of Udayana. In the second series it is the proof based on *pratyayaḥ* that has been elaborated at great length. As mentioned earlier, it is more than one-and-a-half times the length of the fourth Stabaka and occupies more than one-third of the entire length of the fifth Stabaka. This proof provided Udayana an occassion to mention and refute in a long excursus the different Mīmāṃsaka views on the nature of scriptural injunctions (*vidhiḥ*) which form according to them the most important part of the Veda.

3. Concluding Remarks on the Proofs

After going through both these series of proofs for the existence of Īśvara, one may ask oneself what degree of validity or convincing value they possess for the general reader. It should be remembered that they are addressed to thinkers who, though differing from each other in views, belonged to India and shared its specific backgrounds and patterns of thought. Were we to compare these proofs with those proposed by the Western thinkers of the same period, we would find considerable difference between them. The first proof in the first series based on the fact that earth etc. possess the nature of effect (*kāryatvam*) and consequently presuppose the existence of a conscious or intellectual agent, seems at first sight to correspond to the proof brought forward by medieval scholastics to prove the existence of God. But the presuppositions of even this proof are quite different from those of the corresponding argument in Western theodicy; for it presupposes eternally existing atoms and souls which are to be "directed", at the beginning of each creation, so that they may combine into bigger and bigger compounds to form the visible universe. The periodic cycles of creation and dissolution of the universe presupposed by some proofs would also be unacceptable to the Western philosopher. In arguing for the existence of Īśvara from the nature of the Veda, Udayana passes from the domain of philosophy to revelation or theology and his proofs cannot lead to Īśvara himself as the author, except on the presuppositions of the Nyāya-Vaiśeṣika doctrines.

---

[281] Cf. NM I 218, 31—219, 19.

The Nyāya-Vaiśeṣikas hold that the existence of Īśvara can be known through scripture (*śrutiḥ*) and through inference (*anumānam*). However, it is the latter method that has been preferred by them, and scriptural arguments, if any, were introduced only at the close of the purely philosophical arguments by way of confirmation. Through this approach they have followed a path different from that followed by the Vedāntins, for whom the arguments from sacred scripture are more important than those from pure reason. Udayana follows the tradition of his school in this matter. In the first four Stabakas of his Nyāyakusumāñjali we hardly ever come across scriptural quotations[282]. Even in the fifth Stabaka they are employed rarely and sparingly, mostly at the end of the inferential arguments and in confirmation of them. Thus we can regard his Īśvara doctrine as really a natural theology or philosophical theodicy.

At the conclusion of the explanation of the proofs for the existence of Īśvara, Udayana speaks of a third means of cognizing the existence of Īśvara, a means that cannot be reduced to the two we have already referred to. "This Blessed One (= Īśvara)", observes Udayana, "who has thus been known through scriptures and inference, is also directly perceived by some, because he has the nature of an object etc., like a pot"[283].

Three main ideas in this brief statement deserve our consideration. Firstly, Īśvara is here said to be known by immediate perception (*sākṣād api dṛśyate*). The knowledge of Īśvara through scripture and inference is only a mediate cognition which, though convincing under certain conditions, is still weak in comparison with direct perception. Secondly, such a knowledge of Īśvara through direct perception cannot be had by everyone, not even by everyone who inquires after his existence or nature, but only by a few (*kaiścit*). It is clear from a later passage of Udayana that these few are those Yogins who have acquired great merit (*dharmaḥ*) which enables them to enjoy such an experience. Thirdly, the reason why a few persons possessed of extraordinary merits can directly perceive Īśvara is that he has the nature of an object of cognition (*prameyam*). As the pot can be directly perceived when certain conditions of perception are present, so also when a person possesses extraordinary spiritual dispositions, he can directly perceive Īśvara, as he would any other object of cognition. None of the hitherto printed commentaries explain what the other reasons are that are expressed by the term "etc." (*ādi*), but we can include here those reasons of direct perception that are compatible with the nature of Īśvara.

An opponent objects that such a direct perception of Īśvara is impossible, since the causal complex (*sāmagrī*) necessary for it cannot be had. For Īśvara

---

282 In the first four Stabakas we find scriptural passages quoted in NKus 20, 1—4; 302, 3—6; 415, 2—3.

283 NKus 573, 7: *sa evaṃ bhagavān śruto 'numitaś ca, kaiścit sākṣād api dṛśyate, prameyatvāder ghaṭavat.* The term *bhagavān* i. e. "the one who is rich in *bhaga* 'dignity, excellence, majesty, loveliness etc.' ", though sometimes applied to Śiva, was very often preferred by the Viṣṇuites to refer to Kṛṣṇa-Viṣṇu (J. Gonda: Viṣṇuism and Śivaism, pp. 35—36).

would have to be directly perceived either through the external senses (*bahirindriyam*) or through the internal sense (*manaḥ*). But the external senses such as those of sight, hearing etc. have determined objects that are proper to it, and Īśvara does not fall under the proper object of any of them. As to the internal sense called Manas, it is not able to perceive objects that are outside the body it indwells[284]. Thus in the absence of the causal complex, he argues, the effect (viz.: direct perception of Īśvara) cannot be had by any person.

Udayana answers that, the effect (namely, the direct perception of Īśvara by some) being a fact, the causal complex must be present. Although ordinarily the inner sense or Manas cannot operate outside of the body it occupies, nevertheless, it is known that it can, in the dream state, operate even outside its own body, when it is assisted by a special co-operating cause (*sahakāriviśeṣaḥ*). Some of such dream-experiences are true, and though its truth is accidental, it is not without a cause; for it is caused by the merit (*dharmaḥ*) or the person who has such an experience. This merit may be produced either by the performance of actions such as religious rites (*karma*) or by Yoga. In the same way, when the Manas of the Yogin is aided by the merit acquired by Yoga, it can operate, thanks to the power of the special co-operating agent, even with regard to objects that are normally beyond its field of operation, and hence the Yogin can have immediate cognition or experience (*sākṣātkāritvam*) of Īśvara which is the fruit of direct perception (*pratyakṣam*). Its validity is effected by the merit that acts as a co-operating cause of this cognition[285]. Thus Udayana shows his opponent that the causal complex (*sāmagrī*) necessary for the direct cognition of Īśvara can be present in certain persons.

He confirms his argument by pointing out the contradiction that would follow, if such a cognition were not at all possible. For, if Īśvara were not at all to be directly cognized, then the injunctions such as "Two Brahmans are to be cognized" (*dve brahmaṇī veditavye*)[286] would be devoid of meaning, since they would then instruct men to do something that is impossible. The "cognition of the two Brahmans" spoken of in this injunction cannot be under-

---

[284] Cf. Kir 40, 8: *ātmamanasoḥ śarīrāvacchedena vṛttilābhaḥ*. Ibid. 286, 2 and 301, 19: *manaso bahir asvātantryāt*.

[285] Udayana probably utilizes here a doctrine held by Praśastapāda who maintained that dreams about absolutely unknown (*atyantāprasiddheṣu*) objects are caused solely by Adṛṣṭam (PDhS 275, 2—3). Although ordinarily the Manas cannot operate with regard to objects outside the body, nevertheless when it is aided by Adṛṣṭam as special co-operative cause, it can be the instrument of perception also of objects that are not perceptible by the senses, such as Īśvara. The causal complex (*sāmagrī*) of such an intuitive perception will be the Manas of the Yogin which has been assisted by merit (*dharmānugṛhītam*) produced by Karma (i. e. performance of religious rites) or Yoga. See Kir 284, 6—287, 11 where, against the Mīmāṃsakas, Udayana establishes *yogipratyakṣam* of invisible realities through *dharmaḥ* obtained by Yoga. Udayana holds, moreover, that Karma as well as Yoga are equally efficient means for acquiring merit (see Kir 284, 17—19).

[286] Cf. Maitrī Up. VI, 22: . . . *ity evam hy āha: dve brahmaṇī veditavye, śabdabrahma parañ ca yat*, . . .

stood as non-perceptual cognition, continues our author, since such a kind of cognition of Īśvara is already enjoined by other Vedic statements[287]. Hence, since all the Vedic passages are meaningful, the cognition of Brahman which is enjoined by the Vedic passage "Two Brahmans are to be cognized" must be different from the ordinary cognition of Īśvara that can be had from the study of Vedic passages that refer to him and from reflection over them; and such a cognition is direct perception.

Thus, in Udayana's view, Īśvara's existence can be known from sacred scriptures (*śrutiḥ*), from inference (*anumānam*) and, in rare cases, through direct perception (*sākṣād darśanam* or *pratyakṣam*). The three means of cognition of the Supreme Being were already recognized by the Upaniṣadic thinkers and by later philosophers[288], and Udayana himself has referred to them in the opening prose passage of his Nyāyakusumāñjali. But since the last type of cognition of Īśvara is a personal experience limited only to a privileged few, our author does not propose it to his adversaries as an argument for his existence.

---

[287] The commentators Śaṅkaramiśra and Guṇānanda refer to the Vedic statement *svādhyāyo 'dhyetavya* as example (see NKusAm 423, 1; NKusVi 425, 7—8.

[288] Cf. BAUp. II, 4, 5 and IV, 5, 6 where it is said that the Ātmā is *draṣṭavyaḥ, śrotavyaḥ, mantavyaḥ* and *nididhyāsitavyaḥ*. See also NSa 589, 4—590, 2. Śaṅkara in his BSuBh to Sūtra I, 3, 33 remarks that men of ancient times, thanks to their extraordinary merits, had direct dealings with the gods.

Chapter Two

ĪŚVARA'S RELATION TO THE UNIVERSE

The foregoing proofs of Udayana establish the existence of Īśvara in certain relationships with the created universe: as creator, preserver and destroyer of the universe and as teacher of the living beings. These relationships can be considered under two main aspects: his relation to the created universe in general and his relation to the living beings in particular. Briefly we shall now consider these two aspects as they can be understood from his works.

1. Īśvara's Relation to the World in general

Three operations of Īśvara concern the entire created universe consisting of beings, living as well as non-living, and place him in relation to it as its creator, preserver and destroyer. As creator he brings it into being, as preserver he sustains it in existence and as destroyer he causes it to be reduced to the ultimate components out of which it was earlier brought into being.

For all adherents of theism, God is first and foremost the Creator, the maker or the author of the universe. Such is also the case with the Nyāya-Vaiśeṣika theism propounded by Udayana. The most important Nyāya-Vaiśeṣika proof for the existence of Īśvara has been the one in which, from the fact that earth, mountains etc. have the nature of effect, an agent endowed with omniscience is deduced as the guiding cause of their origination.

In what does the creative activity of Īśvara consist? Let it be observed at the very outset that we use the terms "creation", "creator", "creative activity" etc. not in the sense in which Christian philosophy under the medieval scholastics defined them, but in a broader and more general perspective. For these terms cannot be applied in their strict Christian sense to the Nyāya-Vaiśeṣika theism.

The followers of the Nyāya-Vaiśeṣika system maintain that the atoms of the four elements—earth, water, fire and air—that go into the production of the material, inanimate universe are uncreated or eternal. So are also the infinite number of souls (*ātmā*) that, in combination with these material elements, form the universe of living beings. Besides these there are also other eternal realities such as the categories of generality (*sāmānyam*), particularity (*viśeṣaḥ*) and inherence (*samavāyaḥ*); substances such as Time (*kālaḥ*), Space (*dik*), Ether (*ākāśaḥ*) and the inner sense or Manas that plays an important role in the act of cognition of the living beings; and finally the eternal qualities in the eternal substances[289].

This enumeration of realities that exist eternally independent of any action of Īśvara already gives us an idea of the rather limited range of Īśvara's creative activity. Despite the fact that the "materials" necessary for the origination of the visible universe are thus present, the Nyāya-Vaiśeṣikas consider the role of Īśvara indispensable for the origination of the universe. Subject as the world is to periodical dissolutions followed by new creations, a start has to be made at the time of every new creation, and this start can be had only if a conscious or intelligent (*cetana-*) being guides the causes. But none of the realities we enumerated as eternal (and hence existing even during the period of dissolution) are conscious at the beginning of the new creation. The only realities that are capable of conscious activity are the souls; but, in the view of the Nyāya-Vaiśeṣikas, even these remain devoid of any conscious activity when they are separated from their body. As the union of the souls with the bodies already presupposes certain combinations of atoms and the souls, and consequently a conscious being to guide them, the activity of a conscious agent other than these souls would be required. It is on the necessity of such a conscious agent who possesses an eternal cognition of all the causes, that the first and the second proofs for the existence of Īśvara are based. The creative activity of Īśvara will thus consist in "directing" (*adhiṣṭhānam*) the various pre-existing causes in such a way that they combine to produce a universe conformable to the deserts of the living beings for the experience (*bhogaḥ*) of which it is meant.

This last-mentioned idea might require an explanation. The souls find themselves at the time of each dissolution as "bearers" of a certain quantum of merit (*dharmaḥ*) and demerit (*adharmaḥ*) which inheres in them. The universe that is going to originate after the allotted period of dissolution must be one in which the living beings can reap the fruit of their merits and demerits by having experiences conformable to them. In producing such a universe the creator should know all the causes and direct them in such a way that the

---

289 In the second introductory verse of his Kir, however, we read: "We worship that Īśvara from whom (originate) substance, qualities, motion, likewise the lower and the higher generality, the particularities or (*vā*: probably to be interpreted in the sense of *ca* 'and') inherence". Although the verse does not explicitly make use of the word 'origination', nevertheless the term *yataḥ* ('from whom') conveys that meaning. But such a literal interpretation of the verse would go against fundamental doctrines of the Nyāya-Vaiśeṣika school. Hence we have to assume that, by making use of the rhetorical figure of *double entendre* (*śleṣaḥ*), Udayana, on the one hand, offers praise to Īśvara as creator of all realities, and, on the other, means by the words he uses to designate the six categories other things that are compatible with the Nyāya-Vaiśeṣika doctrines. Such an interpretation of this verse is given by Vardhamāna in his commentary on it (see Kiraṇāvalīprakāśa in Kir_1 4, 3—5, 8.

world that comes into being conforms to the requirements of the fruit of deeds of the souls in their past existences.

The fact that Īśvara creates the universe according to certain conditions that are beyond his own choice makes his activity dependent (*sāpekṣa-*). In guiding the origination of the universe he is dependent, not only on Time and Space that are universal causes, but also, and especially, on the merits and demerits of the souls, so that the universe that comes into being is not, properly speaking, planned or ordained by him according to his own choice, but rather conditioned by the deserts of the souls. Although in this way, the Indian philosophers can offer a solution to the "problem of evil"—namely the problem of suffering or inequality of birth, joys etc. of the living beings—without implicating Īśvara in it, nevertheless the Creator is here reduced to a mere director who, endowed as he is with eternal omniscience, causes the pre-existing causes to start at the appointed time their combining action and directs it until the visible universe comes into being.

An important point to be considered here is the manner in which Īśvara fulfils his role of the creator. First of all, like all the Nyāya-Vaiśeṣikas before him, Udayana maintains that in his creative function Īśvara acts without a body (*aśarīrī*). As the question of a body of Īśvara has been raised by the opponents of theism, and since Udayana has dealt with it in his important works while treating the theme of Īśvara, it is necessary to mention here his views on this matter at least in their main outlines.

The problem whether Īśvara acts with a body or without one has been raised and discussed in connection with the proof for Īśvara from the 'nature of effect' (*kāryatvam*) of the visible universe. The opponents had argued that all the agents that fall under human observation are bodied and so Īśvara, too, would have to be considered as possessed of a body, if he is the creator of the universe. Even granting that the Nyāya-Vaiśeṣika proof can establish the necessity of a conscious agent to direct the origination of the universe, they contended, a special kind of agent (*kartṛviśeṣaḥ*), non-bodied and eternally omniscient, as the defenders of theism postulate, cannot be established. Although the discussion on Īśvara's body is found in the context of the proof for the existence of Īśvara and consequently in the general setting of the logical validity of the formal syllogistic proof, we shall consider it here, as far as possible, apart from that context.

In his Ātmatattvaviveka Udayana maintains that body is not pervaded with an agent (*kartravyāpanam*)[290], in other words, an agent need not necessarily be bodied. An agent requires a body for two purposes: either as abode or substratum (*āyatanatayā*)[291], or as procurer of the instruments (*upakaraṇaprāpakatayā*) of his activity. But neither of these purposes can be found in Īśvara. For a body as abode or substratum is required only when the agent

---

[290] Cf. ATV 388, 1—2: *śarīrasya ca nopādhitvaṃ kartravyāpakatvāt.*

[291] On the notion of *āyatanam* see the valuable contribution of J. GONDA in ALB, Vol. 33 (1969) pp. 1—79.

can have experience (*bhogaḥ*). The body then serves as the substratum of the experience of pleasure or pain. But as Īśvara has no experience, he does not require a body for that purpose. Nor does he require it for the purpose of procuring the instruments of his activity; for only an agent that cannot direct the other causes by immediate or direct effort (*sākṣātprayatnaḥ*) requires a body in order to effect the connection between the agent and the other causes[292]. But Īśvara can direct the causes of the universe by his effort without any intermediary (*sākṣāt*)[293].

In answer to the view of the opponent that only a bodied person (*dehī*) can be an agent that directs other causes, Udayana proposes several alternative significations of the term 'bodied person' and shows that none of them can be considered necessarily connected with agency (*kartṛtvam*). The epithet "bodied" may mean, remarks Udayana, either that the self which is the agent directs the causes solely by means of the body (*dehadvāraiva*), or that it does so only by making use of a body (*dehaṃ prayuñjāna eva*). The first alternative cannot be true; for, as the body itself has the nature of a cause, it will itself have to be directed by another bodied being, and thus there will be the defect of infinite regress (*anavasthā*). Nor can the second alternative be correct, since the reverse is observed. It is observed, for instance, that a snake-charmer removes poison from the body of a person bitten by a poisonous snake solely through his mental concentration, without making use of his body at all[294]. At this the opponent proposes a third alternative signification of the term 'bodied', namely 'bearing (or carrying) a body' (*dehaṃ dhārayan*). Udayana shows that such an interpretation, too, is unacceptable. For a body is to be 'borne' (or 'carried') by the agent either as itself a cause (*kārakatayā*), or for the purpose of directing other causes by means of it (*tatkārakāntaraprayogārtham*), or, finally, just because one has acquired it by one's own deeds (*svakarmopāttatāmātreṇa*). He admits that the first alternative is possible; for there are cases of products where the body is necessary as itself a cause (such as, for instance, in teaching, as commentator Nārāyaṇa points out)[295]. In such cases the body itself will have to be directed by the agent. But no sensible person would declare that, even in cases where it is not the cause, it has to be 'borne' as a cause[296]. The second alternative, namely that the body is 'borne' by the agent for the purpose of directing other causes by means of it, is possible in cases where he is not able to direct the causes immediately (*sākṣāt*). In such

---

292 For example, an iron-smith requires tongs as an intermediary instrument, since he cannot directly exert his activity on the burning ball of iron.

293 Cf. ATV 388, 2—5.

294 The commentator Nārāyaṇa, commenting on this passage of ATV, observes that the snake-charmer removes poison by mere meditation alone (*dhyānamātreṇaiva*). He means by *dhyānam* not mere mental concentration, but also probably the recitation of certain magic formulae that are believed to possess the power of removing the poison. Cf. ATV 392, 17—18.

295 Cf. ATV 393, 9—10 see also p. 152ff.

296 According to the commentator Nārāyaṇa the case meant here is the creation of the universe. Cf. ATV 393, 10.

a case the agent takes up and employs something that he can immediately direct by means of which he directs those other causes which he cannot immediately direct. Such is, for example, the case of a potter who is not able to direct the causes of pot such as the potter's wheel, clay etc., or that of a weaver who cannot direct the causes of cloth such as the wheel, cotton etc. without the medium of their bodies. But the fact that the potter and the weaver require a body to direct the causes of pot and cloth, does not mean that every agent requires a body; for there is no rule that what cannot be immediately directed by one agent should necessarily be so also with regard to another. For it is observed that, although Caitra is not able to direct bodies other than his own, say, of Maitra, still he is able to direct his own body. The third explanation, namely that the body is to be "borne" by the agent merely because he has acquired it by his own deeds, is equally objectionable. For if a body is said to be necessarily required by an agent for his action, even though it is neither a cause nor a medium for his action, but merely because the agent in question has acquired it as the fruit of his past deeds, then one would have to concede on the same principle that the maker of a pot who now possesses the body of a potter would be directing the causes such as the potter's wheel, even when he acquires in another birth the body of a young elephant (*karabhaḥ*); for whether the body acquired by the agent is of a potter or of a young elephant does not make any difference, since both have been acquired by the agent in different births as a result of his own deeds. To the rejoinder of the opponent that in effecting the special product called pot the body of a potter is required, though it is not useful in producing the pot, while the body of a young elephant is not required, Udayana points out that the position maintained by the adversary is untenable; for to hold that the body is not useful (*anupayukta-*) in producing the effect (v. g. pot) and that it is necessarily required (*avaśyāpekṣaṇīya-*) implies a contradiction (*vyāghātaḥ*), since only what is useful in producing the effect can be said to be necessarily required. If the opponent is unwilling to accept this contradiction, he would equally have to concede that even a young elephant's body, though not useful for the production of pot, is necessarily required for the origination of the pot.

Udayana brings this discussion to a close with the conclusion that direction by a bodied agent is required only in those cases of effects where the body is required either as a cause or in order to direct the other causes, and not simply because it is a body. But not every effect requires a body either as cause or in order to direct the other causes[297]. Consequently, agency (*kartṛtvam*) does not necessarily require a body.

Udayana comes back to the discussion on the body of Īśvara in a later portion of the Ātmatattvaviveka, but this time in the context of proving that the cognition of Īśvara, being uncaused, is independent of a body. We shall mention this argumentation while dealing with the omniscience (*sarvajñatvam*) of Īśvara, where it is more fitting[298].

---

[297] Cf. ATV 392, 3—395, 4.

[298] Cf. pp. 167f.; 171f.

The problem of how Īśvara could be an agent without possessing a body is raised also in the Nyāyakusumāñjali during the discussion of the first proof for the existence of Īśvara[299]. The whole discussion takes place in the context of the logical accuracy of his proof for the existence of Īśvara as the creator of the universe and is couched in logical terminology. Udayana does not repeat here all the arguments which he had mentioned in his earlier work, the Ātmatattvaviveka, although the main ideas are found here too.

In the Nyāyakusumāñjali we come across an objection which we do not find in the Ātmatattvaviveka. The agent (*kartā*) is the director of the causes (*kāraṇānām adhiṣṭhātā*) either immediately like our soul that directs our body, or mediately like the stick directed by the potter. But he cannot be said to direct the causes immediately, since in that case the atoms and the other causes he directs would have to be considered as his body. Nor can he be said to direct the causes mediately, since mediate direction is possible only with the help of something that is immediately directed, and this is not possible for Īśvara as he has no body. The opponent wants to show by this argument that an immediate direction of the atoms and other causes of creation by Īśvara is not possible and that consequently the existence of Īśvara cannot be established as the intelligent director of the causes of earth etc.

Udayana answers that if "being a body" (*śarīratvam*) means nothing else than "the having to be directed by an agent through immediate effort" (*sākṣātprayatnavadadhiṣṭheyatvam*), then Īśvara may be said to have the atoms etc. as his body[300]. But he adds that in no other sense can the atoms etc. be said to be Īśvara's body. Thus they cannot be said to be his body as the substratum of the senses (*indriyāśrayaḥ*), since, his cognition being eternal, he does not require senses. Nor can they be considered as the subject of experience (*bhogāśrayaḥ*), since Īśvara does not have any experience of pleasure or pain (*bhogaḥ*)[301].

The question of Īśvara's body is again raised by the opponent as an objection to the proof for the existence of Īśvara formulated by Udayana in his Kiraṇāvalī[302]. Here the discussion with the opponent is carried on in the usual logical jargon connected with the correctness of the syllogistic formulation of the proof, but we shall content ourselves with mentioning here the main ideas. An opponent brings forward an objection based on the non-observation of the pervading factor: body etc. (*śarīrādi*, i. e. body and senses) are found to be pervaded with agency (*kartṛtvam*), so that when

---

299 Cf. NKus 485, 1—502, 7.

300 Ibid. 494, 14—15. The same idea occurs in NVTP 5, 3—5 where, commenting on the word *viśvamūrtiḥ* found in the verse of Vācaspati, Udayana remarks: *viśvamūrtir ity atra yāvat kārakagrāmaḥ, tasyaiva sākṣāt tatprayatnādhiṣṭheyatayā 'smadādiśarīrasamānatvāt.*

301 Cf. NKus 493, 7—494, 2 and 494, 13—495, 5.

302 Cf. Kir 100, 7—101, 15.

body is absent, agency should also be absent, just as when one tries to prove that hoar-frost possesses fire because it causes transformations in the grass[303], the absence of fire is established by the non-observation of heat. Udayana answers this objection by enunciating two ways of explaining the pervasion mentioned by the opponent. It can mean either a pervasion of the agent with body etc. (*kartuḥ śarīritvādikam*), or it can mean the pervasion of the effect with an agent that possesses body etc. (*kāryasya śarīrādimatkartṛ-pūrvakatvam*). The meaning of the objection of the opponent according to the first explanation will be that Īśvara is not an agent as he is devoid of body etc. But such an argument implies the logical fallacy called 'non-proved substratum' (*āśrayāsiddhiḥ*), namely assuming in Īśvara body etc.[303a] without accepting Īśvara himself who is the substratum of his body etc. The second explanation of the pervasion postulated by the opponent is rejected by the fact that in the sprout etc. that originate afresh every day, no bodied agent can be perceived. As to the example of hoar-frost said to be possessed of fire due to its capacity to effect changes in grass etc., Udayana shows that it is not at all apt to illustrate a contradiction (*virodhaḥ*). For, if by 'modification of grass etc.' (*tṛṇādivikāraḥ*) is meant merely the changes in colour etc., the fact that hoar-frost does not cause such a change is not unacceptable, since it can be accounted for by the action of the heat of the sun. Indeed a modification of grass into ash would have necessarily implied the presence of fire, but such a modification is never caused by hoar-frost. Hence an argument based on non-perception (*anupalabdhiḥ*) of the pervading factor such as body cannot be used to deny the existence of an agent.

What Udayana wants to show in all the passages where he discusses the question of the necessity of Īśvara's having a body in order to create the universe, is that, although ordinary agents like us require a body for producing effects, there is no absolute necessity that an agent should be bodied, or, to put it in Indian logical terminology, there is no pervasion (*vyāptiḥ*) between 'being an agent' (*kartṛtvam*) and 'having a body' (*śarīravattvam*). The reason why agents require a body for being able to exercise their causality is that they are not able to influence the other causes (such as the material cause or instruments) except through the medium of a body. If a particular agent is able to influence the other causes directly (*sākṣāt*), he does not stand in need of a body in order to fulfil his function as agent[304]. To be an agent means, in the view of our author, nothing else than that a person directs or employs the group of causes that are known to be able to produce a certain effect[305]. Elsewhere Udayana explains agency as consisting in the possession

---

303 Due to cold or hoar-frost grass, undried or wet straw etc. are known to undergo modifications such as are produced by the heat of the fire.

303a Cf. also NKus 328, 5—329, 6.

304 Cf. NVTP 5, 5—7: . . . *sākṣātprayatnānadhiṣṭhiteṣu sā* (= *śarīrāpekṣā*) *syāt, daṇḍādivat, na tu sākṣātprayatnādhiṣṭheyeṣu śarīravat.*

305 Kir 104, 11—12: *paridṛṣṭasāmarthyakārakaprayoktuḥ kartṛśabdavācyatvāt.* See also ibid. 102, 11 and 317, 2—3 where the same idea occurs.

of cognition, desire and effort[306]. In ordinary agents cognition can be produced only through the senses, but senses can be had only if there is a body as their subject (*indriyāśrayatayā*). The cognition produced through the medium of the senses would then give rise to desire which, in its turn, would produce the effort which is the most important factor in the actual causation. Thus it is clear that the ordinary agents require a body in order to be agents, only because their cognition, desire and effort are to be produced through its instrumentality. On the other hand, when agency is defined as the possession of cognition, desire and effort, it follows that a being which possesses these three qualities should necessarily be considered an agent, regardless of the question whether these qualities are produced in him through the medium of a body or whether they are unproduced or eternal. As we shall show later on[307], Īśvara possesses eternal cognition, desire and effort. Hence it follows that the agency (*kartṛtvam*) of Īśvara is satisfactorily explainable without his having to possess a body.

It should, however, be pointed out that, while Udayana emphasizes that Īśvara does not require a body to create this visible universe, he does not altogether exclude the possibility that Īśvara may make use of a body in some other cases on account of the special nature of the action or product (*kārya-vaśāt*)[308].

In defining agency as the possession of the three qualities of cognition, desire and effort, Udayana not only brings out the accidental nature of the body in an agent, but also shows that agency belongs essentially to the domain of the spirit. Of the three qualities it is the last, namely effort (*prayatnaḥ*), that is primarily and immediately related to the agency.

We should have liked to have from Udayana himself an account of the manner in which Īśvara brings this universe into existence. But the only account we can find is in his Kiraṇāvalī where he gives a brief commentary on Praśastapāda's description of creation. Following this commentary the process of creation can be described as follows: At the end of one hundred Brahmā-years[309], there arises in Īśvara, conditioned by this special Time (*kālaviśeṣaḥ*), the desire to create (*sisṛkṣā*), in order that the living beings may have the possibility of enjoying the fruit of their deeds. Consequent upon this desire of Īśvara, the Adṛṣṭam inherent in the souls becomes active. Due

---

306 NKus 496, 8—9: *kārakatvam eva tasya* (= *kuvindādeḥ*) *jñānacikīrṣā-prayatnavataḥ, . . . tad eva cā'dhiṣṭhātṛtvam*. See also NM I, 185, 23—24: *jñāna-cikīrṣāprayatnayogitvaṃ kartṛtvam ācakṣate.*

307 Cf. pp. 170—177.

308 Cf. pp. 152ff.

309 On the number of human years in a Brahmā-day cf. Kir 90, 5—14. We may calculate 100 Brahmā-years in terms of human years as follows: 1 Brahmā-day = 1000 *caturyuga*-s; 1 *caturyuga* = 12000 years of gods; 1 year of gods = 360 human years (Note that 360 days make a year). Thus 1 Brahmā-day = 4, 320, 000, 000 human years. 1 Brahmā-night is as long as 1 Brahmā-day. Thus one full (i. e. day and night) day of Brahmā = 8, 640, 000, 000 human years. 1 Brahmā-year will then be 3, 110, 400, 000, 000 human years. Thus 100 Brahmā-years will amount to a total of 311, 040, 000, 000, 000 human years.

to this activity of the Adṛṣṭam the atoms begin to enter into a process of conjunction on account of which there arise movements (*karma*) in a certain order. It is in the wind-atoms (*pavanaparamāṇuḥ*) that the movement commences. The single wind-atoms form themselves, assisted by the relating cognition (*apekṣābuddhiḥ*) of Īśvara, into dyads and triads and finally into a huge mass of wind blowing in the eternally existing Ether (*nabhaḥ* or *ākāśaḥ*). Thereafter the same process of combination takes place in the water-atoms forming the huge mass of water that remains floating on this mass of wind. The earth, formed according to the same process, now originates and remains as one compact mass over the water. Over the same ocean of water arises also the huge mass of fire, formed in the same manner, spreading its brilliance. When the four gross elements have thus come into being, there originates, through the mere volition (*abhidhyānamātrāt*) of Īśvara, a great Egg formed out of the fire-atoms combined with those of earth. Īśvara then creates in this egg the four-faced Brahmā together with all the worlds, and commissions him to create the living beings. This Brahmā endowed with a superior degree of knowledge, dispassionateness and power, after creating the Prajāpatis, Manus, gods, Ṛṣis and the groups of Pitṛs, brings forth from his mouth, hands, thighs and feet the four social classes, and lastly also the other superior and inferior beings of all kinds, endowing each of his creatures with qualities of merit, knowledge, dispassionateness and power or their opposites, in keeping with its latent fruit of actions[310].

In this account Udayana follows very closely the description of the creation of the universe given by Praśastapāda who, centuries before him, had tried to accomodate and assimilate mythological accounts of cosmogony with the philosophical speculation of his school. Specially noteworthy in this account is the intermediary role given to Brahmā in the creation of the first living beings: instead of himself creating them, Īśvara first creates Brahmā and commissions him with the creation of the living beings. This role of Brahmā could not be easily set aside and so it had to be adjusted in some manner to the philosophical thought of the school. In no case was the account to be interpreted in a way that would make Brahmā the sole creator of the living beings without Īśvara, too, having a part in their creation. Udayana makes this point very clear in his commentary, wherein he says that, when the effects have two agents as causes—Brahmā and Īśvara are meant here—Īśvara, too, is an agent with regard to them[311]. It should not be asked, he tells us, what need there is for Brahmā, if Īśvara is the agent of the living beings; for Īśvara makes use of him for the sake of the effects which are known necessarily to require a bodied agent[312]. In this interpretation the incorporality (*aśarīratvam*) of Īśvara is clearly safeguarded and an explanation is found

[310] Cf. Kir 93, 9—97, 8.

[311] In order to express this double causality Udayana interprets the particle *ca* occurring in this context in the account of the PDhS (95, 4) in a sense apparently not meant in the original text. Kir 95, 11—12: *sa ceti. ca-śabdaḥ samuccaye, dvikartṛkeṣu kāryeṣu maheśvarasyāpi kartṛtvāt.*

[312] Cf. Kir 95, 13—14.

for those activities of Īśvara which would necessarily require a body, since these are performed by Brahmā who possesses a body. As Īśvara is co-agent with Brahmā, he, too, is the creator of the living beings. But such an explanation does not seem to have been acceptable to all. As this theory was felt unsatisfactory, other explanations were probably sought. In any case a new explanation of the passage was given according to which it is Īśvara himself who, on account of the special nature of the effect to be produced (*kāryavaśāt*), takes up the body of Brahmā. Through this interpretation the mediate role of Īśvara in the creation of the first group of living beings is abandoned and, though in the assumed form of Brahmā, he becomes their direct creator. I have not been able to trace this interpretation in the available Vaiśeṣika works prior to Udayana, but the manner in which our author mentions this interpretation[313] inclines me to presume that it may have been proposed even before his time. For Udayana himself such an interpretation brought no problems with it, since he accepted that Īśvara can, on certain occasions and for specific purposes, take up a body[314].

Interesting to note here in this account is also the fact that, although in philosophical explanations the effort (*prayatnaḥ*) of Īśvara is said to be the immediate cause of creation, Praśastapāda does not speak of the effort of Īśvara, but rather of his desire to create (*sisṛkṣā*). A study of his Īśvara doctrine shows that he did not ascribe the quality of effort to Īśvara, but endowed his desire (*icchā*) with such characteristics as implied also those of effort. Udayana, too, does not speak of the effort of Īśvara in his commentary on this passage. However, in explaining the passage wherein Brahmā is said to create *abhidhyānamātrāt* (= 'through mere thinking') he explains this term as *saṅkalpamātrāt* (= 'through mere volition'; 'through mere intention') and contrasts it with the activity effected by means of the body[315]. Such an idea corresponds, at least in substance, to the conception that Īśvara creates by means of his effort (*prayatnaḥ*).

The creative activity of Īśvara is, moreover, eternal (*nitya-*)[316], unlike that of the ordinary agents like the potter, which is dependent upon their causes. Besides, it extends itself to all that is produced, because his cognition, desire and effort have all things as their objects[317]. His eternal and universal causality flows from his nature (*svabhāvataḥ*)[318] and is immediate (*sākṣād adhiṣṭhānam*)[319]. This causality of Īśvara, however, does not do away with the causality of

---

[313] Ibid. 90, 18—19: *yadā tv īśvara eva kāryavaśād gṛhītadivyadeho brahmādyavasthām āpadyata iti pakṣaḥ*, . . .; 96, 17—18: *yadā tv iśvara eva kāryavāśād brahmādiśarīram upādatta iti pakṣaḥ*, . . .

[314] NKus 508, 13—14: *gṛhṇāti hi īśvaro 'pi kāryavaśāc charīram antarāntarā darśayati ca vibhūtim iti*. The same idea occurs also in Kir 317, 7—11 and ATV 414, 2—9.

[315] Cf. Kir 94, 21—95, 6.

[316] Cf. NKus 497, 5; Kir 317, 13.

[317] Cf. NKus 497, 1—2; ATV 429, 5.

[318] Cf. ATV 429, 5. See also NKus 496, 8 where it is implied that Īśvara's *kārakatvam is svarūpataḥ*.

[319] Cf. NKus 494, 13—15.

the living beings; rather his causality is precisely for the sake of permitting the living beings to exercise their causality: "Since a potter etc. would not be able without activity to experience (pleasure or pain: *bhogaḥ*) that is to be obtained from strong movements etc. of the body, Īśvara permits for this purpose their causal activity (*kartṛtvam*); for the (agency of) Īśvara is only for this purpose"[320].

We have so far spoken only of the creative function of Īśvara. The Nyāya-Vaiśeṣikas ascribe to him in addition two other functions closely associated with creation, namely those of preservation (*sthitiḥ* or *dhṛtiḥ*) and dissolution (*pralayaḥ* or *saṃharaṇam*) of the universe. In the introductory verse of the Ātmatattvaviveka which is a salutation to Īśvara, he refers in passing to the preserving function (*pālanam*) of Īśvara and, as we saw before, he establishes in one of his proofs the existence of Īśvara as the supporter or preserver (*vidhārakaḥ*) of the universe[321]. Similarly a reference to his repeated destruction of the universe is found in the concluding verse of the second Stabaka[322], and one of the proofs establishes the existence of Īśvara as the destroyer of the universe[323]. In his commentary on Padārthadharmasaṃgraha's section on dissolution of the universe (*pralayaḥ*), Udayana follows the traditional exposition of Praśastapāda. The role of Īśvara here consists in initiating, at the close of the duration of existence of the created universe, the activity of dissolution whereby the composite universe becomes reduced to its ultimate constituents, the material world being reduced to its atoms[324]. As in his creation, Īśvara is dependent here, too, upon factors extraneous to him, especially the particular Time (*kālaviśeṣaḥ*) which is said to be one hundred Brahmā-years.

In his creative, preservative and destructive functions Īśvara needs to be in contact with the causes he directs. In our study on the qualities of Īśvara, we shall point out that there is such a contact between him and the causes he has to direct[325].

2. Īśvara's Relation to the World of Living Beings

While Īśvara has a relation to the created universe in general as its creator, preserver and destroyer, he has in addition a relation to the universe of living beings in particular as their teacher, a function of his that has been clearly brought out in the important works of Udayana. One can distinguish two aspects of the instructing function of Īśvara. He is, first and foremost, the teacher (*upadeṣṭā*), the proclaimer (*vaktā*) or the author (*kartā*) of the

---

[320] Ibid. 497, 10—12: *na cākurvataḥ kulālādeḥ kāyasaṅkṣobhādisādhyo bhogaḥ siddhyed iti tadartham asya kartṛtvam īśvaro 'numanyate, tadarthamātratvād aiśvarasya.* I read *aiśvarasya* instead of *aiśvaryasya*, as is printed in the text.

[321] Cf. NKus 506, 1—17. Cf. pp. 92—94.

[322] Cf. NKus 309, 1—2.

[323] Ibid. 507, 1—7. Cf. p. 94f.

[324] Cf. NKus 292, 6: *tathā ca brahmāṇḍe paramāṇusād bhavitari* ...

[325] Cf. p. 181f.

Veda. Secondly, he instructs the living beings in the usage of speech as well as in the diverse occupations of the ordinary life (*vyavahāraḥ*).

In his Īśvara doctrine our author has clearly emphasized the role of Īśvara as the author of the Veda. The Nyāya-Vaiśeṣika conception of the periodic dissolutions (*pralayaḥ*) and creations (*sargaḥ*) of the universe necessitates the assumption of a teacher of the Veda at the beginning of each new creation. As we remarked earlier, at the time of the total dissolution of the universe all the composite beings are reduced to their primary, ultimate principles. With the dissolution of the bodies into their constituent atoms, the souls remain devoid of any consciousness. When, at the time of the new creation, the souls have been united with their bodies, they have to be instructed in the Veda, since all the Vedic traditions have been interrupted for a long time during the long period of dissolution, and hence forgotten[326]. Instruction in the Veda is very important, since it is from the Veda that the human beings learn the means of obtaining heaven as well as liberation. In the view of the Nyāya-Vaiśeṣikas the instruction of the living beings in the Veda is done by Īśvara himself, since there is no one else capable of doing it at that time. Once the first human beings have learnt it from Īśvara, they pass it on to others in successive generations, and thus the Veda continues to be studied and practised, though in progressively decreasing quantity and interest[327], through the various cosmic periods (*yugaḥ*) of the universe, until the next dissolution, after which the process repeats itself.

The teacher of the Veda should possess a true knowledge of all that is contained in it. A trustworthy (*āpta-*) teacher is, moreover, one who will not deceive others by wrong teachings. Through his omniscience (*sarvajñatvam*) Īśvara knows all things, even those things that are not ordinarily perceptible to human beings. Free from human passions that may lead one to deceive others, and being a father intent solely on the good of the living beings, he will not deceive anyone by his teaching[328]. Furthermore, at the beginning of the new creation there is no other being that either knows the Veda or is able to teach it to the others. Hence, in the view of the Nyāya-Vaiśeṣikas, it is Īśvara alone that can impart the Veda to the newly created living beings.

The Mīmāṃsakas were the main opponents of the Nyāya-Vaiśeṣika doctrine of Īśvara as the author of the Veda. They maintain that, being eternal (*nitya-*), the Veda does not stand in need of an Īśvara as its author. Moreover, there is no total interruption of Vedic studies and practices, as the Nyāya-Vaiśeṣikas maintain, since there are, in their view, no total dissolutions and creations of the universe, and consequently the eternal Veda is handed down uninterruptedly from generation to generation in endless series of existences without the need of an Īśvara to teach the Veda at the beginning of each new creation.

---

326 The Buddhists object to this theory of the Nyāya-Vaiśeṣikas. See TSP 67, 11—18.

327 Cf. NKus 292, 10—300, 8. Also ATV 423, 7—425, 10.

328 Cf. ATV 427, 11—428, 3.

In a long controversy with the Mīmāṃsakas Udayana shows that the Veda cannot be eternal, but is created[329], that the human power of practising as well as studying the Veda deteriorates in each Yuga so that there will once necessarily be the extinction of Vedic branches as well as of their practices[330], that there are periodical total dissolutions and new creations on account of which the transmission of the Veda taught in the previous Yuga would be completely interrupted[331], and that consequently, at the beginning of every new creation the Veda has to be taught anew to the living beings. As Īśvara is the only being that is able to teach them at that time, he should be considered as the author of the Veda.

Although the Mīmāṃsakas in general denied the existence of Īśvara and his authorship of the Veda, there seems to have been, already during the time of Udayana, a group of them who had accepted, in some modified form, the doctrine of Īśvara. In Udayana's Ātmatattvaviveka we come across the theory of some Mīmāṃsakas who admit Īśvara (*seśvaramīmāṃsāpakṣaḥ*), although we are not further informed about them. What role was allotted to Īśvara in their doctrine is not clear, except that the Vedic tradition (*vedasaṃpradāyaḥ*) was believed to be effected by him, and this, in their view, was done only in dependence upon the Veda of the previous creation. In this way they seem to have reached a compromise between the Mīmāṃsaka and Nyāya-Vaiśeṣika views, advocating the eternality of the Veda as maintained by the classical Mīmāṃsakas, but slightly modified by the acceptance of Īśvara who, though in dependence upon the Veda of the previous creations, is said to be its author. Such a view is rejected by Udayana; according to him, Īśvara is not dependent upon the Veda of the previous creations, as there is no need of it. Being endowed with eternal omniscience, he knows, even without dependence on any previous Veda, all its contents[332].

The Sāṃkhya theory of the transmission of Veda has also been rejected by Udayana on the ground that it cannot adequately account for the trust placed in the Veda by the people. It is true that the followers of Sāṃkhya admitted periodical total dissolutions and new creations of the universe. But they maintained that sages like Kapila who had acquired, through the performance of religious rites and ascetical practices, the power to perceive even those realities that are beyond the senses, could perceive the contents (*arthaḥ*) of the eternally existing Veda[333]. Moved to great compassion at the sight of

---

[329] In NKus 233, 4—280, 2 Udayana argues that sound (*śabdaḥ*) is non-eternal or produced, and then 280, 3—5 he applies this view to the Veda and argues that, if the sounds of the alphabet (*varṇāḥ*) are not eternal, the words composed of them could also not be eternal; even less the sentences arising from the combination of such words, and still less the Veda which is a collection of such sentences. Cf. also ATV 416, 3.

[330] Cf. NKus 292, 10—301, 1. Also ATV 424, 9—12.

[331] Cf. NKus 280, 6—300, 8; see also ATV 422, 7—426, 9.

[332] Cf. ATV 429, 1—8.

[333] Cf. NKus 306, 1; See also STK to Sāṃkhyakārikā 5.

the living beings "being burnt in the fire of mundane existence"[334], they favour them by communicating to them the Veda at the time of the new creation, and hence, in their view, there is no need of assuming an Īśvara as its author. Udayana repudiates such a theory on the ground that, even if sages like Kapila may have a special intuition (*bhāvanā*), this is nevertheless unable to produce true perception (*satyam eva sākṣātkāram*), and consequently the Veda based on such an imperfect kind of perception would not be able to elicit absolute and unshakable confidence of those who accept it as infallibly authoritative[335].

In this connection Udayana disposes of a theory brought forward by some opponents that, even without assuming the existence of an Īśvara, the transmission of Vedic practices can be explained through the migration of Brāhmins and other social classes from another universe (*brahmāṇḍāntaram*) to the newly created earth, who would then teach the Veda and spread among the newly created human beings on earth the religious rites and duties proper to each caste. Our author answers that such a migration of Brāhmins and other social classes is impossible, since it is beyond their power. "For even the passing over (from one) continent (*varṣaḥ*) to another is difficult; how much more (difficult will it be) to pass (from one) world (*lokaḥ*) to another? But how very much more (difficult will it be) to go (from one) universe (*brahmāṇḍaḥ*) to another?"[336]. Nor can it be argued that, on account of their special powers, such as are ascribed to yogins[337], they are able to go from one universe to another; for there is no proof of their possessing such powers; mere supposition (*saṃbhāvanā*) of such powers in them would not be able to produce the absolute certainty in the Vedic traditions[338].

The teaching function of Īśvara is not restricted, as we remarked earlier, to the communication of the Veda, but it also extends itself to the instruction of the newly created human beings in the usage of speech as well as in the different trades or occupations of the ordinary life such as the making of pots, weaving of cloth etc. We have already seen that Udayana has made the necessity of a teacher of these human usages the basis for an argument for the existence of Īśvara. What we said earlier with regard to the Nyāya-Vaiśeṣika theory of the need of Īśvara for the transmission of the Veda holds good also here; the newly created beings have forgotten, during the long period of dissolution, their usage of words and the different crafts and arts of ordinary life and, unless someone teaches them these things anew, they will not be able to exercise these human usages. Udayana maintains that Īśvara himself

---

334 NKus 306, 2: . . . *saṃsārāṅgāreṣu pacyamānān prāṇinaḥ paśyantaḥ paramakāruṇikāḥ priyahitopadeśenānugrahīṣyanti* . . .

335 Ibid. 306, 3—308, 4.

336 Ibid. 308, 6—7: *varṣāntarasañcaraṇam eva hi duṣkaraṃ, kuto lokāntarasañcāraḥ, kutastarāñ ca brahmāṇḍāntaragamanam?*

337 Reference is to the well-known eight powers acquired by Yoga (cf. YSu III, 45 and the YBh to it, see YBh 301, 10—302, 7), one of which is *prāptiḥ* through which all things become very near to the Yogin.

338 Cf. NKus 308, 7—8.

is this teacher. He conceives of Īśvara as the foremost of the first teachers (*pūrvagurūttamaḥ*)[339], an idea found earlier in the Yogasūtras[340], indeed, as the teacher of even the teacher of Indra (*amareśaguror guruḥ*)[341].

But the function of Īśvara as the teacher of the living beings poses the problem as to the manner in which he is able to fulfil it, if he does not possess the organs of speech and consequently a body[342]. We have earlier shown that Udayana maintained with great emphasis that Īśvara does not stand in need of a body for his function of creating the universe. We mentioned, however, that he was willing to accept the necessity of a body in Īśvara when the particular nature of the action or effect to be produced required it (*kārya-vaśāt*), that is to say, when the necessity of a body was established through the methods of concomitance and non-concomitance (*anvayavyatirekābhyam*) as absolutely indispensable for the production of the effect. The action of teaching is such a case, and when Udayana admits that Īśvara assumes a body now and then (*antarāntarā*) for the purpose of a special action (*kāryavaśāt*), he includes also this action of teaching the living beings. This body by which he manifests himself is merely an 'instrumental body' (*upakaraṇaśarīram*)[343], also called a 'body of artifice' or 'body of manifestation' (*nirmāṇakāyaḥ*)[344] assumed for a specific purpose, and it cannot be considered to have all the qualities or functions of the body of an ordinary living being. For, unlike the body of ordinary living beings, the body assumed for a specific purpose by Īśvara does not serve him as the subject of the senses (*indriyāśrayaḥ*), nor as the substratum of experiences of pleasure and pain (*bhogāśrayaḥ*)[345]. It is, as it were, something "put on" extrinsically by Īśvara without its being a real part of himself, though necessary as a condition for the performance of certain actions.

The necessity of assuming a body in Īśvara arose, no doubt, for the Nyāya-Vaiśeṣika philosophers, from theoretical reasons in connection with his instructing function. He is said to be the "speaker" of the Veda (*vedavaktā*), and, in order to communicate or teach the Veda to the first living beings, vocal organs were considered indispensable as inseparably connected with the activity of speaking or teaching. The already existing beliefs also came in as a help to support the ascription of a body to Īśvara in certain cases. In the

---

339 Cf. ATV the last line of the introductory verse.

340 Cf. YSu I, 26.

341 Cf. NKus 576, 7.

342 Cf. Kir 317, 2—7.

343 Ibid. 317, 7—8.

344 Cf. NKus 15, 1; see also YBh to YSu I, 25 (YBh 72, 5—7). L. Schmithausen, speaking of the concept of *nirmāṇakāyaḥ* in Buddhism, defines it as follows: "Ein *nirmāṇakāyaḥ* ist (soweit *kāyaḥ* nicht in einem übertragenden Sinn verstanden wird) ein nicht auf natürliche Weise entstandener, sondern durch übernormale Macht künstlich hergestellter oder manifestierter Leib, der eben deshalb nicht der eigentliche Leib der betreffenden Person und meist nur eine unwirkliche Erscheinung, ein Scheinleib ist". (Cf. Der Nirvāṇa-Abschnitt in der Viniścayasaṃgrahaṇī der Yogācārabhūmiḥ. p. 172, Anmerkung 205).

345 Cf. Kir 317, 11—13; NKus 494, 15—495, 10.

Bhagavadgītā (IV, 7—8), for example, it was taught that God becomes born (*saṃbhavāmi*) in each Yuga to protect the good, to destroy the evil-doers and to re-establish righteousness (*dharmaḥ*). Similarly, the epic and Purāṇic literature had described with popular charm the descents (*avatāraḥ*) of Viṣṇu on earth in different visible bodily forms in order to fulfil a special function. The Nyāya-Vaiśeṣikas could thus build up into their philosophical theory this religious conception of Īśvara taking up a body, with a qualifying clause "when the special nature of the action or effect to be produced requires it" (*kāryavaśāt*). This view is traceable with certainty at least as early as Jayantabhaṭṭa[346].

Udayana himself does not give us any detail as to the manner in which Īśvara assumes such a body. In the view of the Nyāya-Vaiśeṣikas a body is obtained as the result of merit and demerit of the soul it is meant to embody, but in the view of our author neither merit nor demerit is found in Īśvara. No justification of the manner in which Īśvara acquires a body seemed to him necessary; after all, it does not form a real part of Īśvara, nor does it serve him as the subject of senses or as substratum of experiences, as ordinary bodies do. Although ordinary bodies are fashioned according to the merits and demerits of the soul that are destined to inhabit them, Īśvara's body of manifestation has only a purely extrinsic function and hence it could be assumed by him even regardless or independent of any merit or demerit of his own. But some commentators of Udayana tried to give a philosophic explanation of the causes of this body of Īśvara. Thus Vardhamāna, the author of Prakāśa, remarks that, although Īśvara does not possess merit or demerit, he produces for himself a body of manifestation, making use of the Adṛṣṭam of the living beings themselves[347].

Another problem connected with the teaching function of Īśvara is how he actually instructs the living beings. The view of Udayana as well as the interpretation of different commentators how the different Vedic branches have been transmitted by Īśvara have been mentioned earlier while explaining the manner in which the names of Vedic branches such as Kāṭhaka, Kālāpaka etc. are to be understood. Iśvara himself is said to have taken up the bodies of the authors of the different Vedic branches and taught them to the living beings. This can be applied to all the Vedic texts. The bodies of the authors of these Vedic texts were thus merely bodies of manifestation (*nirmāṇakāyaḥ*). A similar explanation was given also concerning the manner in which Īśvara communicates the usage of speech as well as the different human trades such as making pots or weaving cloth. In his proof for the existence of Īśvara based

---

346 Cf. NM I 218, 13—15. Śaṅkarasvāmin who probably lived at the time of Śantarakṣita (cf. E. STEINKELLNER: Die Literatur des älteren Nyāya, p. 156; G. OBERHAMMER thinks that he lived between the period of Dharmakīrti and Śāntarakṣita. See his paper: On the Sources in Jayanta Bhaṭṭa and Uddyotakara, p. 149) seems to have held such a theory. Cf. AP 69, 8—12; A. THAKUR: Some Lost Nyāya Works and Authors, p. 390.

347 Cf. NKusPr 508, 27—28. Śaṅkaramiśra commenting on the same passage follows the same view. Cf. NKusAm 350, 19—20.

on the need of a teacher of these human usages of daily life, Udayana states that Īśvara takes up a body from time to time when the special action to be performed necessarily requires it. In the conclusion of that proof he observes that the Yajus passages such as "Reverence to the artisans, the potters" are to be understood as applying to Īśvara. The commentators explain these passages in the sense that Īśvara himself takes up the body of the potter, the weaver etc. and teaches the human beings the art of making these things.

Udayana himself has been rather reserved in his statements about the manner in which Īśvara teaches the first living beings. In the second Stabaka of the Nyāyakusumāñjali, however, he gives us some idea of it. In his view Īśvara instructs men in the usage of words through action (*vyavahārataḥ*) by directing (*adhiṣṭhānam*), as a single magician does, diverse bodies that stand in the relation of to-be-taught and teacher (*vyutpādyavyutpādaka-bhāvena*). He explains this statement by a comparison. When a magician orders a puppet, which he directs by a string, to bring a certain object and it does so, the children watching this are instructed as though the action of bringing the object were done by a conscious being. In the same way is also the instruction of the first living beings by Īśvara to be thought of. What is said of the usage of words can be applied, *mutatis mutandis*, also to the actions of making pots, weaving cloth etc.[348].

There is no doubt that for Udayana Īśvara is first and foremost the creator, sustainer and destroyer of the universe and the instructor of the living beings in the Veda and in the traditional arts of ordinary life. It might be interesting to inquire whether he ascribes to Īśvara also some other functions in relation to the living beings, which are often wont to be ascribed to God. It should be pointed out at the very outset that some of the functions we are going to consider are, according to Western systems of thought, of a theological nature, not forming part of a philosophical study of God. Although Udayana deals with the doctrine of Īśvara primarily from the philosophical stand-point, we noticed that he makes use of and argues from the testimony of the Vedic scriptures, a method which would be considered by the Westerners as pertaining to the domain of theology.

The final aim of human existence on earth, according to all Indian thinkers, is liberation termed variously as *mokṣaḥ*, *muktiḥ*, *apavargaḥ*, *niḥśreyaḥ* etc. The state of liberation consists, to put it in rather general terms, in the freedom of the soul from its bondage to the cycle of existences or *saṃsāraḥ* and from all kinds of pains, not only actual but also possible[349]. Most of the people who believe in God ascribe to him in some way or other a role in the final destiny of man. Has Īśvara, in the opinion of Udayana, any role in the liberation of the souls ?

---

[348] Cf. NKus 286, 5—9. See also ATV 428, 3—7: Śaṅkaramiśra commenting on the words *vyutpatteḥ karaṇam* found in the opening verse of the ATV remarks in ATVK 2, 13—15: *vyutpatter iti. yathā pitā adhyāpanādinā putrān vyutpādayati, tatheśvaro 'pi prayojyaprayojakadehabhedam āśritya prāṇino gavādipadajāte paṭādinirmāṇe ca vyutpādayatīty arthaḥ.*

[349] Kir 6, 14: *niḥśreyasaṃ punar duḥkhanivṛttir ātyantikī.* See also ibid. 8, 11.

The author of the Nyāyakusumāñjali follows the traditional view of the Nyāya-Vaiśeṣika school with regard to the causes of rebirths and the means of liberation from them. Rebirths are, in the last analysis, rooted in or caused by false knowledge (*mithyājñānam*)[350]. Since the law of causality is applied even to the process of liberation, freedom from rebirths is conceived to be realisable through the removal of its cause by its opposite, namely through true knowledge (*tattvajñānam*) or the knowledge of realities as they are[351]. When false knowledge has been thus removed, passion (*rāgaḥ*) etc. disappear and actions prompted by them also cease to be, and consequently there would be no more births and deaths or sufferings caused by them[352].

Although religious performances (*karma*) are conducive to final liberation as remote help, the immediate cause of liberation is, in the view of Udayana, the knowledge of the true nature of realities[353]. With regard to the means of obtaining this true knowledge, he observes: "And this knowledge of the true nature of things is to be obtained by the efforts of the person (who is desirous of obtaining liberation)"[354]. According to this statement he conceives of liberation as directly effected through the efforts of the person himself who strives after it without any aid of Īśvara.

There is, on the other hand, another passage where Udayana ascribes a certain, though mediate, role to Īśvara in the soul's liberation. Commenting upon a passage of the Padārthadharmasaṃgraha, he states that an indirect (*parokṣa-*) knowledge produced by argumentation (*upapattiḥ*) or verbal testimony (*śabdaḥ*) is incapable of removing the false knowledge in question; rather it is only that kind of true knowledge which is of a stronger type (*balavattara-*), direct or perceptual (*aparokṣa-*) and unerring (*avyutthāyi-*), that is able to remove the false knowledge and produce liberation. Such a true knowledge, however, he observes following the author of the Padārthadharmasaṃgraha, arises only from the Dharma taught by Īśvara in the Veda. The liberating knowledge arises from the Dharma practised continuously for a long period of time according to what is taught in the works of Śruti, Smṛti, Itihāsa and Purāṇa[355]. In this passage Īśvara is said to have at least a mediate role in the process of liberation, in as far as it is he who is the author of the Veda which teaches men the Dharma that finally leads to the liberating knowledge.

This idea of a mediate role of Īśvara in the process of liberation can be traced also in some occasional references of Udayana in his other works. Thus in the concluding section of the Ātmatattvaviveka he remarks that the Supreme Soul (= Īśvara) is to be worshipped by means of yogic practices for the extirpation of rebirths (*bhavocchittiḥ*)[356]. In the opening lines of his Nyāya-

---

350 Kir 9, 6: *tathā hi mithyājñānaṃ savāsanam iha saṃsāramūlakāraṇam.*
351 Ibid. 9, 6—7.
352 Ibid. 9, 7—8.
353 Ibid. 12, 5—7.
354 Ibid. 9, 8—9: *tac ca tattvajñānaṃ puruṣaprayatnasādhyam iti.*
355 Ibid. 11, 7—12, 2.
356 Cf. ATV 447, 1—4.

kusumāñjali he remarks with approval that wise men consider the worship of the Supreme Soul to be the path to heaven and liberation[357]. Similarly, in the concluding verses of the same work he seems to ascribe to Īśvara some role in the liberation of the souls; for in these verses he prays that, moved by mercy, Īśvara may draw to himself by his supreme power the stony hearts of even the unbelievers who are not convinced of his existence through rational arguments[358]. There is, finally, the opening verse of his Lakṣaṇamālā, a verse that occurs also at the beginning of the Guṇapadārtha-section of his Kiraṇāvalī, where Īśvara is said to liberate souls from the bondage of existences when he is pleased and to bind them when displeased[359]. With regard to all these verses it should be remembered that they belong to a genre different from the philosophical and that, being verses of salutation or prayer, they do not admit of strict philosophical interpretation. However, even leaving aside such verses, we have come across at least one passage in the Kiraṇāvalī which, as we saw, allows us to conclude that our author ascribes to Īśvara a mediate role in the liberation of the souls from the cycles of existences.

Closely connected with the role of God in the attainment of the final destiny of man is also the concept of that activity or relation of his usually designated by the term "providence". "The notion of providence sums up God's relationship to the world as he knows, wills and executes his plan of universal salvation and leads the world to the end decreed by him"[360]. According to this definition which, despite its predominant Christian signification, can be said to correspond to a large extent to the notion of divine providence found also in non-Christian conceptions of God, the creator of the universe is believed to direct the creatures to their final end by means of his foreseeing disposition of events in the universe and, when necessary, even by his free intervention in the course of events. The question may be raised whether Udayana admits in his theodicy such a providence of Īśvara.

The providence of Īśvara in the sense of a free intervention in the course of events in the universe of created beings does not have a place in a system where his activity with regard to the creatures is conceived of as conditioned and dependent upon the merit and demerit of the living beings. It is true that Udayana admits that, for the sake of the living beings, Īśvara maintains the universe in existence after creating it and destroys it afterwards. It is also true that, like his predecessors of the school, he, too, admits that Īśvara is like a father towards his creatures. Nevertheless, the fact remains that, while the conception of providence of God as it is generally understood presupposes in him absolute liberty in his dealings with his creatures, irrespective of their deserts, the Īśvara of the Nyāya-Vaiśeṣika system is not absolutely free in

---

[357] Cf. NKus 11, 1—12, 1. See also NKusBo 11, 3—12, 3.

[358] Cf. NKus 575, 15—18.

[359] LM opening verse; Kir 159, 4—5:
tuṣṭer mocayato baddhān atuṣṭer badhnataḥ punaḥ /
kārāgāram idaṃ viśvaṃ yasya naumi tam īśvaram //

[360] Sacramentum Mundi, Vol. 5, p. 130.

his dealings with his creatures, but rather dependent (*sāpekṣa-*) upon their merits and demerits.

On the other hand, we may be allowed to speak of the "providence" of Īśvara over all his creation in general and of the living beings in particular in a restricted and analogous sense, since he maintains the universe in being and, like a loving father, engages himself in activities that are meant for the good of the souls. We shall show below that all his activities with regard to the world are, in the last analysis, guided by the motive of helping the living beings to attain liberation which is the final end of existence (*puruṣārthaḥ*). Being endowed with omniscience, he is able to direct the living beings to their final end, though he is limited and conditioned in his "providence" by the merits and demerits of the souls. Moreover, he helps the living beings to bring their actions to a successful conclusion. Commenting on the introductory verse of the Padārthadharmasaṃgraha wherein Praśastapāda offers his reverential salutation to Īśvara, Udayana remarks that such a salutation, marked by an abundance of devotion and faith (*bhaktiśraddhātiśayalakṣaṇa-*) leads to success and brings the undertaking to a good conclusion free from hindrances[361].

Finally, the Creator of the universe is mostly conceived also as the rewarder of the good deeds and the punisher of the wicked acts of man. In a system of thought like the Nyāya-Vaiśeṣika according to which retribution of one's deeds takes place with automatic causal necessity through the law of Karma, such an idea of Īśvara is hardly conceivable[362]. On the other hand, Īśvara can be said to help the souls in enjoying the fruit of their good as well as bad actions by providing them with the conditions under which the law of Karma may operate. Thus, himself conditioned by the Karma of the living beings, he creates the universe in which the living beings will be enabled to enjoy the reward or the punishment of their actions.

---

[361] Kir 3, 10—12.

[362] The idea of a god who rewards the good and punishes the wicked is, however, not completely foreign to Indian thought. Before the development of the doctrine of Karma, Varuṇa who was regarded "as the embodiment of a fair number of the characteristics ascribed to the Supreme Being" was looked upon as the guardian of morality and the upholder of order, especially *ṛtam*. Cf. J. GONDA: The Concept of a personal God in ancient Indian religious thought, pp. 111—112.

Chapter Three

MOTIVES FOR THE ACTIVITY OF ĪŚVARA

The relationship of Īśvara to the created universe which we discussed in the preceding chapter raises a question: what, indeed, is the motive that prompts Īśvara to his diverse activities? For it is generally accepted also by the Indian thinkers that no intelligent agent does anything without an end in view[363]. What is the purpose which makes Īśvara engage himself in activities with regard to the universe?

One of the topics of controversy in the earlier period of the development of the Nyāya-Vaiśeṣika Īśvara doctrine was precisely the motive of his activity. The objection of the opponents can be thus summarily formulated: On the one hand, being an agent (*kartā*), Īśvara should have some motive for his activity, since every agent acts with an end in view. On the other hand, to ascribe a purpose to Īśvara's activity seems to be incompatible with his nature. For the motives that prompt an agent to an action can be classed under two main groups: motive of gaining something for one's own self (*svārthaṃ*) or the motive of doing something for the sake of another (*parārtham*). But were Īśvara to act in order to gain something for himself, he would be lacking that which he seeks to gain by his activity, and consequently he would not be Īśvara; if he acted for the sake of others, he ought to have created a universe free from pains and sufferings[364].

The advocates of the Īśvara doctrine prior to Udayana had brought forward various answers to this objection. The author of the Nyāyakusumāñjali himself does not deal *ex professo* with this subject, probably because during his time the opponents of the Īśvara doctrine had attached less importance to this objection than to those relating to the logical aspect of the proofs for his existence. What will be said below concerning his view on this matter is gleaned from the occasional passing references or expressions found in his works.

Udayana is at one with his predecessors[365] in refusing to ascribe to Īśvara any motive of self-interest (*svārthaḥ*) for his action[366]. Himself lacking

[363] To quote Udayana only: NKus 312, 2: *ko hi prayojanam antareṇa kiñcit kuryāt?* Also Kir 5, 16—17.

[364] Cf., for example, NV 949, 18ff.; NM I 176, 17—177, 13.

[365] Among the Nyaya-Vaiśeṣikas Bhāsarvajña is, however, known to have held that the motive of *svārtham* may be ascribed to Īśvara. Cf. NBhu 459, 17—24.

[366] Cf. ATV 409, 6: . . . *na syāt pramāṇābhāvāt. . . . parārthaṃ ca.* The edition of the ATV to which all our references are made has unfortunately omitted the line *parārthaṃ ca pravṛttiḥ, svārthābhāvāt* which comes immediately after *na syāt pramāṇābhāvāt.*

in no desirable perfection, he has nothing to acquire for himself. He is not only self-contented, but the very repository of all bliss (*ānandanidhiḥ*)[367]. Having nothing to gain for himself, and being endowed with unconditioned compassion (*nirupadhiḥ kṛpā*)[368], his activity is prompted solely by the motive of helping the beings that are caught in the stream of existences.

Among the works of Udayana it is the Ātmatattvaviveka that offers us the most material on the problem under consideration. In answer to an objection[369], our author observes that the presence of pain in this world does not go against the fact that Īśvara is full of compassion and that he acts solely for the good of the living beings. For the causing of pain does not necessarily imply absence of compassion in the agent that causes it, "since there is exception in the case of father, teacher, physician etc."[370]. What Udayana means is that, just as when an affectionate father, or a benevolent teacher or a beneficent physician causes on occasion some pain to his son, disciple or patient respectively, it is meant for the sake of a future good that exceeds the present pains, so also when Īśvara causes—one ought to say more correctly, 'permits'—suffering in this world, it is in view of the greater good of the living beings. The infliction or permission of sufferings, far from being acts of injustice or cruelty, thus becomes rather tokens of compassion, benevolence and love on the part of the person that causes or permits them.

Such a statement is quite consonant with one of the basic concepts accepted by most of the schools of Indian philosophy. The souls find themselves "affected by" or "loaded with" the fruit of the actions of their earlier existences for which there is no beginning (*anādi-*). This fruit—or Adṛṣṭam, as it is often termed in Nyāya-Vaiśeṣika philosophy, or the sum total of merit (*dharmaḥ*) and demerit (*adharmaḥ*)—has necessarily to be "enjoyed" or "experienced" (*bhogaḥ*) in order that it may disappear and thus lead the soul to liberation[371]. The "enjoyment" of the fruit of good and bad actions is through the experience of pleasures and pains. And, as we said earlier, Īśvara directs the origination of the universe and thus creates the milieu or conditions in which the souls are enabled to experience the fruit of their actions[372]. In doing so, Īśvara helps the souls on their path to liberation, and consequently the sufferings in this world not only do not contradict the attributes of compassion or love or justice of Īśvara, but even positively reveal his goodness or compassion towards the living beings. Udayana rejects any attempt of the opponent to impute the

---

367 Cf. NKus 576, 2.

368 Cf. ATV 1, 6.

369 Ibid. 408, 4—5.

370 Ibid. 409, 6—8: *na ca duḥkhasṛṣṭyā kāruṇyāpavādaḥ, janakādhyāpakacikitsakādiṣu vyabhicārāt.*

371 Cf. NVTP 377, 4—9: . . . *tathā ca prayogaḥ. vivādādhyāsitāni karmāṇi bhogād eva kṣīyante, acīrṇaprāyaścittakarmatvāt, ārabdhaśarīrakarmavat.* See also ibid. 381, 11—13.

372 Cf. Nar 409, 14—15: *janakādivat parameśvaro 'pi hitabuddhyaiva jantūnāṃ pūrvakṛtaśubhāśubhakarmaphalopabhogena tatkṣayāya duḥkhamayam api jagat sṛjatīti bhāvaḥ.*

creation of a universe in which there is suffering to wickedness or cruelty (*daurjanyam*) on the part of Īśvara; for wickedness and cruelty can be found only in those persons who are tainted with the quality of "faults" (*doṣaḥ*). But, since Īśvara is free from infatuation (*mohaḥ*) on account of his omniscience (*sarvajñatvam*), there cannot be "faults" in him[373].

Such an explanation of the sufferings in this world is at the same time Udayana's answer to one of the important problems of the philosophers of all times and of all places, especially when they deal with the existence of a just, compassionate and loving God, in fact the object of theodicy properly so called. The Indian philosophers look for the solution of this "problem of evil" in the subjects that endure the sufferings rather than in Īśvara or any other agent outside the enduring subjects themselves. The irrevocable law of Karma operating with unalterable causal necessity[374], though guided by the activity of Īśvara, requires that every living being should reap the fruit of its actions either in the form of pleasure (*sukham*) or in that of pain (*duḥkham*) in accordance with the merit (*dharmaḥ*) or demerit (*adharmaḥ*) resulting from its actions. In the view of Udayana Īśvara himself cannot go against this law[375]. Moreover, in the creation of the universe in which the living beings have to experience the fruit of their actions, he is conditioned by their Karma, so that, in the last analysis, it is the living beings themselves that earn for themselves, as their due, pleasures or pains in each of the existences they have to pass through.

Although there is such a finality in the sufferings of this existence, in as far as they help the living beings towards their ultimate purpose, it is possible that it is not known to or properly understood by us mortals; for, as Udayana remarks, "We who (perceive things) through the earthly (lit.: 'fleshy') sense of sight, do not perceive the purpose of all the things that come into being"[376]. Nevertheless, whether we know it or not, there is, in fact, a purpose even behind every suffering, a purpose that is directed towards the final aim of mundane existence of the living beings.

That Īśvara acts, not for any motive of self-interest, but solely for the good of the living beings is further evident from Udayana's conception of Īśvara as a father (*pitā*), an idea expressed much earlier by Pakṣilasvāmin and continued to be recognized, at least implicitly, by all the later Nyāya-Vaiśeṣika exponents of the Īśvara doctrine. In the opening verse of the Ātmatattvaviveka our author speaks of Īśvara as father and points out that all his activities with regard to the universe are directed towards the good of the creation.

---

[373] Cf. ATV 409, 9—410, 2.

[374] We leave out of consideration here the religious Bhakti schools according to which Īśvara can and does overlook the *karma* of his devotees.

[375] Cf. NVTP 381, 7: *na hi īśvaro 'pi karmaṇāṃ svabhāvaṃ viparyāsayitum arhati.*

[376] Ibid. 552, 5—6: *na tāvat sarvasyaivotpattimataḥ prayojanaṃ piśitacakṣuṣaḥ sākṣātkurmaḥ.*

That the motive of compassion underlies the activity of creation of the universe has been already mentioned. The same motive is also the reason for the dissolution of the universe[377]. But Udayana sees the motive of Īśvara's compassion in particular in the instruction of living beings in the Veda. Īśvara is the author of the Vedas, he says, "because, while there is (in him) the power of speech, his mind is fixed on one object only, namely the good of the others. For he who aims at the good of the others (and) knows the distinction between that which is salutary and that which is not salutary, would, if he has the skill of the instruments of uttering sounds (i. e. if he has the organs of speech), necessarily give instruction to the ignorant, just as even an ordinary person (would instruct) a blind man (going unguided along a road that may be dangerous for him, telling him) 'Go by the right (side); do not go by the left'. And in the same manner (does) the Blessed (Īśvara give instruction to the living beings who are on the path to liberation)"[378]. In this passage Udayana clearly brings out the motive of Īśvara's compassion for the living beings. But he goes further in explaining this motive in a more revealing manner by associating it with the fatherhood of Īśvara; for he says: "Or the instruction (of the living beings by Īśvara) is inferred from (his) being a father (to them)"[379]. The compassion of a father towards his own children who are in difficult or dangerous situations and who are ignorant of the way of getting out of them is, generally speaking, much greater than the compassion of a person towards another who is not related to him by paternal bond. Udayana wants to point out here that the solicitude of Īśvara for the good of the living beings is that of an affectionate father and that he does all he can to help them attain their final end. Udayana who has persistently refused to admit a body in Īśvara for his creative activity is even willing to concede that he may assume a body for his activity of instructing the living beings.

In the concluding verses of the Nyāyakusumāñjali the author refers no less than three times to the compassion of Īśvara. There he addresses him as the compassionate one (*kāruṇika-*) and entreats him to make, out of compassion (*kṛpayā*), the unbelievers thoughtful of him; and finally he beseeches him to be compassionate (*karuṇām vidhehi*) towards him and to fix his wavering mind upon him[380]. Although the verses wherein these ideas are found are more of a religious or devotional nature than strictly philosophical, nevertheless we can see in them a reflection of the compassion of Īśvara spoken of in the other passages of Udayana which we have already discussed. When we recall that our author defines compassion as "the desire to remove the pains of others" and characterizes it further as "being without any cause"[381]

377 Cf. Kir 93, 11—14 and 91, 5—7.

378 ATV 413, 8—414, 2: *vacanaśaktau satyāṃ parārthaikatānatvāt. yo hi hitāhitavibhāgaṃ vidvān parārthābhiprāyaḥ sa sthānakaraṇapāṭave saty aviduṣe "dakṣiṇena yāhi, vāmena mā gā" iti pṛthagjano 'pi, tathā ca bhagavān iti.*

379 ATV 414, 9: *pitṛtvād vopadeśānumānam.*

380 Cf. NKus 575, 18 and 576, 3.

381 Cf. NVTP 20, 3: *niṣkāraṇam eva hi paraduḥkhaprahāṇecchā kāruṇyam.*

—with the phrase (*niṣkāraṇam eva*) is probably meant 'without any conditioning factor on the part of the person on whom compassion is taken'—and apply this definition to Īśvara, we find that it clearly brings out the motive of compassion in his activity.

In the earlier Indian literature, philosophical as well as religious, we come across passages wherein sport or play (*līlā* or *krīḍā*) is spoken of as one of the motives of God's actions[382]. While dealing with the motive of Īśvara's activity, Udayana has nowhere spoken of this motive. In fact, the Nyāya-Vaiśeṣikas in general were against the ascription of such a motive to Īśvara[383]. However, we find two passing references to it, both of them in the concluding verses of the second and third Stabakas of his Nyāyakusumāñjali. In the first passage the creative and destructive activities of Īśvara are spoken of as his play. The second passage refers to Īśvara as enjoying in sport at his own will[384]. Even leaving aside the fact that these references are found among the concluding verses of his work, an interpretation of these passages in the sense that Īśvara performs his creative or other activities for the sake of deriving some pleasure from such a sport or play would be unjust. Being self-contented and free from even the least pain, he cannot be assumed to be seeking any satisfaction for himself or as trying to get rid of or forget any pain by such sport or amusement. Such an interpretation would, moreover, imply that Īśvara acts for gaining something for himself (*svārtham*), an idea that has been explicitly repudiated by Udayana. It would, therefore, be more correct to interpret the term 'play' here in the sense that Īśvara acts with that spontaneity and absolute ease that characterize what we term 'play'.

Concluding our brief consideration of the motives of the activity of Īśvara we can say that Udayana agrees with the general Nyāya-Vaiśeṣika view, according to which Īśvara is not guided in his activities in relation to the universe by motives of self-interest, but rather by those of compassion towards the living beings.

---

[382] Cf., e. g., NV 949, 20—22; TSP 98, 19—21.

[383] Jayanta, however, seems to have accepted the motive of *krīḍā* as an alternative motive for the creative activity of Īśvara. Cf. NM I 186, 6—7.

[384] Cf. NKus 309, 1—2 and 449, 3.

Chapter Four

ONTOLOGICAL DETERMINATION OF ĪŚVARA

1. The Nature of Īśvara

One of the most fundamental doctrines of the Nyāya-Vaiśeṣikas is that of the categories (*padārthaḥ*) or classes of realities. All realities, visible or invisible, eternal or non-eternal, were brought under one of the six categories set up by the system. Whatever could not be classed under any of these did not belong to the domain of reality. When we speak of the nature of Īśvara, we use the term 'nature' in a limited and special sense here, namely to indicate the particular class of reality under which Īśvara can be grouped.

The first and foremost among the six categories of the school is that of substance (*dravyam*). Nine substances are admitted, some of which are only one in number, while others admit more individuals and thus form a class or group. To this last belongs the substance called soul (*ātmā*) comprising innumerable, eternal souls. Even a casual study of the doctrine of categories of the school will show that Īśvara can be grouped only under the category of substance. The Nyāya-Vaiśeṣikas have, in fact, always maintained such a view from the early beginnings of their Īśvara doctrine. But there seems to have been a divergence of opinion among them as to whether Īśvara was to be classified under the class of souls as one among them (*ātmāntaram*) or whether he was to be thought of as a substance *sui generis* (*dravyāntaram*), in other words, as a tenth substance. Although the details of this controversy are unknown to us, we have sufficient indications that warrant a surmise that such a problem was raised, at least in the earlier stages of the development of the Īśvara doctrine[385]. The Nyāya-Vaiśeṣikas whose works are available to us maintained that Īśvara belonged to the class of substance called soul (*ātmā*), although they taught at the same time that he was different from the ordinary souls by virtue of his special qualities.

Udayana follows the traditional doctrine of the school that Īśvara is not a separate substance *sui generis* (*dravyāntaram*), but belongs to the class of soul (*ātmā*). In his Lakṣaṇāvalī he classifies souls into two groups: the soul that is Īśvara and the souls that are not Īśvara (*anīśvaraḥ*), a classification which is found also in the Kiraṇāvalī in the context of proving the multiplicity of souls[386]. Such a division shows, on the one hand, that Īśvara is grouped

---

[385] Cf., e. g., NV 951, 2ff.; TSP 51, 17—20; NM I 185, 16.

[386] Cf. LV 14, 13—14; Kir 150, 9—12.

under the class of souls, and, on the other, that he differs from the ordinary souls. In what way he differs from the ordinary souls will be spoken of below.

Another question that was raised in this connection in the earlier period was whether Īśvara was to be considered as bound (*baddha-*) or free (*mukta-*)[387]. Such a formulation of the problem can be understood only from the conception of Īśvara as soul; for souls were considered to be of two kinds, those that are 'bound', that is to say, entangled in the Saṃsāra or cycle of existences, and those that have freed themselves from this bondage. While the question had a meaning as far as the ordinary souls are concerned, the consideration as to whether Īśvara is bound or free arose more out of dialectical considerations than from real doubt; for a bound Īśvara could not be the creator of the universe, and to be freed, he ought to have been bound before he became free. If we remember that false knowledge (*mithyājñānam*) is, in the eyes of the Nyāya-Vaiśeṣikas, the root of bondage to Saṃsāra, it is clear that an eternally omniscient (*nityasarvajña-*) being like Īśvara could at no time have been bound, and consequently never freed from bondage. In this he distinguishes himself from the liberated souls (*mukta-*) who are, indeed, now free, but were once bound or subject to the bondage of cycle of existences. In commenting upon a passage of the Padārthadharmasaṃgraha, Udayana observes that the expression "at the time of the liberation of Brahmā" (*brahmaṇo 'pavargakāle*), if it is interpreted as applying to Īśvara himself in as far as he assumes, for the sake of a particular action or effect, a divine body, it should be explained to mean "at the time of the liberation from the body"; for "he in whom there is absolute absence of pain is eternally free (*nityamukta-*)"[388]. The expression 'eternally' (*nitya-*) makes it very clear that Īśvara was at no time under the bondage of the law of cycle of existences and can never be.

In conclusion we can say that, although Udayana conceives of Īśvara as belonging to the class of souls (*ātmā*), he allots to him a very special place and marks him off from the ordinary souls. The main reason for the pre-eminence of Īśvara over other souls are his qualities to which we shall now turn our attention.

2. The Qualities of Īśvara

The fact that Īśvara belongs to the class of souls (*ātmā*) gives us some general idea of the qualities (*guṇaḥ*) that will be ascribed to him. But as he is in some respects different from the ordinary souls, it is necessary for us to examine more particularly his qualities and see which of the qualities predicated of soul are found in him and which are not, and whether he possesses qualities other than or in a mode different from that of the qualities found in the ordinary souls. But this task is not very easy; for, while the earlier Nyāya-Vaiśeṣikas like Pakṣilasvāmin, Praśastapāda, Uddyotakara, Bhāsarvajña and Jayanta have dealt with the qualities of Īśvara as an important part of their

---

[387] Cf., e. g., NV 952, 15—16; NKand 142, 8—11.

[388] Kir 90, 18—91, 5: *tasyātyantaduḥkhābhāvavato nityamuktatvāt.*

theistic doctrine, Udayana has not treated this aspect of the Īśvara doctrine as a separate theme. One can, however, glean from his works certain expressions and, in some cases, certain passages on the basis of which one can reconstruct in some manner the general outlines of the qualities of Īśvara according to him. The following pages are an attempt at such a reconstruction. As is only to be expected, such a procedure can claim to give neither a complete nor an adequate picture of the qualities of Īśvara as our author had conceived them.

The early Vaiśeṣikas had classified the twenty-four qualities they admitted into several groups according to various view-points such as their perceptibility, their origination, their products, the nature of the substratum on which they inhere, etc.[389]. One of the most important classifications is that into specific qualities (*viśeṣagunaḥ*) and generic qualities (*sāmānyaguṇaḥ*). The former are proper or specific to certain classes of substances in such a way that they can never be common to two classes of substances, while the latter can inhere in more than one class of substances. Only nine specific qualities are ascribed to the soul, namely cognition (*jñānam* or *buddhiḥ*), pleasure (*sukham*), pain (*duḥkham*), desire (*icchā*), aversion (*dveṣaḥ*), effort (*prayatnaḥ*), merit (*dharmaḥ*), demerit (*adharmaḥ*) and mental impressions (*saṃskāraḥ*). Similarly, the Nyāya-Vaiśeṣikas ascribe five generic qualities to the soul, namely number (*saṃkhyā*), size (*parimāṇam*), individuality (*pṛthaktvam*), conjunction (*saṃyogaḥ*) and disjunction (*vibhāgaḥ*)[390]. We shall now enquire how many of these qualities, specific as well as generic, ascribed to the soul as a class are attributed to Īśvara by Udayana. Since the specific qualities are more important than the generic, we shall consider them first.

Even a cursory glance at the list of the specific qualities of the soul shows that not all of them can be found in Īśvara; for some of them such as pain or demerit imply imperfection, and hence are incompatible with the nature of Īśvara.

a) Cognition (*jñānam*) of Īśvara

Among the specific qualities of Īśvara it is his cognition that has been the most emphasized and the most extensively dealt with by all the protagonists of philosophical theism. Such an emphasis is easily understandable when one recollects that it is this quality that is most essential to Īśvara for fulfilling his important functions as creator of the universe and as the author of the Veda. This explains also why it is this quality that has been the special target for objections. It is on this quality that we have the most abundant information in the works of Udayana.

The Nyāya-Vaiśeṣikas had maintained from the earlier stages of their acceptance of the Īśvara doctrine that his cognition was eternal omniscience. The opponents of theism, on their part, brought forward several objections against this attribute of Īśvara. Prominent among these opponents were the

---

[389] Cf. PDhS 162, 1ff.; E. Frauwallner: Geschichte II, pp. 212ff.
[390] Cf. PDhS 148, 1—2.

Mīmāṃsakas and the Buddhists. The great Kumārila had subjected the eternal omniscience of Īśvara to a severe criticism[391]. His followers continued this criticism in their commentaries. The Prābhākaras, on their part, joined the Bhāṭṭas in their attack on the eternal omniscience of Īśvara, denying the very possibility of eternal cognition[392]. The Buddhists, though ardent advocates of the omniscience of the Buddha, raised objections against the omniscience of Īśvara. We can find these objections in the Tattvasaṃgraha of Śāntarakṣita and in its commentary by Kamalaśīla[393]. Jñānaśrī also made serious objections to the omniscience of Īśvara[394]. Under such circumstances it is quite understandable that the author of the Nyāyakusumāñjali attaches special importance to this foremost quality of Īśvara and vindicates it with singular interest.

Like all the advocates of theism, Udayana maintains that the cognition of Īśvara is omniscience (*sarvajñatvam*). His arguments for Īśvara's omniscience are based on two important functions of Īśvara, namely on his being the creator of the universe and his being the author of the Veda.

There is an important passage in the Ātmatattvaviveka dealing with the cognition of Īśvara which deserves to be quoted here in full:

"It is also beyond dispute that (Īśvara) being the sole producer of the dyads[395] certainly knows the ultimate atoms, the Adṛṣṭam, the (souls) that are benefitted (*upakāryam*), (the intended result) beginning from the triads and ending with the experience (of pleasure and pain by the living beings), and the sixfold categories (of reality) beginning with substance[396]; for these have the nature of material cause etc. (of the universe). Or because the thorough knowledge of the material cause etc. is not possible without the thorough knowledge of the relation of that which determines and that which is deter-

---

391 Cf. ŚV 79, 4ff. (II, 111ff.); 650, 5 and 673, 3 (= Sambandhākṣepaparihāraḥ, verses 44b and 114a respectively).

392 Cf. ṚP 144, 29—31: *yā yā buddhiḥ sā sā utpattimatī vināśinī ca. teneśvarasyāpi dhiyā tathāvidhayaiva bhavitavyam.* See also PrP 307, 10—11: *athākāraṇā nityaiveśvarabuddhir iti cet, tad apy asundaram, buddhitattvasya nityatvābhāvāt. nityā satī buddhir eva na syāt.*

393 Cf. TS 63, 1—66, 3 (= Īśvaraparīkṣā, verses 72—82) and TSP 63, 9—66, 18.

394 Cf. JMN 260, 19ff.

395 The translation of the term *ekadvyaṇukakārī* presents some difficulty, as it suggests different interpretations. To take it as "one who produces the single atoms and the dyads" would be incorrect, since the single atoms, being eternal, are not produced. Other possible interpretations are: "one who produces (something, namely, the universe) out of the single atoms and the dyads", or perhaps even "one who operates with single atoms and dyads". I have, chosen the interpretation "one who is the sole (*ekaḥ*) producer of the dyads", because it seemed to me the best in the context.

396 I find it difficult to explain satisfactorily the reading *upakāryatryaṇukādibhogaparyantaṃ dravyādipadārthaṣaṭkañ ca.* The translation "and (he knows) the sixfold categories of substance etc. beginning with (their forms as) triads etc. that are to be helped and ending with the experience" does not, as far as I see, explain the passage properly. Hence I have translated it in a manner that would fit in with the traditional Nyāya-Vaiśeṣika argument for the omniscience of Īśvara from his cognition of all the causes of the universe.

mined. And the general rule is that he who is capable of producing or knowing one (individual thing) belonging to a certain class, (is capable of producing or knowing) all things without exception (*eva*) belonging to that class; for capacity is determined according to class. (It might be objected that) although he may be capable by himself alone (to produce or to know things), he may not produce or know when the co-operating (causes) are not present. Of these, the first (alternative) is indeed accepted; for we see that the effect is determined as to place and time. But the second (alternative) would only be possible, if his cognition were produced; but such is not that (= cognition of Īśvara). How (it may be asked, is Īśvara's cognition not produced)? (It is so) because, when body is absent, senses etc. which have it (= body) as the substratum are also absent. Nor can it be (supposed) that, even in the absence of that which has been established by means of the (methods of) concomitance and non-concomitance to be the cause, the effect can come into being from some other cause; for it would (then) be devoid of cause. And there cannot at all be an effect without (its) cause. Consequently, his power of cognition, desire to produce and effort which are necessarily (*eva*) connatural (i. e. unproduced), having a certain thing as its object, have all things belonging to that class as its object. Thus is established that (he is) omniscient"[397].

Despite the length of the passage and the inclusion of the qualities of desire and effort of Īśvara in the last part, it has been quoted here in full, since it throws much light on our author's conception of the nature of Īśvara's cognition. Two essential aspects of Īśvara's cognition are here specially brought out, namely that it extends itself to all objects and that it is unproduced or eternal.

In the first part of the passage Udayana argues for the all-comprehending nature of Īśvara's cognition from the fact that every agent should have an adequate knowledge of all the different causes he makes use of in his activity of producing an effect. Being the agent or maker (*kartā*) of this universe Īśvara, too, should have an adequate cognition of the different causes he "directs", namely, the ultimate atoms which are the material causes (*upādānakāraṇam*), the Adṛṣṭam or the invisible fruit of the actions of the living beings which is the instrumental cause (*upakaraṇam*), the souls or living beings for whom the created things are intended (*saṃpradānakāraṇam*) and finally the intended purpose of the created things (*prayojanam*) which is the experience of pleasure or pain (*bhogaḥ*) by the living beings. He possesses, moreover,

---

[397] ATV 410, 2—411, 5: *ekadvyaṇukakārī paramāṇum adṛṣṭam upakāryatryaṇukādibhogaparyantaṃ dravyādipadārthaṣaṭkañ ca jānāti nūnam ity api avivādam, eṣām upādānādirūpatvāt, avacchedyāvacchedakabhāvāparijñānena vopadānādiparijñānānupapatteḥ. yaś ca yajjātīyakam ekaṃ kartuṃ jñātuṃ vā samarthaḥ sa tajjātīyaṃ sarvam eveti niyamaḥ, sāmarthyasya jātiniyatatvāt. kevalaṃ samartho 'pi sahakāryasannidher na kuryāt na jānīyāt. tatra prathamam iṣyata eva, kāryasya deśakālaniyamopalambhāt. dvitīyas tu sambhaved api yadi kāryam asya jñānaṃ syāt, na ca tat tathā. katham iti cet? śarīrāpāye tadāśritānām indriyādīnam apāyāt. na ca anvayavyatirekasiddhahetubhāvasyābhāve 'pi hetvantarāt kāryajanma, nirhetukatvaprasaṅgāt. na cāhetukaṃ kāryaṃ nāma. tataḥ svataḥsiddhaivāsya jñānacikīrṣāprayatnaśaktir yadgocarā tajjātīyasamastagocareti sarvajñasiddhiḥ.*

a knowledge of the six categories which comprise the totality of reality. In maintaining that an agent who possesses the knowledge of all the causes of the universe or a person who has the knowledge of all the six categories of reality must be omniscient, Udayana was following a tradition already accepted in the school much before him[398]. One should not think that the cognition of Īśvara extends itself only to some individuals belonging to each class, but not to all. For first of all, an adequate cognition of the causes presupposes that he cognizes properly the causes in their relation as determining and determined, and consequently that he cognizes the generality contained in them. Secondly, the general principle is that he who is able to produce or to know a single individual belonging to a class is able to produce or know all the individuals of that class, since capacity for something is determined with regard to the class, and not the individual. He concedes that this capacity has to be actuated or determined in some cases through the presence of co-operating causes where these are required. Such is the case even with regard to the creative activity of Īśvara in as far as his capacity for producing the universe becomes actuated or effective only when the other co-operating causes are present. The capacity to know, too, may require the presence of such causes in order to be actualised. For example, in the case of the living beings, although the soul possesses the capacity to know, its actual cognition is necessarily conditioned by the presence of a body, so that, in the view of the Nyāya-Vaiśeṣikas, when it is separated from the body either temporarily during the time of the dissolution of the universe or permanently after attaining liberation, the soul remains devoid of any cognition whatsoever. Such a restriction of cognition through extrinsic factors or co-operating causes, however, is possible, Udayana reminds us, only in the case of a cognition that is produced (*kāryam*), but not in the case of a cognition that is not produced, as is the case with the cognition of Īśvara. As we shall soon see, he shows by means of several arguments that the cognition of Īśvara cannot be produced, but must be unproduced or eternal (*nitya-*). Were it produced, it would be produced in dependence upon a body which, in as far as it is the substratum of the senses, is the cause of cognition. It cannot be thought that Īśvara's cognition is produced from a cause other than body; for it has been established by the methods of concomitance and non-concomitance that body is the cause of cognition. Hence given the facts that, on the one hand, Īśvara has cognition and, on the other, that his cognition cannot be produced, it follows that it is connatural to or co-eternal or co-existent with himself. Since this cognition of his comprehends all the objects, it cannot but be omniscience.

The argument for the omniscience of Īśvara on the ground that he is the creator of the universe occurs in another form in a passage of the Nyāya-

[398] Such are the proofs for the omniscience of Īśvara brought forward by Praśastapāda, by some hitherto unidentified author(s) and by Trilocana. Cf. G. Chemparathy: The Īśvara doctrine of Praśastapāda, pp. 77—79; also: Two little-known fragments from early Vaiśeṣika literature on the omniscience of Īśvara, pp. 125—130: JMN 239, 17—24.

vārttikatātparyapariśuddhi where Udayana observes: "... For, in the (proof for the existence of Īśvara:) 'Earth etc. have a maker, because they are products', the very fact of the earth etc. having a maker is impossible without (his) being omniscient; for, if he does not know the ultimate atoms, Adṛṣṭam etc., he cannot direct them (in the process leading to the formation of the universe). On the other hand (*vā*), if he does direct them, he cannot be non-omniscient. Hence, since the meaning (expressed) in the statement (of the proof cited above) (*pratijñātārtham*) would be inconclusive without the omniscience (of the maker), it is pervaded with that (= omniscience of the maker); and, since there is such a meaning (implied), it falls within the domain of being the quality of the subject of the thesis"[399]. We have earlier referred to the same idea found in his Kiraṇāvalī[400].

Attention of the reader may be drawn also to the proof for the existence of Īśvara based on number (*saṃkhyā*), where it was stated that the relating cognition (*apekṣābuddhiḥ*) to be applied to the ultimate atoms in order to produce the dyads and to the dyads in order to form the triads was impossible to intellects such as ours and that the cognition of a being that can have such a relating cognition must necessarily be omniscience[401].

In these passages Udayana wants to convey with all emphasis the idea that the acceptance of a maker of the universe necessarily implies the admission that such a maker is also omniscient. As he observes elsewhere: "It is not possible that a non-omniscient (agent) be the maker of the universe"[402]. For, were he not omniscient, he could not have the cognition necessary for being the creator of the universe, and consequently the universe would not have come into existence. Only an omniscient agent could have the cognition of the ultimate atoms, Adṛṣṭam etc., and direct them to form the universe.

The omniscience of Īśvara is also established from the fact that he is the author of the sacred scriptures. If the Vedas were composed by a non-omniscient author, remarks Udayana, they would not be accepted, as they in fact are, by the large multitude of people (*mahājanaḥ*)[403]. Moreover, what is not composed by an omniscient person, cannot be Veda[404].

But why should the author of the sacred scriptures be necessarily omniscient? An answer to the question can be found in a short statement of

---

[399] NVTP 753, 1—6: *kṣityādikaṃ sakartṛkaṃ kāryatvād ity atra sarvajñatvam antareṇa kṣityādīnāṃ sakartṛkatvam eva nopapadyate paramāṇvadṛṣṭādīnām ajñāne tadadhiṣṭhānānupapatteḥ. tadadhiṣṭhāne vā 'sarvajñatvānupapatteḥ. tasmāt sarvajñatvam antareṇa pratijñātārthānupapattau tadabhiprāyavyāptam, ābhiprāyikatvāc ca pakṣadharmatāgocaraḥ.* See also ibid. 752, 3—4.

[400] See above p. 89.

[401] Cf. NKus 517, 1—518, 1. See also above pp. 106ff.

[402] NKus 415, 5: *na cāsarvajñasya jagatkartṛtvam asti.* Note that the text is misprinted in the KSS edition.

[403] Cf. ATV 421, 2—4: ... *so 'yam īdṛśo mahājanaparigraho vedasyāsarvajñapūrvakatve 'sambhavan sarvajñapūrvakatvena vyāpyate.* See also ibid. 416, 5—6 where the same idea recurs.

[404] NKus 509, 7—8: *yat punar na sarvajñapraṇītaṃ nā'sau vedo, yathetaravākyam.*

Udayana in his Nyāyakusumāñjali where, in answer to the objection that there are scriptural passages that contradict the existence of an omniscient creator of the universe, he observes: "The utterance of one who is not trustworthy is not a means of valid cognition. There is no trustworthiness at all with regard to a thing that has not been perceived (by the speaker). If (a person) has the perception of that which is not perceptible (to ordinary persons) he is omniscient"[405]. In his explanation of these lines, he brings out his idea more clearly: "If, indeed, the sacred scriptures (*śabdaḥ*) which (as you, opponent, assert) teach the absence of an omniscient maker, is not the utterance of a trustworthy person, then they are not a means of valid cognition; but if their speaker (*vaktā*) is trustworthy, how can it be that he does not see their objects? If he perceives objects that are beyond (the perception of) the senses, how can he be non-omniscient?"[406]. These passages show that, in the author's view, one who is able to perceive objects that are supra-sensible cannot but be omniscient, an idea which he shares with the other Nyāya-Vaiśeṣikas who ascribe omniscience also to the perfect yogins who are able to perceive things such as the atoms, Manas etc. that are imperceptible to the ordinary human beings. As "the seer of all the Vedas and their contents" (*sakalavedavedārthadarśī*)[407] and the "knower of the contents of all the Vedas" (*sarvavedārthavid*)[408], it is but natural that Īśvara should have perception of all that is spoken of in all the Vedic scriptures. He cognizes even the Vedic usages of the earlier creations (*pūrvasargāntaravedavyavahāraḥ*)[409]. Since the Vedas speak of realities like heaven that are beyond the perception of the senses of the ordinary people, their author must necessarily be omniscient[410]. Īśvara is, therefore, said to be "all-perceiving" (*sarvānubhāvī*)[411], "all-knowing" (*viśvavid*)[412] and "supreme knower" (*paramavidvān*)[413].

The omniscience of Īśvara cannot be separated from its nature as unproduced (*akārya-*) or eternal (*nitya-*). When the Nyāya-Vaiśeṣika authors speak of the cognition of Īśvara they often use the terms 'eternal' and 'omniscience' together (*nityasarvajñatvam*)[414], and this is not without a good reason. For, in their view, the yogins assisted by merit can attain omniscience and perceive objects imperceptible to ordinary human beings, and consequently

---

[405] NKus 415, 6—7:
na pramāṇam anāptoktir nādṛṣṭe kācid āptatā /
adṛśyadṛṣṭau sarvajño . . . //

[406] Ibid. 416, 1—2: *yadi hi sarvajñakartrabhāvāvedakaḥ śabdo nāptoktaḥ, na tarhi pramāṇam. athāpto 'sya vaktā, kathaṃ na tadarthadarśī? atīndriyārthadarśīti cet, katham asarvajñaḥ?*

[407] Cf. NKus 522, 15.

[408] Ibid. 522, 19.

[409] Cf. ATV 429, 9—10.

[410] Ibid. 416, 3—6.

[411] Cf. NKus 209, 5 and the NKusBo to it.

[412] Ibid. 479, 8.

[413] Cf. Kir 151, 3.

[414] To speak only of Udayana, see NKus 495, 4; ATV 429, 4—5; Kir 104, 17.

omniscience need not necessarily be eternal. The specific feature that distinguishes the cognition of Īśvara from that of the omniscient yogins is that, while the omniscience of the latter is acquired, that of Īśvara is not acquired[415], but belongs to his very nature as self-existent (*svataḥsiddha-* or *sāṃsiddhika-*)[416]; he was ever omniscient and so will he ever be.

The eternity (*nityatvam*) of the cognition of Īśvara follows from the fact that it is not produced. The production of cognition necessarily requires as cause, as we said earlier, a body. In order to establish that Īśvara's cognition is not produced, our author argues that Īśvara possesses no body. He denies in Īśvara any kind of body that might serve as the cause of his cognition. A visible (*dṛśya-*) body of his is contradicted by direct perception, since it is not perceived. Nor can it be supposed that he has an invisible (*adṛśya-*) body; for even such a body will have parts (*sāvayava-*) and material form (*mūrta-*), and consequently it will not be able to enter unbroken or without injury (*abhagna-*) the crevices of rocks or the interspace between two compact stones in order to create there bodies of frog etc. It cannot be thought that he possesses a body which is atomic in size; for such a body cannot serve as the substratum of senses, since, in the absence of space, it would not be able to contain Manas, the inner sense, which is absolutely necessary as cause of produced cognition. And a Manas that exists outside of a body cannot be of use in the production of cognition. For, if the Manas were able to produce cognition even independent of a body, then body would be of no use for cognition. Nor can it be thought that a bodied Īśvara will be able to act, like the sun, even from a very great distance (*daviṣṭha eva*); for the direction (*adhiṣṭhānam*) of the causes that produce even the frog etc. in the space between compact rocks is impossible without his effort (*prayatnaḥ*) reaching to them. But the effort of a bodied agent cannot be such. And it cannot be thought that, even without reaching the causes through effort, an agent can create through the contact of mere intention (*uddeśamātrasaṃbandhaḥ*), since, in that case, we too would have been able to produce effects through mere intention or desire. Moreover, when Īśvara is said to direct the causes, what is meant is an immediate direction (*sākṣād adhiṣṭhānam*), and not a mediate direction of causes through a body. Udayana concludes his arguments with the short but significant remark: "But, as there is not even the smell of a body at the beginning of creation, there is absolute absence of body (in Īśvara, and his) cognition being (thus) uncaused, omniscience is inevitable, because of the special nature of the one cause"[417].

Important for us to note in this context is not so much the arguments themselves for the absence of body in Īśvara as the reason why Udayana brings them forward. He wants to make it clear that, in the absence of a

---

[415] Cf. NM I 99, 24—26.

[416] Ibid. 100, 1 (= *sāṃsiddhika*); ATV 411, 3 (= *svataḥsiddha*).

[417] Cf. ATV 411, 5—413, 6: ... *sargādau tu na śarīragandho 'pīti sarvathā kalevaravigamād akāraṇatayā buddheḥ sarvajñatvam anivāryaṃ viśeṣāt kartur ekasyeti.*

body in Īśvara, his cognition cannot be considered as produced; for, as he points out in an earlier passage which we have already quoted, it has been established by concomitance and non-concomitance that a body is absolutely necessary as the cause of every produced cognition.

There is a small passage in the Lakṣaṇamālā which, though occurring in a different context, also shows that Īśvara's cognition is unproduced. While enumerating and defining the objects of cognition (*prameyam*), Udayana defines soul (*ātmā*) as "the substratum of (qualities such as) cognition etc."[418]. After commenting on the words contained in the definition, he adds: "One should not make (that is: 'define') it as the inherent cause of cognition, since (such a definition of soul) would not include Īśvara"[419]. The definition of soul (*ātmā*) must be such as to be applicable to all the souls, and since, as we have seen, Īśvara is a soul, it should be applicable also to him. With regard to all the souls (including Īśvara) it can be said that they are the substratum of their specific qualities such as cognition etc. Although the ordinary souls possess nine specific qualities, not all of them are found in Īśvara, and when Udayana defines 'soul' as the substratum of cognition etc., the expression 'etc.' (*ādi*) should not be interpreted to include all the specific qualities of the soul, but only those that are common to the ordinary souls and Īśvara, namely cognition, desire and effort. More important for us here than this definition itself is his remark that the soul should not be defined as the inherent cause (*samavāyikāraṇam*) of cognition, since such a characteristic is not applicable to Īśvara. By this remark our author wants to point out that, although the ordinary souls are not only the substratum, but also the inherent cause of cognition, the soul called Īśvara has no relation of a cause, but only that of a substratum, with regard to his cognition. A cognition that has no relation to the soul as its inherent cause cannot be said to be produced; it must be eternal.

The idea that Īśvara is only the substratum of cognition but not its cause, occurs also in a passage of his Nyāyakusumāñjali. An opponent objects that Īśvara's cognition cannot be said to be a valid cognition (*pramā*), since, being eternal, it is not the fruit of an act of cognition. Nor can it be said to be a means of valid cognition (*pramāṇam*) since it does not produce cognition. Consequently, he concludes, there is no cognizer (*pramātā*) that is its substratum[420]. In his answer Udayana defines valid cognition as correct experience (*samīcīno 'nubhavaḥ*) irrespective of the fact whether it is eternal or non-eternal. He concedes that the act of cognition of Īśvara does not produce valid cognition in himself, since it has no causal relation with his cognition. But he points out that the 'nature of cognizer' (*pramātṛtvam*) of Īśvara consists only in this that valid cognition inheres in him[421]. "It is, indeed, the inherence of valid cognition that is the cause of the usage (of the term) 'subject of valid cognition'; but the cause of the usage (of the term) 'means of valid cognition' is the relation to valid cognition through inseparable associa-

[418] LM 20, 25: . . . *tatra jñānādyadhikaraṇam ātmā.*
[419] Ibid. 20, 27: *jñānasamavāyikāraṇam iti na kartavyam, īśvarāvyāpakatvāt.*
[420] Cf. NKus 475, 1—2.
[421] Ibid. 475, 7—476, 2.

tion. And both these are (found) in Īśvara"[422]. It is in this sense—and in this sense alone—that Īśvara can be said to be the subject of valid cognition (*pramātā*) and his cognition a means of valid cognition (*pramāṇam*). Here again Udayana shows that the cognition of Īśvara has no cause, but that it is unproduced. The relation between Īśvara and his cognition is not that of cause and effect (*kāryakāraṇabhāvaḥ*), but merely that of inherence (*samavāyaḥ*) in as far as his eternal cognition inheres in him as its substratum.

The cognition of Īśvara is not only an eternal omniscience, but it is also one single act. In the fourth Stabaka of the Nyāyakusumāñjali we come across a passage where the Mīmāṃsakas argue that, even granting for argument's sake that there is an Īśvara, his cognition would not be valid (*pramā*), since it would lack the characteristic mark of a valid cognition, namely that it should be the cognition of what has not already been cognized (*agṛhīta-grāhitvam*). But such a cognition of what has not already been cognized, they maintain, is not possible in the case of Īśvara, since he is said to be eternally omniscient[423]. After refuting the definition of valid cognition as proposed by these opponents, Udayana observes that even supposing that their criterion of valid cognition is correct, the cognition of Īśvara cannot be said to be invalid, since it does not have the nature of a cognition of what has already been cognized (*gṛhītagrāhitvam*); "for the universe is not the object of another (i. e. a second) cognition of his"[424]. In other words, due to the absence of a second act or successive acts in the cognition of Īśvara, it cannot have the characteristic of a cognition of what has already been cognized which, in the eyes of the Mīmāṃsakas, would render it invalid. For 'cognition of what has (already) been cognized' (*gṛhītagrāhitvam*) presupposes at least two acts of cognition: an anterior act by which an object is cognized and a posterior act which cognizes the very object of the first cognition. The denial of such a cognition in Īśvara is at the same time the denial of anteriority and posteriority, in other words, the denial of a plurality of acts in the cognition of Īśvara. The opponent might still object that, even if Īśvara has no plurality of acts of cognition, there is nevertheless the defect of its being a cognition of what has already been cognized, since Īśvara would cognize in the second moment what he has already cognized in an earlier moment. Foreseeing such an objection our author remarks: "Nor does that same (single) cognition of Īśvara cease to be valid through difference of time; for it does not cease to be independent. Or, if it would nevertheless be invalid, then there would be too wide an application of the principle"[425]. Udayana means that Īśvara's cognition, which is accepted to be valid, cannot lose its characteristic of validity

---

422 Ibid. 476, 5—6: *pramāsamavāyo hi pramātṛvyavahāranimittaṃ, pramayā tv ayogavyavacchedena sambandhaḥ pramāṇavyavahāranimittaṃ, tad ubhayañ ceśvare.*

423 Ibid. 450, 4—6.

424 Ibid. 458, 4—459, 2: *na ca gṛhītagrāhitvam īśvarajñānasya, tadīyajñānāntarāgocaratvād viśvasya.*

425 Ibid. 459, 1—2: *na ca tad eva jñānaṃ kālabhedenāpramāṇam, anapekṣasyāparāvṛtteḥ. tathāpi vā aprāmāṇye 'tiprasaṅgād iti.*

at another point of time, since it is independent of the time-factor, as it is independent of all causes. Were it not so, the opponents would be obliged to accept that every valid cognition would become invalid in the succeeding points of time, a consequence which they would not be ready to accept. Udayana thus shows that Īśvara's cognition, being eternal, has neither a before nor an after, but is an ever-existing single act that embraces all objects of cognition. Although the intention of the author of this passage was to point out to the opponent that the cognition of Īśvara could not but be valid, his explanation shows that he conceives of it as a single act, an idea expressed also, though in another context, in a passing remark in his Kiraṇāvalī[426].

An important direct consequence of the eternal omniscience of Īśvara is that it embraces all objects of cognition[427], for a cognition that is limited to certain objects is necessarily non-eternal[428]. An opponent brings forward an objection against the all-embracing nature of the cognition of Īśvara. If Īśvara were to know all cognizable objects he would cognize also the erroneous cognitions (*vibhramaḥ*) of people like us, whereby his own cognition would turn out to be erroneous. Udayana answers this objection by pointing out that the conclusion of the adversary is incorrect. The cognition of Īśvara does not become vitiated by cognizing the erroneous cognitions of people like us, since he cognizes them as well as the objects that occasion them, as they really are. Thus he knows the erroneous cognition of a person who mistakes nacre as silver; but he cognizes it as an erroneous cognition and the nacre as nacre. Thus he cannot himself be said to be in error[429].

The most important characteristic mark of Īśvara's cognition is that it is eternal omniscience; all other details flow from this central fact. We have already spoken of the singleness (*ekatvam*) of the cognition of Īśvara. Other minor traits of it can be met with in brief remarks of Udayana. That Īśvara's cognition has no beginning follows from its eternality; for the same reason it will also have no end. But our author speaks of the cognition of Īśvara as endless (*ananta-*) also in another sense, namely in as far as its object is without end[430]. It is also said to be uninterrupted since it is always in conjunction with its object[431], an idea that is intimately related to the conception of the singleness of his act of cognition. It cannot be considered as inference or verbal testimony, since it is not produced by means of a logical reason (*liṅgam*) or words of others. On the other hand, it has the nature of a direct perception of the object (*sākṣātkāraḥ*). Hence it is to be considered as the means of valid cognition called direct perception (*pratyakṣam*), and not as any other of the means of valid cognition recognized by the school[432]. This does not, however, mean that Īśvara's direct perception of things is effected in

---

426 Cf. Kir 259, 10.
427 Ibid. 213, 15—16.
428 Cf. ATV 390, 3—6.
429 Cf. NKus 477, 3—11.
430 Cf. Kir 259, 13—14.
431 Cf. NKus 478, 1—2.
432 Ibid. 476, 13—497, 2.

dependence upon senses, as is the case with our direct perception of things. For, on the one hand, due to the absence of a body, he cannot possess senses; on the other, being unproduced or eternal, his cognition does not stand in need of senses. Moreover, the direct perception of Īśvara, unlike ours, goes even beyond the realm of objects that can be perceived by the senses. Hence it can be said to be direct perception (*pratyakṣam*) only in an analogical sense[433]. It is, in short, an immediate cognition which is co-eternal with Īśvara himself and has for its object all things.

b) Other specific qualities (*viśeṣaguṇaḥ*) of Īśvara.

Two other specific qualities ascribed to the souls in general are also attributed to Īśvara by the author of the Nyāyakusumāñjali, namely the qualities of desire (*icchā*) and effort (*prayatnaḥ*). Although we have no explanation of the nature of these qualities in his hitherto published works, we can glean from his occasional remarks as well as from the tradition of the school how he conceived of them.

Desire is defined by Praśastapāda as "the longing for that which is unobtained, be it for one's own self or for another"[434]. It is produced through the conjunction of the soul and Manas, in dependence upon pleasure or remembrance of pleasurable things. While the nature of desire given in the above definition is applicable to the desire of Īśvara, the explanation of its origin cannot be applied to it. For, though his desire has the nature of a longing to make other beings attain something that they do not possess, it has no cause, as it is unproduced (*svataḥsiddha-*) or eternal[435]. Being eternal, the desire of Īśvara is also one (*eka-*). When we speak of his desire to destroy (*sañjihīrṣā*) or of his desire to create (*cikīrṣā*), as though there were more acts of desire in Īśvara, we impute to it a distinction merely on the basis of the difference of external conditioning factors (*upādhibhedāt*)[436]. Thus when the external conditioning factors are those that determine the creation of the universe, the eternal desire of Īśvara becomes specified as desire to create (*cikīrṣā*). Similarly when the external conditioning factors are those that determine the dissolution of the universe, the eternal desire of Īśvara becomes specified as desire to destroy (*sañjihīrṣā*). In the same manner, when we speak of the origination (*utpattiḥ*) of the desire of Īśvara to create or to destroy, what is meant by it is that the external conditioning factor determining his one and eternal desire, either as desire to create or as desire to destroy, has come into being. This external conditioning factor is the particular time (*kālaviśeṣaḥ*) described in the scriptures as the end of one-hundred Brahmā-

---

[433] An essential feature of *pratyakṣam* is *indriyārthasannikarṣotpanna(tva)m* (cf. NSu I, 1, 4), and this is absent in the perception of Īśvara, since he has no *indriyāṇi*.

[434] PDhS 348, 16: *svārthaṃ parārthaṃ vā'prāptaprārthanecchā*. Cf. E. Frauwallner: Geschichte II, p. 232.

[435] Cf. ATV 411, 3.

[436] Cf. Kir 91, 12—13.

years[437]. In a passage of the Ātmatattvaviveka which we studied in connection with the cognition of Īśvara we came across a statement according to which, even when an agent is capable of producing the effect, actual production may not take place if the co-operating causes are absent[438]. Although the desire of Īśvara is eternal, the absence of continuous dissolution (*pralayaḥ*) and creation (*sargaḥ*) is accounted for by the fact that the co-operating causes are absent.

Desire to obtain something that one does not already possess leads to a striving or effort (*prayatnaḥ*) to attain it. According to the Vaiśeṣikas, effort is of two kinds: that which presupposes life (*jīvanapūrvaka-*) and that which presupposes desire or aversion (*icchādveṣapūrvaka-*)[439]. The first kind of effort which impels a person to breathe while asleep and, when he is awake, causes the union of the Manas with the other senses is produced by the conjunction of the soul and Manas and in dependence upon the merit and demerit (*dharmādharmāpekṣa-*) of the person. The second kind is the cause of an operation capable of attaining a desired object or of avoiding what is undesired, and it supports the body; it is produced by the conjunction of the soul and Manas and in dependence upon desire or aversion. In speaking of the effort of Īśvara we have to modify these definitions so as to be applicable to it. It goes without saying that it is only the second kind of effort that is to be ascribed to Īśvara and that too with certain qualifications.

Like his cognition and desire, the effort (*prayatnaḥ*) of Īśvara is unproduced or eternal[440]. As it is eternal and consequently one act in itself, any distinction that we may attribute to it is merely based on the external conditioning factors or objects. It is solely through his effort, though guided by cognition and desire with regard to its object, that Īśvara creates, maintains and destroys the universe, and, as we have seen, not through the medium of a body.

In the Ātmatattvaviveka an opponent poses a problem: although the body is a necessary presupposition for ordinary cognition, the Nyāya-Vaiśeṣikas maintain that where cognition is eternal, a body is of no use. If that is so, one could argue in a similar manner that, though ordinary effort presupposes cognition as its cause, an effort that is eternal, such as that of Īśvara, would not require cognition and desire[441]. In his answer Udayana points out that effort has a double property, first in as far as it is the effect of cognition (*jñānakāryam*) and secondly in as far as it has for its object only the cognition (*jñānaikaviṣayaḥ*). It is true that the effort of Īśvara, being eternal, does not stand in need of cognition for its origination; but it does depend upon cognition for its object[442]. For effort, of its own nature, does not have an inclination

[437] Ibid. 91, 13—15.

[438] Cf. ATV 410, 8—9.

[439] Cf. PDhS 349, 14ff.; Cf. E. Frauwallner: Geschichte II, pp. 232—233.

[440] Cf. ATV 411, 3—4.

[441] Cf. ATV 380, 5—7; Kir 101, 15—19.

[442] NKus 499, 4—5: *na ca prayatna ātmalābhārtham eva matim apekṣate, viṣayalābhārtham apy apekṣaṇāt.*

towards any specific object. As a matter of fact, the distinction between effort and cognition consists in this that the former has an inclination towards an object (*viṣayapravaṇaḥ*), while the latter has not. An effort that is not directed towards a determined object is inconceivable. Hence, even though the effort of Īśvara is eternal, it requires cognition, also eternal like itself[443], in order that it may be inclined towards a determinate object. A non-eternal cognition would not be able to determine an eternal effort, since it would not have its object in that way. Nor can it be maintained that Īśvara's effort will have its determination of object in the same manner as in the case of the effort that presupposes life (*jīvanapūrvakaprayatnaḥ*); for this latter is of a different kind, since its determination towards an object is effected without desire, while the effort of Īśvara is guided by his desire which in its turn is specified by his cognition.

The Nyāya-Vaiśeṣikas have recognized an intimate relationship between the three qualities, cognition (*jñānam*), desire (*icchā*) and effort (*prayatnaḥ*)[444]. When these qualities are non-eternal, cognition is produced in dependence upon senses and objects; desire is produced in dependence upon cognition; and effort in dependence upon cognition and desire. As these qualities are eternal in Īśvara they have no dependence on other causes or on each other for their being; the desire and effort of Īśvara, however, need determination or specification as far as their objects are concerned.

So far we have seen that, in the view of Udayana, Īśvara possesses three of the nine specific qualities (*viśeṣaguṇaḥ*) ascribed to the souls (*ātmā*) by the Nyāya-Vaiśeṣikas. It now remains to see whether he ascribes to him also some other of the remaining six specific qualities: pleasure (*sukham*), pain (*duḥkham*), aversion (*dveṣaḥ*), merit (*dharmaḥ*), demerit (*adharmaḥ*) and mental impressions (*saṃskāraḥ*).

Like the Nyāya-Vaiśeṣikas before him, Udayana denies in Īśvara the qualities of demerit, pain, aversion and mental impressions. The root cause for the absence of these qualities in him is his omniscience; for these qualities originate ultimately from false knowledge (*mithyājñānam*) which consists, according to the Nyāya, in identifying the self with what it really is not. Since Īśvara is omniscient, he is free from all false knowledge[445]. Being free from false knowledge, he possesses no 'faults' (*doṣaḥ*) which are considered to be the source of human actions. In the absence of 'faults' in him, there is no activity that results from them. As there is in him no activity that results from 'faults', he does not have demerit (*adharmaḥ*)[446], nor pain (*duḥkham*) that results from demerit. Being free from pain, he is also free from aversion (*dveṣaḥ*). Since his cognition is an eternal perception, there arise in him no mental impressions (*saṃskāraḥ*), nor does he require them.

---

[443] Ibid. 499, 7—9.
[444] Cf. NVTT 956, 20—22.
[445] Cf. NKus 495, 4—5; ATV 410, 1—2.
[446] Cf. NKus 495, 5.

There remain only two more specific qualities, namely merit (*dharmaḥ*) and pleasure (*sukham*) the presence of which in Īśvara we have still to consider. It is to be borne in mind that, while no Nyāya-Vaiśeṣikas are known to have ascribed the qualities of demerit, pain, aversion and mental impressions to Īśvara, there were some who maintained that he possessed merit and pleasure[447]. Udayana himself denies both these qualities in Īśvara. On account of the absence of 'faults' in him, he has, as we observed, no activity resulting from them, and consequently he is devoid of merit, as he is of demerit[448]. Pleasure has been conceived of as the fruit of merit, and, as he has no merit, he cannot have pleasure[449]. Udayana traces back the absence of the experience of pleasure and pain (*bhogaḥ*) in Īśvara to his eternal omniscience[450]. The absence of pleasure in Īśvara is also accounted for by the fact that pleasure presupposes not only the direct perception of the object (*viṣayasākṣātkāraḥ*), but also the contact of the object with the senses (*indriyārthasannikarṣaḥ*); but, since such a contact is impossible in the case of Īśvara, he cannot have pleasure[451]. Though he has no pleasure, there is in him absolute absence of pain (*atyantaduḥkhābhāvaḥ*)[452]. When Udayana speaks of Īśvara as the repository of bliss (*ānandanidhiḥ*) in one of his concluding verses[453], the term should not be interpreted as meaning that he possesses pleasure (*sukham*). The concluding verses, as we said, belong to a genre different from the purely philosophical. The author here refers to one of the attributes ascribed to Brahman in the Upaniṣads. Although he identifies the Supreme Brahman with the Īśvara, still the attributes of one cannot be transferred to the other without some modifications. The term *ānandaḥ* (bliss) in the expression *ānandanidhiḥ* should, therefore, be interpreted here in the context of the Nyāya-Vaiśeṣika philosophy, only as meaning the absence of pain (*duḥkhābhāvaḥ*). Īśvara can in this sense be said to be *ānandanidhiḥ*, since he is absolutely free from any kind of pain. Perhaps it is even better to interpret this expression in terms of the other beings; it would then mean that he is the source of bliss for the other beings, in as far as he helps them to attain liberation and thus reach the state of absolute freedom from pain.

Concluding our inquiry into the specific qualities of Īśvara, we see that Udayana ascribes to him only three of the nine specific qualities ascribed to the ordinary soul, namely the qualities of cognition (*jñānam*), desire (*icchā*) and effort (*prayatnaḥ*). All these three qualities are eternal in him and have all things for their object.

---

447 E. g., Pakṣilasvāmin (5th century A. D) admitted *dharmaḥ* in Īśvara (cf. NBh 943, 7). Jayanta (9th century A. D) ascribed to Īśvara both *dharmaḥ* and *sukham* (cf. NM I 185, 4—6.

448 NKus 495, 5: *doṣānutpattau dharmādharmayor asattvāt.*

449 ATV 422, 5: . . . *dharmābhāve tu tatkāryasya sukhasyāpy abhāve* . . .

450 NKus 495, 4: *na ca nityasarvajñasya bhogasaṃbhāvanā 'pi.*

451 Cf. NVTP 527, 10—530, 9.

452 Cf. Kir 90, 20: *tasya* (= *īśvarasya*) *atyantaduḥkhābhāvavataḥ* . . .

453 Cf. NKus 576, 2.

In the first verse of the fifth Stabaka our author speaks of Īśvara as immutable (*avyayaḥ*). Later on he explains what he means by this term: "Immutability consists in the absence of adventitious specific qualities"[454]. In other words, he excludes from Īśvara all specific qualities that are produced or non-eternal.

c) Generic qualities (*sāmānyaguṇaḥ*) of Īśvara.

Although Udayana has not dealt with the qualities of Īśvara as a theme for itself, we were able to reconstruct his conception of the specific qualities of Īśvara from his occasional remarks. The situation is more difficult with regard to his generic qualities which have practically not been touched upon in any of his available writings. However, we have every reason to believe that, like his predecessors, Udayana ascribed to Īśvara all the five generic qualities ascribed to the souls, namely number (*saṃkhyā*), size (*parimāṇam*), individuality (*pṛthaktvam*), conjunction (*saṃyogaḥ*) and disjunction (*vibhāgaḥ*); for these qualities are predicated of all individual substances and hence can be attributed also to Īśvara.

Of these five qualities, number (*saṃkhyā*), that is to say, the question how many Īśvaras there are, seems to be the most important and it has been in an earlier period the object of much discussion. Thus the earlier exponents of the Nyāya-Vaiśeṣika theism such as Praśastapāda, Uddyotakara, Vācaspatimiśra, Jayanta etc. have dealt at some length with this quality of Īśvara and established that Īśvara is only one (*ekaḥ*). Although Udayana has devoted a whole book to establish the existence of Īśvara, he does not specifically deal with this quality, a fact that strikes us all the more for two reasons. First, Jñānaśrī who was one of the formidable antagonists of the Nyāya-Vaiśeṣika theism, had brought forward some arguments against this particular quality of Īśvara[455], an objection to which our author himself probably refers very briefly in his Ātmatattvaviveka[456]. Secondly, in the introductory lines to his short excursus on Īśvara in his Kiraṇāvalī our author remarks that he will speak there not only of Īśvara's existence (*sattvam*), but also of how many Īśvaras there are, or, as he puts it, "of his many-ness"[457]. He does later deal with the existence of Īśvara, but we look there in vain for a separate treatment of the question of the number of Īśvaras.

That Udayana admitted Īśvara to be only one (*ekaḥ*) goes without saying[458]; for the theism which he advocates, and which has been traditionally maintained by the Nyāya-Vaiśeṣika school, is monotheism. It is also quite understandable that he does not speak specifically of this aspect of the Īśvara doctrine in his works. But as a matter of fact his arguments for the existence

---

454 NKus 506, 15—16: *avyayatvam āgantukaviśeṣaguṇaśūnyatvam.*
455 Cf. JMN 258, 26—260, 18; 269, 8—272, 22.
456 Cf. ATV 408, 5—6.
457 Kir 97, 10: *tadbahutve 'pi kiñcid ucyate.*
458 Cf. ATV 413, 5—6: ... *sarvajñatvam anivāryam, viśeṣāt kartur ekasya.*

of Īśvara as the creator of the universe necessarily imply that Īśvara is one, and not many. Likewise, the qualities that are ascribed to him, especially eternal omniscience, make it clear that a second (or more) Īśvara is not only not necessary, but also incompatible with the functions of Īśvara[459]. Hence, he did not, really speaking, need to treat separately of the one-ness of Īśvara.

The fact that Udayana offers, at the beginning of some of his works, his salutation to deities other than Īśvara does not go against his conception of Īśvara as one. It is true that in the opening verse of his Pariśuddhi he bows again and again (*punaḥ punaḥ*) to Mother Sarasvatī and prays her so to guide him that he may not err while commenting upon the Nyāyavārttikatātparyaṭīkā of Vācaspati. Such a prayer is easily understandable, since this goddess is venerated among the Hindus as the patroness of learning and wisdom. In the same manner, Udayana's worship of god Sūrya (*viśvatastviṭ*) in the opening verse of his Kiraṇāvalī can be accounted for by the fact that the worship of this god seems to have been current among the Śaivites of his period[460]. It should, moreover, be borne in mind that a perfect and pure monotheism without any other subsidiary deity by the side of the Supreme God has never been the tradition of Hinduism and that even philosophic thinkers who accepted only one Supreme Being as the creator and master of the universe did worship other deities, especially those of popular devotion. But these thinkers make a clear distinction between Īśvara and the other minor deities. A passage in Kiraṇāvalī shows very clearly that Udayana does not place Īśvara on a par with the other gods, not even as a *primus inter pares*, but above them all and superior to them all. Explaining the word *maheśvaraḥ* which occurs in the section on creation and dissolution of the universe in the Padārthadharmasaṃgraha, he observes that, while the other gods such as Indra, Varuṇa and Yama are lords, each of a particular part of the universe, the Maheśvara or the Supreme Lord is the lord of the universe in its entirety[461]. In the same vein he also calls Īśvara "God even of the gods" (*devānām api devaḥ*)[462].

As regards the second generic quality, namely the size (*parimāṇam*) of Īśvara, I have come across no statement of Udayana. But it is beyond all doubt that he conceived of it as absolute greatness (*paramamahattvam*) or, as it is often termed, all-pervasiveness (*vibhutvam*). Such is the size that has

---

[459] There is close relationship between omniscience and one-ness of Īśvara. Cf. ATV 408, 5—6; 410, 6—8 (cf. Nārāyaṇī to it); JMN 258, 27—259, 3.

[460] J. GONDA points out that, from the sixth century onwards, the god Sūrya came to be worshipped by certain groups of people as a very important deity together with Viṣṇu, Śiva and Brahmā (Die Religionen Indiens, Vol. II, p. 60), that in the post-epic Hinduism the number of Sun-worshippers must have been large (ibid. pp. 63—64), and that in the Saura-Purāṇa (12th century ?) Śiva is even identified with the Sun-God (ibid. p. 56). The same author remarks elsewhere: "Those who adore the Sun are for instance said actually to worship Śiva" (Viṣṇuism and Śivaism, p. 13).

[461] Cf. Kir 91, 9—11: *anye hīśvarā jagadekadeśapataya indravaruṇayamādayaḥ. sa punaḥ kṛtsnasyaiva jagataḥ, ato mahān īśvaraḥ.*

[462] Cf. NKus 449, 4.

been ascribed to the souls in general by Udayana[463]. It is through his all-pervasiveness that Īśvara is present everywhere and can operate everywhere. More details about his omnipresence are unfortunately lacking.

The individuality (*pṛthaktvam*) of Īśvara is that quality on account of which he is distinct from all other substances[464], and it follows from his being numerically distinct from them.

The last two generic qualities of Īśvara are conjunction (*saṃyogaḥ*) and disjunction (*vibhāgaḥ*) in as far as he becomes conjoined to or disjoined from other substances. The Nyāya-Vaiśeṣikas have never accepted *actio in distans*; rather they insisted that the efficient cause must be, directly or at least indirectly, in contact with the other causes so that it can guide their activity[465]. But this view poses certain problems. The conjunction and disjunction of all-pervasive (*vibhu-*) substances such as Ether, Time, Space and Soul with the substances of limited size (*mūrta-*) such as the atoms can be explained, according to the Vaiśeṣika view, by the movement on the part of the substance of limited size[466]. But the contact between the all-pervasive substances among themselves posed a great problem, since due to their all-pervasiveness no movement whatever can be had on the part of the substances in question. This problem was of special importance in the Īśvara doctrine, since Īśvara who is all-pervasive has to come into contact with the souls, which are also considered all-pervasive, in order to guide the Adṛṣṭam inhering in them. Udayana does not tell us how this contact is brought about, but we can infer it from his statements concerning the conjunction and disjunction of the other all-pervasive substances. We shall here touch upon only the essential points without entering into the details of this intricate problem.

Following the view of Praśastapāda, he rejects the possibility of conjunction (*saṃyogaḥ*) between the all-pervasive substances[467]. A conjunction between them would be unproduced and eternal; for a movement that would disjoin them is impossible since they are all-pervasive. But an unproduced conjunction (*ajaḥ saṃyogaḥ*) is denied by the Vaiśeṣikas[468]. Although there is thus no possibility of a direct conjunction of Īśvara and the souls, the Nyāya-Vaiśeṣikas have assumed that there is an indirect conjunction effected by means of substances of limited size (*mūrta-*) such as the atoms which are eternal. The individual souls are in conjunction with the atoms and these atoms are in conjunction with Īśvara, so that there is an indirect conjunction between the individual souls and Īśvara. This indirect conjunction may also

---

[463] The view held by S. RADHAKRISHNAN (in his Indian Philosophy Vol. II, p. 149, footnote 2) that Udayana views the soul "not bigger than an atom in size though capable of pervading the body" is untenable. Cf. ATV 368, 6f. where Udayana explicitly states that *ātmā* is *vibhuḥ*. See also Kir 223, 10—11.

[464] Cf. Kir 218, 2—5.

[465] Udayana himself rejects the view that Īśvara could produce effects from a distance without contact. Cf. ATV 411, 11ff.

[466] Cf. Kir 223, 10—13; NKand 349, 1—2.

[467] Cf. Kir 228, 20—22; 229, 11—14.

[468] Cf. PDhS 226, 3; Kir 26, 5; 228, 16—22. See also E. FRAUWALLNER: Geschichte II, p. 223ff.

be explained by taking the Manas, which is also eternal, to be the connecting link between the individual souls and Īśvara[469].

What we said of conjunction applies, *mutatis mutandis*, also to disjunction (*vibhāgaḥ*). As he rejected an unproduced conjunction, Udayana denies also an unproduced disjunction (*ajo vibhāgaḥ*)[470]; the disjunction between the eternal all-pervasive substances takes place only indirectly through the medium of limited (*mūrta-*) substances like the atoms[471].

While speaking of the qualities of Īśvara, Śrīdhara who was probably a contemporary of Udayana, mentions two theories, one holding that Īśvara possesses only six qualities (*ṣaḍguṇādhikaraṇa īśvaraḥ*) and the other maintaining that he has eight qualities (*aṣṭaguṇādhikaraṇa īśvaraḥ*)[472]. In both views five of the qualities are the five generic qualities (*sāmānyaguṇāḥ*), namely number (*saṃkhyā*), size (*parimāṇam*), individuality (*pṛthaktvam*), conjunction (*saṃyogaḥ*) and disjunction (*vibhāgaḥ*). Thus the upholders of the first view admitted in Īśvara only one specific quality (*viśeṣaguṇaḥ*), namely cognition (*jñānam*). They, however, seem to have ascribed to this cognition also functions of desire and effort. Those who admit eight qualities in Īśvara—and most of the Nyāya-Vaiśeṣikas we know follow this view—ascribe to him, in addition to the five generic qualities enumerated above, three specific qualities of cognition (*jñānam*), desire (*icchā*) and effort (*prayatnaḥ*). From our study of Udayana's view of the qualities of Īśvara it is clear that he follows this second view.

At the close of our study of the nature and qualities of Īśvara, we can say in summing up that Udayana has followed the tradition of the school as regards these aspects of the Īśvara doctrine. Īśvara is indeed to be brought under the class of soul (*ātmā*), but he does not resemble the ordinary souls in all respects. In spite of the fact that Īśvara and the ordinary souls belong to the same class through the possession of 'soul-ness' (*ātmatvam*), there are differences between them that mark them off from each other. First of all, Īśvara is but one (*eka eva*), while the ordinary souls are many (*nānā*) in number. There are, in fact, endless numbers of ordinary souls. Furthermore, not all the specific qualities found in the ordinary souls are found in Īśvara; for, as we saw, while these possess no less than nine specific qualities, Īśvara possesses, according to Udayana, only three of them. Finally, even these three specific qualities that are found in Īśvara, though found also in the ordinary souls, are found in him in a mode more perfect than in them; for in Īśvara these qualities are eternal (*nitya-*) or unproduced (*akārya-*), while they are non-eternal or produced in the ordinary souls. Since the qualities of cognition, desire and effort are inseparably present in Īśvara, he possesses them at all times, while these qualities, being produced in the ordinary souls in dependence upon body, will be absent in them during their separation from the body, be it during the periodical dissolutions or in their state of final liberation.

[469] Cf. NV and NVTT 957, 4—7 and 957, 18—19 respectively; NVTP 5, 1—3; Kir 223, 10—13; 228, 14—16.

[470] Cf. Kir 233, 12—13.

[471] Ibid. 228, 14—16.

[472] NKand 142, 1—8.

Chapter Five

CONCLUDING REMARKS

In the preceding pages we have tried to give a brief account of Udayana's doctrine of Īśvara. We have exposed the different proofs for the existence of Īśvara and considered his relation to the universe, the motives of his action, his nature and qualities. It would be interesting now to take account of the personal contribution of our author to the Nyāya-Vaiśeṣika Īśvara doctrine. We shall first consider his contribution to the establishment of the existence of Īśvara, not only because it forms the central theme of the Nyāyakusumāñjali, but also because some scholars question Udayana's personal contribution precisely on this point. Their view in its most pronounced form can be thus stated in brief: the arguments for the existence of Īśvara found in the Nyāyakusumāñjali are, all of them, traceable in their basic form in the extant works of his predecessors such as Pakṣilasvāmin, Uddyotakara, Vācaspati and Bhāsarvajña or in the lost works of Aviddhakarṇa, Praśastamati, Śaṅkarasvāmin, Śatānanda and Trilocana, fragments of which can be found in the works of Buddhist authors like Śāntarakṣita, Kamalaśīla, Jñānaśrī and Ratnakīrti. Udayana has merely taken the arguments of his predecessors and given a clear exposition of them with the addition of some details such as new examples. He is thus said to be a mere compiler of the arguments that were already proposed before him and not a proponent of new, original proofs[473].

It would be incorrect to deny this contention as absolutely untrue. But in the opinion of the present writer the dependence of Udayana on the already existing material should not be so exaggerated as to minimize his own positive contribution. While pointing out his indebtedness to his predecessors we must also give him his due. We shall, therefore, consider briefly what materials he had before him and what contribution he himself has made.

The first proof based on *kāryatvam* of the earth etc. has been the traditional proof of the school, and it is not Udayana's as regards both its form and its content. But when one compares the elaborate discussion of the proof that follows its very brief formulation with the material given by previous Nyāya authors, one can certainly see that Udayana has not been reproducing old material, but really contributing something of his own. A survey of the history of the development of the Īśvara doctrine shows that it was not merely a matter of bringing in additional doctrines or proofs, but also of adapting the

---

[473] Such is the view maintained by Kishore Nath Jha in his (Sanskrit) article *nyāyakusumāñjalau prācīnācāryaprabhāvaḥ* in Ṛtam Vol. I (1969), pp. 1ff.

existing material, by means of necessary explanations and modifications, to the current standard of content and form, so that it might keep pace with the general advancement of the philosophical thinking of the time. The development of the Nyāya-Vaiśeṣika Īśvara doctrine can be understood only in the context of the controversy with the opponents, and re-adjustment of arguments was necessary according to the stage of progress of the controversy. In the discussion after the first proof Udayana meets the objections of the opponents of his own time—it is especially the Buddhists that are refuted there—and answers them. Thus even granting that the proof in itself has been formulated by earlier thinkers of the school, our author has built and improved upon it and brought it up to date.

The idea of the second proof can be traced back to earlier thinkers[474]. In fact it is very closely related to the first proof in as far as it considers the process of origination of the earth etc. as produced. The term *āyojanam*, however, in this context is, as far as can be verified from the available works, found in Udayana for the first time.

The third and fourth proofs based respectively on *dhṛtiḥ* and *saṃharaṇam* can be said to be Udayana's own contribution. The underlying ideas of these proofs, no doubt, were essential parts of the cosmology of the Nyāya-Vaiśeṣika school, but no earlier author is known to have formulated proofs for the existence of Īśvara based on these two ideas.

The fifth proof based on *padam* can be found, though in another formulation, in a fragment ascribed by Kamalaśīla to Praśastamati[475]. Whether the passage of Praśastamati contained more materials than what has been handed down by Kamalaśīla is not known. In any case, Udayana's treatment of the proof gives us some material on the controversy about the proof which cannot be traced in earlier writers.

The ideas behind the proofs based on *pratyayaḥ* and *śrutiḥ* can be traced in the works of previous authors, but an earlier formulation of proofs for the existence of Īśvara is not known to me.

The last two proofs based on *vākyatvam* and *saṃkhyā* can be traced back to earlier thinkers[476]. But when we compare the material offered by the author of the Nyāyakusumāñjali with that found in the works of his predecessors, it seems fair to conclude that, here also he does not just repeat the ideas that were already current, but rather works them out and formulates them anew according to the needs of his time.

Thus, although the fact that Udayana made use of the material offered by his predecessors cannot be denied, we should not lose sight of the perfection the author has brought to each of these proofs. He has assimilated the proofs for the existence of Īśvara that were current before him and made them

---

[474] Cf. NV 945, 11—14.

[475] Cf. TSP 54, 18—23: G. Chemparathy: The Īśvara doctrine of Praśastapāda, p. 68f.

[476] For the proof based on *vākyatvam*, see above pp. 99ff. The proof based on *saṃkhyā* is found in a fragment ascribed to Trilocana. Cf. RKN 36, 7—13. Note that Trilocana bases his proof only on the *dvitvasaṃkhyātvam*.

his own by formulating them anew in his own words and exposed them together with the discussions on them, thus bringing them up to date. It is precisely in this that the contribution of Udayana in the first series of proofs consists.

But a more positive and original contribution of Udayana can be noted in his second series of proofs for the existence of Īśvara. It is regrettable that those scholars who call in question or minimise the original contribution of our author to the proofs for the existence of Īśvara apparently do not take into account this series. It is true that in the works of Vācaspati and more especially of Jayanta the aspect of Īśvara as the author of the Veda has been dealt with[477]. It is also true that Jayanta has brought forward a proof to establish, against the view of the Mīmāṃsakas, that the Vedas must have an author[478]. But no Nyāya-Vaiśeṣika author before Udayana has brought forward a whole series of proofs based on the various aspects of the Veda to prove the existence of Īśvara as its author.

Passing now from the proofs for the existence of Īśvara to the other aspects of the Īśvara doctrine such as his nature, motives of activity or qualities, it can be conceded that Udayana hardly brings in any new idea which his predecessors had not touched upon. In his discussion on the cognition of Īśvara, however, we find ideas and arguments that are not found in works of the earlier authors[479]. But, as we said in the beginning of our study, since his main purpose in writing the Nyāyakusumāñjali was to defend the existence of Īśvara which was the aspect of the Īśvara doctrine most attacked by the opponents of his time, the other aspects of that doctrine are either neglected or made subservient to the aspect of the existence of Īśvara.

Concluding our consideration of Udayana's personal contribution to the doctrine of Īśvara we can say that it consists in a re-thinking of the problems of the Īśvara doctrine and a new understanding and formulation of them.

A fitting conclusion to our study of Udayana's Īśvara doctrine would be a reference to the introductory verse of the Ātmatattvaviveka which can be said to contain an epitome of his Īśvara doctrine:

"Salutation to that Father, the Lord of the worlds, the foremost of the ancient teachers, whose lordship is innate (to him); who, having at the beginning created the worlds, thereafter maintains (them); who causes (in the living beings) proficiency (in the usages of words etc.); who effects the injunctions with regard to what is salutary and the prohibitions with regard to what is not salutary; whose truthfulness of speech is congenital (i. e. natural) (to him); whose compassion is unconditioned; whose effort has the nature of having (only) that (= the worlds, especially the living beings) as its aim"[480].

---

[477] Cf. NVTT 566, 5ff.; NM I, 213, 18ff.

[478] Cf. NM I, 213, 23—214, 4.

[479] I have in mind especially the arguments for the eternity of Īśvara's cognition as mentioned above on pp. 171—173.

[480] ATV 1, 4—7:

svāmyaṃ yasya nijaṃ jagatsu janiteṣv ādau tataḥ pālanam
vyutpatteḥ karaṇaṃ hitāhitavidhivyāsedhasambhāvanam /
bhūtoktiḥ sahajā kṛpā nirupadhir yatnas tadarthātmakas
tasmai pūrvagurūttamāya jagatām īśāya pitre namaḥ //

Diverse functions of Īśvara with regard to the created universe, functions that characterize him as a father (*pītā*), are mentioned in this verse of salutation. Īśvara is the lord of all the worlds, and this lordship is not something acquired by him or adventitious to his nature, but connatural (*nija-*) to him. He is the creator and sustainer of the worlds. He is, besides, the foremost of ancient teachers and, being endowed with compassion, imparts his teachings to the living beings, instructing them not only as to what they should perform or refrain from, but also in all those usages of daily life necessary for this mundane existence. His instruction can be relied upon and accepted with absolute confidence; for his words are true (*bhūtoktiḥ*). Having no reason for deceiving others and being endowed with unconditioned or natural compassion, he will teach only what is true. Above all, he is a father towards his creatures and, like a good father, he desires nothing but the good of his children, the living beings. Having nothing to gain for himself, he directs his effort solely towards the good of the living beings.

APPENDIX

Editions, Commentaries and Translations of the Nyāyakusumāñjali:

The Nyāyakusumāñjali, as we remarked earlier, consists of Kārikās with elaborate prose explanations of them by Udayana himself. Some later writers have commented only on the Kārikās, while others commented on both the Kārikās and the prose explanations. Thus we have two kinds of commentaries on the work.

A) Editions of the Nyāyakusumāñjali with only the Kārikā Portion and Commentaries on them

The following editions are known to me:

1) Kusumāñjaliḥ śrīmad udayanācāryyaviracitaḥ. śrīharidāsabhaṭṭācāryyakṛtavyākhyānasahitaḥ. "government"-saṃsthāpitasaṃskṛtapāṭhaśālādhyakṣa śrīyuta vāvu rasamaya datta mahodayānām anujñayā saṃskṛtayantre mudritaḥ. Calcutta Śakābdaḥ 1769 [= A. D. 1847].

2) The same was reprinted in Bengali script in the Samvat year 1916 [= A. D. 1859].

3) The Kusumánjali, or Hindu proof of the existence of a Supreme Being, by Udayana Achárya, with the commentary of Hari Dása Bhaṭṭáchárya. Edited and translated by E. B. Cowell, assisted by Paṇḍita Maheśa Chandra Nyáyaratna. Calcutta 1864.

4) Kusumāñjaliḥ śrīmad udayanācāryaviracitaḥ śrī haridāsabhaṭṭācāryakṛtaṭīkayā samudbhāsitaḥ. vi e upādhidhāreṇa śrī *jīvānanda vidyāsāgara bhaṭṭācārya*eṇa saṃskṛtaḥ prakāśitaś ca. Calcutta 1885.

5) Kusumāñjali by Udayanācārya with commentary Kusumāñjaliṭīkā by Haridāsa Bhaṭṭācārya, with commentary Kusumāñjalikārikāvyākhyānam by Candrakānta Tarkālaṅkāra Bhaṭṭācārya. Calcutta 1888. [I could not consult this edition].

6) Kusumāñjalikārikā by Udayanācārya with commentary Kusumāñjalivyākhyāvivṛtiḥ by Kāmākhyānātha Tarkavāgīśa. Calcutta 1892; second edition: Calcutta 1917. [I could not consult this edition.]

7) Kusumanjali. A treatise on the Proof of the existence of God by Nyayacharya Sri Udayanacharya, with the commentary of Hari Das Bhattacharya; edited with his own notes by Pandit Ambadas Sastri. Benares 1913.

8) The Nyāya Kusumāñjali of Śrī Udayanāchārya with the Sanskrit commentary of Śrī Haridās Bhaṭṭāchārya. Edited with the 'Kusumāñjali Parimal' Hindi commentary by Āchārya Viśveśvar Siddhānta Śiromaṇi (= The Vidyabhavan Sanskrit Granthamala, No. 74), Varanasi 1962.

9) Śrīmad udayanācāryaviracitaḥ nyāya-kusumāñjaliḥ. śrīharidāsa-bhaṭṭācārya-viracitayā vṛttyā prabhākhyayā saṃskṛta-vyākhyayā ca vibhūṣitaḥ. vyākhyākāraḥ śrī*nārayaṇamiśraḥ*. Varanasi 1968.

10) Kusumāñjalikārikā of Udayanācārya. With the commentary Kusumāñjalivyākhyā of Rāmabhadra Sārvabhauma and Sanskrit Notes compiled by Chandidasa Nyaya-Tarkatirtha. Edited by NARENDRACHANDRA Vedantatirtha (= ASS, No. 2), Calcutta 1944.

Among the commentaries on the Kārikās the most popular one, as the above list of editions shows, is that of Haridāsa Bhaṭṭācārya, popularly known as Haridāsī. There is no absolute certainty about the date of its author, but it is generally believed that he wrote it in the sixteenth century.

Rāmabhadra Sārvabhauma is believed to have flourished in the seventeenth century. His commentary which is known, according to GOPINATH KAVIRAJ, as Āmoda in Mithila and Rāmabhadrī in Bengal, is not the work of a single author, but it was begun by Śaṅkaramiśra and completed by Rāmabhadra Sārvabhauma. In this way KAVIRAJ explains the parentage of the author mentioned in the second introductory verse of this commentary where the author is said to be the son of Bhavānī and Bhavanātha who are known to have been the parents of Śaṅkaramiśra.

It is specially to be noted that all the above editions of the Kārikās also contain the introductory prose passage of Udayana (NKus 14, 1—41, 1).

UMESHA MISHRA in his History of Indian Philosophy II, p. 194 gives a list of other less known commentaries on the Kārikas of the Nyāyakusumāñjali which are of a later date. See also NARENDRACHANDRA Vedantatirtha's edition of the Rāmabhadrī, Introduction, p. xlix where other commentaries are mentioned. Unfortunately I did not have the opportunity of consulting them. As far as I know, these exist only in manuscript form.

B) EDITIONS OF THE COMPLETE TEXT (I. E. KĀRIKĀS AND PROSE EXPLANATIONS) OF THE NYĀYAKUSUMĀÑJALI AND COMMENTARIES ON IT

The following editions are known to me:

1) The Nyaya-Kusumanjali Prakaranam by Udayanácharya. First Part containing the 1st, 2nd and 3rd Stavakas with the commentary of Varddhamána and the gloss of Ruchidatta, edited by CHANDRAKÁNTA Tarkálankár. Calcutta 1891. Second Part containing the 4th and 5th Stavakas with the commentary of Rucidatta and the gloss of Varddhamana, edited by CANDRAKĀNTA Tarkālaṅkāra. Calcutta 1895 (= BI, No. 123).

Remarks: This edition is based on 5 MSS. of the text of the NKus (Cfr. Sanskrit Introduction in Part II, p. 2—3), 6 MSS. of Prakāśa (Ibid. p. 3) and 3 MSS. of Makaranda (Ibid. p. 3).

2) Nyâya Kusumânjali, by Nyâyâchârya Sri Udayanâchârya. With the commentary of Mahâmahopâdhyâya Varddhamânopâdhyâya and the Gloss of Mahâmahopâdhyâya Ruchidatta. Edited by Pandit LAXMAN SHASTRI DRAVID. Benares 1912.

Remarks: There is neither Preface nor Introduction and hence nothing is known about the nature and number of the MSS. used. This edition has a great disadvantage for scientific reference, since each Stabaka, except the fifth, begins with a new pagination commencing with 1, so that reference to the text is made difficult. Even the fifth Stabaka starts with new pagination, but after page 2 the next page is numbered 31, to be more or less a continuation of the numeration of Stabaka four which had ended with page 29.

3) Nyāyachārya Sri Udayana's Nyayakusumanjali with commentary of Kusumanjalivisthara by Tarkarnava Panditaratna T. VIRARAGHAVACHARYA Siromani. Tiruvadi [= Tirupati] 1941.

Remarks: The editior did not make use of any MSS., but only the two earlier editions (see Bhūmikā, p. iii). It was printed in two separate parts. Stabakas 1 to 3 numbered consecutively come up to 246 pages; Stabaka 4 begins a new pagination and with Stabaka 5 runs to 114 pages.

4) The Nyāya Kusumāñjali of Śrī Udayanāchārya with four commentaries—the Bodhanī, Prakāśa, Prakāśika (Jalada) and Makaranda by Varadarāja, Vardhamānopādhyāya, Megha Thakkura and Ruchidaṭṭopādhyāya and Notes by Śrī Dharmadatta (Bachchā Jhā) edited by Pt. Śrī PADMAPRASĀDA UPĀDHYĀYA & Pt. Śrī DHUṆḌHIRĀJA ŚĀSTRI. With Foreword by Dr. GOPINĀTH KAVIRĀJ and Introduction by Śrī Rājeśwara Śāstri Drāviḍa (= KSS, No. 30), Varanasi 1957.

Remarks: The text of the NKus is based on the edition of 1912. Two MSS. of the Prakāśika have been used. For the text of the Bodhanī the editor used the previous edition of the same in the Saraswati Bhavana Texts Series, No. 1 by GOPINATH KAVIRAJ (Allahabad 1922). Note that the Bodhanī is printed only for the first three Stabakas.

5) Udayanācārya's Nyāyakusumāñjali. With the commentaries of Śaṅkara Miśra and Guṇānanda Vidyāvāgīśa. Edited by NARENDRACHANDRA Vedantatirtha. (= ASS, No. 4) Part I [containing only the First Stabaka] Calcutta 1954. Part II [Stabakas II—V preceded by a long "An Introduction to the Nyāya System" (89 pages) by the editor himself] Calcutta 1964.

Remarks: The text of the NKus has been based on the printed editions of BI and of 1912. The commentary of Śaṅkaramiśra, the Āmoda, is based on one single MS. while that of Guṇānanda, the NKusVi, is based on 2 MSS., the concluding portion of one of which is missing. The text of the NKus has been interrupted at short intervals for printing the commentaries. This interruption of the text has occasionally been badly done, for example, in the middle of or before the conclusion of a discussion.

In spite of the fact that we have hitherto at least five editions of the NKus, it is greatly to be regretted that a faultless edition of the work is still a desideratum.

c) Translations of the Nyāyakusumāñjali:

The following translations are known to me. None of them is complete.

1) The Kusumánjali, or Hindu proof of the existence of a Supreme Being by Udayana Achárya, with the commentary of Hari Dása Bhaṭṭáchárya. Edited and translated by E. B. Cowell. Calcutta 1864.

Remarks: This translation covers the entire text of Haridāsa Bhaṭṭācārya: that is to say, all the Kārikās of the NKus with the commentary of Haridāsa Bhaṭṭācārya on them.

2) Gopinath Kaviraj: Nyāya Kusumāñjali (English Translation). In: PWSBS, ed. by Ganga Nath Jha and Gopinath Kaviraj, Vol. II, Benares 1923, pp. 159—191.

Remarks: The translation which was planned to be published serially, covers only up to NKus 60, 2 of the KSS edition of 1957. Although at the end of the first part of the translation (with elaborate annotations) there was appended a "to be continued", as far as I know, the translation was not continued.

3) The Nyāyakusumāñjali of Udayanācārya (A presentation of theistic doctrines according to the Nyāya system of philosophy). Translated into English by Swami Ravi Tirtha. Vol. I—Books i and ii. (= The Adyar Library Series, No. 55), Adyar 1946.

Remarks: This work contains, besides a Foreword by C. Kunhan Raja, the English translation of the first two Stabakas of the NKus with some notes at the end. From the Bibliography of C. Kunhan Raja published in ALB, Vol. 27 (1963) p. 296 we know that the name Swami Ravi Tirtha is a pseudonymn assumed by C. Kunhan Raja in this case.

Note that the last two mentioned translations, though incomplete, are based on the complete text of the NKus.

4) There is a Bengali translation by Rāmakṛṣṇa Tarkatīrtha, which covers the Kārikās and is in the form of verses. It is called Kusumāñjali-saurabha and was published in Tripura in Bengal year 1330.

Some brief Notes on the Commentaries of the complete Text of the Nyāyakusumāñjali

1) Nyāyakusumāñjalibodhanī (often simply called Bodhanī): This commentary is probably the oldest and the most helpful for the understanding of the text of Udayana. Written in a lucid style, it explains, in most cases, all the difficult passages of the NKus. As a matter of fact, the student of the NKus becomes aware of the importance of this commentary while studying the fourth and the fifth Stabakas, the Bodhanī-commentary to which has unfortunately not yet been published. It is, however, known that the complete Bodhanī is available. In view of the extreme importance of this commentary for the study of the NKus it is to be hoped that it will soon be published.

The author of the Bodhanī is Varadarāja who wrote the Tārkikarakṣā and has written a commentary on Udayana's Kiraṇāvalī. Scholars are inclined to place him in the eleventh century.

Editions of the Bodhanī:

The following editions are known to me:

a) The Kusumāñjali-Bodhanī of Varadarāja Miśra: Edited with Introduction etc. by Gopinath Kaviraj. (= The Princess of Wales Saraswati-Bhavana Texts, No. 1), Allahabad 1922.

This edition is based on a single incomplete MS.

b) It is published together with the NKus by Padmaprasāda Upādhyāya and Dhundhirāja Śāstri (Cf. p. 189 Editions of the complete text of the NKus . . ., No. 4).

2) Nyāyakusumāñjaliprakāśa (often simply called Prakāśa): No doubt an important commentary on the NKus, it is nevertheless, in my opinion, less helpful than the Bodhanī for the study of the NKus. Unlike the Bodhanī which explains most of the passages of the original text, the Prakāśa does not explain all the important words of Udayana and, when confronted with a difficult word or passage in the original, one not infrequently looks in vain for help from the Prakāśa. Moreover, the Prakāśa is often not easy to follow unless one is well grounded in the terminology of the Navya-Nyāya.

Vardhamāna, its author, is believed to have lived in the thirteenth or beginning of the fourteenth century.

Editions of the Prakāśa:

Three editions—all complete—are known to me: Cf. p. 188f. Editions of the complete text of the NKus . . . Nos. 1, 2, and 4.

3) Nyāyakusumāñjalyāmoda (often simply called Āmoda): The author of this commentary is the renowned commentator Śaṅkaramiśra who most probably lived in Mithila in the fifteenth century. Like all his commentaries, the Āmoda is written in a very lucid style. However, its author follows too closely—often *verbatim*—the author of the Prakāśa. It is of great help, especially in the absence of the complete Bodhanī, for the understanding of the NKus.

Editions of the Āmoda:

A single edition of this commentary is known to me. Cf. p. 189 Editions of the complete text of the NKus . . ., No. 5.

4) Nyāyakusumāñjaliviveka: The colophons at the end of the first four Stabakas—there is no colophon at the end of the fifth—name this work Kusumāñjalitātparyaviveka or simply Viveka. G. Kaviraj informs us (Cf. his: Gleanings p. 63) that the work is called Tātparyaviveka in the MS of the Government Sanskrit Library, Benares. Its author, Guṇānanda Vidyāvāgīśa is believed to have lived about the end of the sixteenth century. Like Āmoda, this also is a very lucid commentary.

Editions of the Viveka:

For the only edition known to me, cf. p. 189: Editions of the complete text of the NKus. No. 5.

Besides these four published commentaries, the following unpublished commentaries on the full text of the Nyāyakusumāñjali are known to me.

5) According to the information given by E. P. RADHAKRISHNAN (in: The Poona Orientalist Vol. 4, January 1940, pp. 170—173), a complete MS of a commentary to the NKus, called Nyāyakusumāñjalinibandha, by a certain Vāmadhvaja has been discovered. According to RADHAKRISHNAN this Vāmadhvajācārya flourished towards the close of the sixteenth century.

6) UMESHA MISHRA (History of Indian Philosophy II, p. 442) informs us that Gadādhara Bhaṭṭācārya (whom D. C. BHATTACHARYA dates 1604—1709; cf. HNNM, p. 126) commented upon the NKus, a MS of which has been discovered and mentioned by KIELHORN (in his: Search of Manuscripts in Central Provinces, 1874, p. 144). G. KAVIRAJ also speaks of this commentary (Gleanings, p. 71). The exact nature of this commentary is not known.

7) UMESHA MISHRA (History of Indian Philosophy II, pp. 194—195) informs us that a MS of the commentary on the Kusumāñjaliprakaraṇam by a nineteenth century author, Arjuna Jhā, of the village of Maṅgarauṇī in the district of Darbhanga has been discovered.

8) D. H. H. INGALLS in his "Materials for the Study of Navya-Nyāya Logic" p. 19, while enumerating the works of Raghunātha Śiromaṇi, mentions also a commentary of his on Udayana's Nyāyakusumāñjali. In a footnote on the same page he remarks: "The only listing of this work that I can quote is that noticed by AUFRECHT, viz. Cat. Benares, p. 160". (See also G. KAVIRAJ: Gleanings, p. 59). So far nothing more is known about this work.

9) The Nyāyakusumāñjaliparimala mentioned in the third introductory verse of the Rāmabhadrī is, according to D. C. BHATTACHARYA, not a sub-commentary on the Nyāyakusumāñjaliprakāśa, as is sometimes believed, but a direct commentary on the NKus (HNNM pp. 72—74; 133). Its author, Divākara, is believed to have lived ca. 1200—1250 A. D. (HNNM p. 74).

The above-mentioned commentaries—certainly the first four, probably the others too—are all directly on the text of Udayana himself. Mention may here be made also of two sub-commentaries on the NKus which have so far been published. One of these is the Kusumāñjaliprakāśikā, commentary on the Nyāyakusumāñjaliprakāśa of Vardhamāna. Its author is Bhagīratha or Megha Ṭhakkura who wrote this commentary about A. D. 1500. It is also known by the name of Jalada. The second sub-commentary is called Nyāyakusumāñjalimakaranda (or simply Makaranda). Scholars are not agreed as to the nature and the author of this work. D. C. BHATTACHARYA is of the view that there are two Makarandas, one written by Tvantopādhyāya who lived before Śaṅkaramiśra and the other written by Rucidatta who was a disciple of Jayadevamiśra and was at least one generation later than Śaṅkaramiśra (Cfr. Tvantopadhyāya in: JGJRI 5 (1947), pp. 16—20; HNNM p. 133). Bhattacharya believes that the Makaranda mentioned in the introductory verse of the Rāmabhadrī is "an earlier commentary directly on the Kusumāñjali" and is written by Tvantopādhyāya during the period 1375—1400 A. D., while the Makaranda of Rucidatta is a sub-commentary on the Nyāyakusumāñjali. The edition of Makaranda published in the Nyāyakusumāñjali editions of LAXMAN SHASTRI DRAVID (Benares 1912) and later in that of Padmaprasāda Upādhyāya and Duṇḍhirāja Śāstri (Benares 1957) is not a direct commentary on the Nyāyakusumāñjali, but a commentary on the Nyāyakusumāñjaliprakāśa of Vardhamāna.

INDEX